agents or bosses?

patronage and intra-party politics
in argentina and turkey

Özge Kemahlıoğlu

ecpr PRESS

ECPR – Monographs

Series Editors:
Dario Castiglione (University of Exeter)
Peter Kennealy (European University Institute)
Alexandra Segerberg (Stockholm University)
Peter Triantafillou (Roskilde University)

Please visit www.ecprnet.eu/ecprpress for information about new publications.

contents

To my father, Ömer Kemahlıoğlu

'Unhappy the land that is in need of heroes.'
Bertolt Brecht, *Galileo*

| list of figures and tables

Figures

Tables

| list of abbreviations

ARI	Alternative for a Republic of Equals (Alternativa por una Republica de Iguales)
JDP	Justice and Development Party (Adalet ve Kalkinma Partisi, AK Parti)
DLP	Democratic Left Party (Demokratik Sol Parti, DSP)
MP	Motherland Party (Anavatan Partisi, ANAP)
NAP	Nationalist Action Party (Milliyetci Hareket Partisi, MHP)
PJ	Peronist Party (Partido Justicialista)
RPP	Republican Peoples Party (Cumhuriyet Halk Partisi, CHP)
UCR	Radical Party (Union Civica Radical)
SPP	Social Democratic People's Party (Sosyaldemokrat Halk Partisi, SHP)
TPP	True Path Party (Dogru Yol Partisi, DYP)
VP	Virtue Party (Fazilet Partisi)
WP	Welfare Party (Refah Partisi)

| acknowledgements

Without the support and friendliness of many Argentineans, this project would not have been possible. I would like to first thank academics in Argentina who have showed enthusiasm about my project, shared their vast knowledge on Argentinean politics, and helped me in every other way that they can. Valeria Brusco was the person who introduced me to this circle, spent hours with me talking about Argentinean politics, and helped me to get an idea on how to move forward with finding the data when I was almost completely lost in the labyrinth of public offices and websites. I would like to thank her for this generous support. In the various stages of the research many others provided guidance and feedback: Marcelo Cavarozzi, Marcelo Leiras, María Inés Tula, Mario Maurich, Catalina Smulovitz, Ernesto Calvo (who continued to provide helpful questions and feedback later in the US), Mariano Tommasi, Héctor Zimmerman, Daniel Arzadun, and Susana Gelber. I would like to thank them for sharing their knowledge and ideas on Argentinean politics with me. I also had an opportunity to present the earliest version of the project at CEPyS, Córdoba. I would like to thank the participants of this seminar for their feedback.

Many other people and institutions helped me collect the data for this project. I am grateful first and foremost to my interviewees. Due to confidentiality I am not able to list their names here, but without the information that they provided I could not have written this book. I would like to also thank el 'Pato' Gustovo, Guido Bordachar, Gabriela Sosa, Joly Arismendi, Eduardo Luque and many bureaucrats at the provincial administration of Chaco for introducing me to the local politics of La Matanza, Pilar and Chaco and for helping to contact the interviewees. Then, many shared with me their own statistical data or helped me to access the data from public offices. First, I would like to thank Horacio Cao for not only his guidance with the existing data, but also for giving me the excellent idea of looking at provincial budgets for information on temporary personnel. I am also grateful to Daniel Turraca, Christian Vaernet, and Oscar Alderete for providing me very helpful data on Chaco and to Mario Baressi for sharing with me his provincial level data. Many librarians at the National Library, Library of Argentinean Congress, Provincial Archive of Chaco, Congressional Library of Chaco, Congressional Library of Mendoza, the Legislative Library of the City of Buenos Aires helped me with the research. I would like to thank them for their experienced guidance. I also used the archive of the newspaper, *Resumen*. I am grateful to them for making their archive accessible. Finally, I would like to thank Julia Maskivker, Marisol Yakimiuk, and Ana Lia and Raul Cabrera for their friendliness.

Turkey was a more familiar territory for me, but still the research was not that easy. Many friends and family members pulled out their clientelistic ties in order to help me to get data or contact interviewees. I would like to thank my uncle, Utku Onan, (who also has always been an unexpected example of an academic for me),

Havva and Raif Ziya (who gave up all his time and energy to travel to Bilecik and Bozüyük just for this research), Ersen Sozener, Sevim Altug, Ali Ihsan Ilkbahar, Yildiz and Eser Alptekin, Hayriye Suvarierol, Bilgen Kemahlıoğlu, Ali Sagsoz, and Gokhan Gunaydin for all their help. The research would not have been possible without their support. I am also grateful to Ahmet Kesik for his guidance with data, to Tuba Eyicil Akin for her help in accessing the Turkish National Congress Library, to Mehmet Ozgur for making the archive of his newspaper, Yarın, available to me and sharing very sincerely his immense knowledge of politics in Bilecik. I also benefitted from the support of many librarians in Turkey: National Congress Library, Bogazici Library and Ataturk Library. I would like to thank them all here. As in Argentina, interviewees in Turkey provided invaluable information for this research. Unfortunately, due to confidentiality I cannot thank them individually here, but I am grateful to them for giving their time and energy to this project.

I have presented different versions of this project at many conferences and universities, but unfortunately I cannot thank individually all the colleagues who gave very useful feedback and helped the project to evolve. I would like to single out some of the support that I received from faculty at Columbia, though, who not only asked valuable questions in the presentations, but followed up on their comments afterwards: Pablo Pinto, Nisha Fazal, Douglas Chalmers, Michael Ting, David Epstein, Greg Wawro, Macartan Humphreys, and Shigeo Hirano.

I would like to give my sincerest thanks to Bob Kaufman for his open-mindedness and boundless knowledge on politics and social science, Vicky Murillo for her dynamism, intelligence, and the continuous careful feedback on my work, and John Huber for giving me support starting from the first day of the program at Columbia, teaching me how to do research in political science, and most importantly for being the excellent example of an honest, hard working, and creative academic.

Many friends and colleagues read and listened to many different versions of this project with patience. I would like to thank them for the fun, emotional support and all the feedback that they gave to this project: Semin Suvarierol, Mary McCarthy, Baris Balcioglu, Amy Widsten, Rebecca Weitz-Shapiro, Monika Nalepa, Georgia Kernell and Ali Carkoglu.

My colleagues at the Florida State University gave feedback in revising the manuscript. I thank Bill Berry, Jeff Staton, Sona and Matt Golder, Chris Reenock, and David Siegel for their comments. I would also like to thank Liz Nyman for editing an earlier version of the manuscript. I made the final touches to the research and the manuscript at Sabanci University. I thank my colleagues and the administration for their encouragement and support.

This research is based upon work supported by the National Science Foundation under Grant No. 0318036. I am grateful to the financial support provided by the NSF and Tinker fellowships. I would also like to thank the Center for Globalization and Governance at Princeton University and Rice University for providing excellent intellectual environments at different stages of this research. I am also grateful to Ildi Clarke for the final editing of the manuscript and Mark Kench from the ECPR Press for his valuable input. Parts of Chapters Four and

Five appeared as 'Jobs in politicians' backyards: Party leadership competition and patronage' in *Journal of Theoretical Politics*, October 2011. I am grateful to the *Journal of Theoretical Politics* for allowing me to reprint parts of the article in this book.

I am most grateful to my family who continued to provide their endless support all throughout this project. My brother-in-law, Serhan Ziya, patiently listened to all my complaints and crazy stories about Argentina and Turkey, and gave me advice on all kinds of academic and non-academic issues. My sister, Eda Kemahlıoğlu-Ziya, has always been an inspiration with her intelligence. I would like to thank her also for being the voice of reason all throughout and for always being at the end of the phone line, laughing, chatting, and listening. My deepest gratitude goes to my parents, Ediz and Ömer Kemahlıoğlu, for being supportive in every way throughout all these years, for always believing in this project, and most importantly for raising a kid with intellectual curiosity. Unfortunately my father could not see the book published. I dedicate this book to him, to his endless support, encouragement, and cheerful presence. Finally, I thank Reşat Bayer for his humor, patience, compassion, and hugs. These tough times would be unbearable without his support.

chapter one | introduction

Fall of 1983 was a critical time for the two countries analysed in this book. After seven years of a turbulent military rule, elections were scheduled for October in Argentina. In Turkey, the transition took place in the following month with the first competitive elections that were held after the three-year-long military intervention. Besides this coincidence in the timing of the democratic transition, these two countries share similarities in their political system, the most notable being the problems they still face with the quality of democracy. Social scientists, as well as the general public, frequently question the ability of the citizens in either country to elect representatives that truly pursue the interests of voters, or to hold these representatives accountable for their performance in government. One obstacle that stands in the way is the prevalence of particularism in the citizen-state relationships.

The purpose of this book is to focus on one type of such particularism, patronage jobs, and to shed light on mainly the political factors that shape how elected public office holders *supply* public jobs through particularistic relationships to some selected citizens. In both Argentina and Turkey, personal and direct relationships with politicians are thought to help the chances of getting employment in the public sector. These political networks supplement and sometimes even replace universal criteria like education and merit. Striking data was available on the website of the President of the Turkish Republic: Out of the 3220 citizens' requests that were handled by the office of the president, 1348 involved personal demands for employment and monetary help.[1] This example helps to illustrate the particularistic nature of the state-citizen relationships in this country. Citizens seem to believe that contacting a (high-level) public official is a means to have access to state resources. In this book, I approach the problem from the perspective of politicians and try to understand what shapes the politicians' incentives to hire people in the public sector through personal networks.

The explanation emphasises the internal dynamics of political parties. Without full bureaucratic or judicial oversight over their actions, politicians who hold administrative positions in government have the leeway to employ people at their own discretion. When politicians or parties do not have independent financial resources, they are likely to take advantage of this opportunity and fill public positions with their supporters and party activists in order to pay back for their political

---

1. President's website, http://www.cankaya.gov.tr/tr_html/VERILER/yurutme.html (accessed 11 December 2007). According to Sayari (2011), there were 11,973 such requests for assistance in total from the President in the period between 2007 and 2009, 4,542 out of these individuals wanted help with finding a job.

work. I find, however, that the use of this clientelistic strategy might be contained by intra-party politics because the members of a political party simultaneously compete and depend on each other. Politicians who depend on their party to advance their political career have the incentive to refrain from too aggressive efforts to build their independent political power base with the fear that this might threaten their fellow party members, especially their party leaders. Party leaders who care about their own survival are likely to be suspicious of too strong fellow party members when their position as leader is susceptible to challenges. When the party leaders are not dominant in their parties and when leaders control important material or symbolic resources that can impinge on the careers of their fellow party members, politicians might restrict patronage efforts in order not to lose their party leader's support. Therefore, under two conditions – if the parties play a critical role in elections and if party leadership selection processes are competitive – the internal politics of parties can help reduce incentives for patronage in public employment. Lower levels of patronage, in turn, improve the quality of democracy by providing a real possibility of choice among candidates and depoliticising the public administration as I discuss in the following section.

Why Study Particularism in Citizen-Politician Relationships?

The particularistic exchange of public jobs between politicians and citizens can be characterised as a form of a patron-client relationship. The immense literature on clientelism, patronage, and patron-client relationships, has discussed the possible consequences of these particularistic exchanges for the characteristics of the inter-personal relationships, the legitimacy of the political system, the distribution of economic resources, and the efficiency of the public administration.

The earlier literature that focused on the characteristics of the inter-personal interaction (Lemarchand and Legg 1972; Kaufman 1974; Eisenstadt and Roniger 1984) discusses how clientelism leads to the dependency of those that receive the material benefits on those who distribute them. As Zuckerman (1979) argued, in democratic settings where there is competition among patrons for clients this competition empowers the clients to some degree. However, in exchanges between elected political representatives and citizens where the representatives are the ones who are supplying the material goods, and hence become the patrons, citizens become dependent on their representatives, especially if other (private) alternatives for resources are bleak. Then these particularistic exchanges have significant consequences for mechanisms of democratic accountability.

One desired and critical characteristic of democratic political systems, even in the most limited conception of democracy with competitive elections for public office (Schumpeter 1975), is the ability of citizens to evaluate the performance of their elected representatives and to vote them out of government if they are not satisfied with their performance (Powell 2001; Manin 1997; Przeworski, Stokes and Manin 1999). However, the dependency of clients (voters) on their patrons (representatives) hamper the ability of citizens to replace their representatives with alternative candidates if they are not satisfied with their overall (policy) performance in government. Therefore, particularism in state-citizen linkages contribute to the major problem that most developing democracies face with the lack of political accountability (O'Donnell 1996; Smulovitz and Peruzotti 2002; Rose-Ackerman 2005; Stokes 2007; Lyne 2007; Lyne 2008).

In addition, depending on the breadth of these particularistic networks, clientelism might affect citizens' perceptions of the political system's legitimacy. Even though a robust empirical analysis on the impact of patronage on political legitimacy has yet to be conducted, a considerable debate exists in the literature on this issue. While, especially in the literature that has focused on modernisation and patron-client relationships, it has been argued that these direct and personal clientelistic networks have been useful for linking citizens in the periphery with the state and hence helped to legitimise the political system (Huntington 2002; Kalaycioglu 2001[2]; James 2005[3]), it has also been claimed that particularism hurts the legitimacy of the system because it is perceived as a form of corruption and violation of the rule of law (Adaman and Carkoglu 2000; Piattoni 2001).

One of the key reasons why particularism has a negative impact on legitimacy is that it leads to the exclusion of some citizens from having access to the goods provided by the state. However, the share of those that are excluded would be expected to influence citizens' perceptions. In two cases the negative impact on legitimacy would be expected to be lower: When the financial resources that are provided by the state are so extensive that clientelistic networks cover a large part of the population, very few are excluded. In the contrasting case where the clientelistic networks are formed only with a minor share of the population, in the end patronage does not affect the distribution of important financial resources.

The consequences of particularism in citizen-state relationships are not limited to the political arena, but also affect the quality of public administration and economic performance. Again, even though an empirical analysis of the extent of the inefficiencies it creates in the public administration and economic production has not yet been conducted (probably partly due to the difficulties of such a research design), the manner through which particularism would lead to inefficiencies is very clear. First of all, the distribution of state goods and services in a particularistic way leads to obstructions in the ranking of recipients according to need or merit. A clear and widely discussed example, on which this book focuses, is the particularistic distribution of jobs in the public administration for political support. Since in this case the hiring decisions are made according to the political networks of the applicants rather than education or merit, most of the time unqualified individuals end up doing the jobs, leading to a loss in efficiency and deterioration in the quality of public services.

---

2.   While pointing out one positive consequence of clientelistic linkages, Kalaycioglu (2001) actually discusses the problematic nature of such a patronage based democracy and discusses the dilemmas that clientelism poses for the rule of law and governance.

3.   In the case of the US that James (2005) discusses, the patron-client linkages helped legitimising parties in an anti-party environment.

This, in turn, has negative effects on the economic performance because scarce and valuable resources are wasted (Baland and Robinson 2007). Again, in the case of particularism in public employment, for example, a large share of the public budget is allocated to the spending on personnel. This leads to the loss of resources, first, because, with the same number of employees, the output in terms of production ends up being lower than would be the case if qualified individuals were hired and second, because the public sector expands due to political reasons even if there is no economic need.

Why Focus on Public Employment?

We can ask this question at two levels: First, why not take clientelism in general as the dependent variable and try to explain the political factors that shape patron-client relationships? Second, among different types of particularistic exchanges, why focus on this specific form of particularism, that is, exchanges within public employment, as opposed to other types?

The answer to the second question is easier to frame conceptually. We can talk about different types of particularistic exchanges that vary along two key dimensions: the political or social position of the actors who are involved, and the nature of the benefit that is exchanged. In this book, the analysis focuses on the type of exchange where the patron is an elected public office holder and the benefit that she distributes to the client(s) is a job in the public sector. I chose to focus on patron-client relationships where the patron is a public office holder as opposed to, for example, a private businessman who uses his own financial resources to establish a power base because such elected patrons persist in most developing democracies even though the earlier literature on development and modernisation [4] had predicted that these types of patron-client relationships would disappear from public life. Also, as I already discussed in the previous section, these patron-client relationships between elected officials and citizens have significant political consequences. Therefore, I find it important to have a better understanding of them if we care about the quality of democracy in developing countries.

Given that the patrons are the elected public office holders and the clients are some selected group of citizens, we know that different type of benefits that are distributed by the state can be exchanged in the particularistic relationships. These material benefits include contracts, subsidies, social assistance goods (that have become more widespread recently in Argentina and Turkey as in other developing countries), health services, scholarships and jobs, just to name a few examples. Among all these types of benefits why do I focus on the distribution of public jobs? First of all, patronage jobs are one of the most frequently cited types of ben-

---

4. See Gellner (1977); Mouzelis (1978); Boissevain (1966,1979); White (1980) on explanations related to the socio-economic level of a society and Huntington (2002); Boissevain (1966); Weingrod (1968); Gellner (1977) on explanations that are related to political development and modernisation.

efits in the literature on patron-client relationships that cover various countries and hence seems to be a general form of patronage across different cases (Wolfinger 1972; Schuler 1999; Robinson and Verdier 2002; Gordin 2002; Calvo and Murillo 2004; Freedman 1994; Shefter 1994; Geddes 1994; James 2005). Second, it is relatively easy to have access to data on public employment. Finally, I focus on public employment because, as I discussed previously, particularism in the hiring of public employees leads to significant economic inefficiencies. It might be argued that both countries, Turkey and especially Argentina, went through a period of economic crises that have eliminated the opportunity for new patronage hirings in the public employment and hence shifted patronage relationships to the distribution of other types of benefits such as social assistance goods (Stokes 2005). However, as can be seen in the case of Turkey, as soon as the emergency situation is over, the same patronage politics are likely to move back into the hiring decisions in the public administration. Therefore, it is important to understand the political factors that would lead to a public administration that has less particularistic hirings, which would then be more efficient economically.

However, the question remains as to why I choose to frame my question as what are the political factors that shape the particularistic exchange of public jobs between politicians and their selected supporters as opposed to for example, what are the factors that lead to political clientelism. A large part of the previous literature used more broadly defined dependent variables such as the concepts of clientelism, patronage, and corruption (i.e. Piattoni 2001; Kitschelt 2000; Gunes-Ayata 1994; Huntington 2002; Medina and Stokes 2002). Among these works, those that were motivated to introduce an explanation of variation across cases either focused on the impact of development (Huntington 2002) or on the characteristics of electoral competition among parties (Kitschelt 2000; Medina and Stokes 2002). Studies that focused on economic or political development can explain the widespread existence of particularistic linkages between state and citizens in relatively less developed countries (Wantchekon 2003; Gobel 2001; Kim 1999) and poorer regions within countries (Desposato 2003). However, they cannot explain why particularism has not been replaced by universalism in countries such as Argentina and Turkey that developed economically and politically (even though in relative terms they remained as developing countries) or these arguments cannot explain why we see variation across countries with similar levels of development. For example, their theoretical predictions contradict the empirical observations of particularistic exchanges in economically and politically developed countries such as Japan, Italy, and Austria (Kitschelt 2000).

Even though the economic context clearly shapes the demand and supply of particularistic goods from the state, in addition to these structural explanations it is helpful to introduce an analysis of political mechanisms behind these particularistic exchanges. Who are the actors involved in the exchange? What are the conditions under which they have incentives to engage in these particularistic exchanges? Although the literature that focuses on electoral competition takes a step forward in this direction, most of this literature still treats different types of particularistic exchanges under one category of patronage or clientelism. However, as Rose-Ackerman (1999) argues in the case of corruption, different types of corruption or particularism involve different actors with different incentive structures. As such, it is helpful to focus the analysis on one type of exchange where the defining dimension can be the nature of the material benefit that is exchanged, such as a public job.

Puzzle with the Electoral Explanation

Clearly electoral competition forms the basic frame that shapes politicians' incentives in democracies (or even in hybrid regimes). However, when I analyse particularistic exchanges within public employment in Argentina and Turkey with a focus on the distribution of jobs by politicians to citizens in return for their votes in general elections, I am faced with two problems. First, as there would be with any type of benefit that is exchanged in any context with a secret ballot, politicians are faced with monitoring problems. After giving out these benefits, politicians find it very difficult to make sure that citizens who receive these benefits really vote for them. As Stokes (2005) argues, there are different ways through which politicians can put some pressure on voters. For example, small sizes of voting departments or the lack of officially printed ballots can make citizens believe that their vote choice is observed whether in reality it is or not.[5] However, these constraints work only to a degree. Politicians and parties can cut back on the quantity of benefits to the neighbourhood where the share of votes turned out to be lower than expected (Magaloni 2006), but it is very hard to single out individuals who have defected and in cases where the exchange involves a job, this is the level at which monitoring should work.

The literature recently recognised that the exchange does not need to influence the vote choice because material benefits might instead be used to merely get the clients to vote on the election day (Dunning and Stokes 2008; Nichter 2008; Lyne 2008; Schaffer 2007; Vicente 2007). If the motivation behind clientelism is mobilisation for turn-out, then politicians and parties can easily monitor whether the recipients have fulfilled their obligation by participating in the elections. As long as the politicians are able to target potential supporters when allocating material benefits, they do not have to worry about the effectiveness of these clientelistic exchanges.

However, whether the politicians' goal is influencing vote choice or mobilising potential supporters to turn-out to vote, a second problem remains with respect to the effectiveness of exchanging patronage jobs for votes. If the number of public jobs were plenty, as in the case of Argentina and Turkey prior to the neo-liberal reforms that involved privatisations and reductions in the size of the state, politi-

---

5.   See Lyne (2008: 74–82) for a discussion of the innovative strategies that parties and politicians developed to monitor voting behaviour in secret ballot elections.

cians would be able to hire a large number of potential supporters in the government. As in the case of small benefits such as baskets of foods or incomes from social assistance programs,[6] this could then lead to a difference in the electoral results. However, the fact that only a small pool of public jobs is available to the politicians (as I will discuss in Chapter Two) has made it an inefficient strategy for politicians to hire voters before or after elections (as a promise) in order to change their voting behaviour.

Jobs for party members: the role of internal party politics

The literature that analyses particular cases of politician-citizen linkages (patron-client relationships) has illustrated that there are various forms of particularism and that the nature of particularistic exchanges is transformed with changes in the surrounding political and socioeconomic context (Auyero 2001; Gunes-Ayata 1994; Eisenstadt and Roniger 1984). In the case of Argentina and Turkey, starting with the 1980s, the neo-liberal economic reforms that reduced the number of public jobs have also led to such changes. In the new context, politicians and parties, rather than using patronage jobs for influencing voting decisions for general elections, distribute them within their own parties to party members (activists). In return, they expect the activists' participation in electoral campaigns and in mobilisation efforts for internal party elections as well as their votes in internal party elections.

Three characteristics of Argentinean and Turkish parties make this an efficient strategy: the lack of financial resources provided by the party to conduct campaigns at the local or provincial level, the subsequent reliance of parties on party members and activists in campaigns for general and intra-party elections, and the rules of selecting candidates for public positions and party posts that are not truly participatory. Since parties and politicians have to rely on non-paid participation of party members, they have an incentive to use selective rewards such as public jobs in order to mobilise party members for campaigns. In addition, in contrast to general elections where the number of voters is high, a small number of people participate in internal party elections for nominations or for choosing party leadership either due to low turn-out in the case of primaries or inherently small number of electors in indirect elections through delegates. This gives additional incentives to politicians to distribute patronage jobs in order to increase their support within their own parties.

Therefore, in order to shed light on the political factors that affect levels of particularism in public employment, we have to analyse two stages of political competition: among parties in general elections and within parties for nomination and leadership. A critical interaction between members of the same party takes place between politicians of hierarchical position: a lower level politician (fol-

---

6.   These are the types of goods that a public opinion survey finds to be exchanged for votes in elections (Stokes 2005).

lower) and a higher level politician (leader). The follower's ambitions to move up in the party hierarchy poses threats to the leader's position in the party. Since the leader and follower both need their party to be successful, they are in an interdependent position and the leader who is facing a potential challenger has to decide whether to support the follower symbolically or financially. I argue that in this context, patronage jobs, in addition to their role of building support in the party and in public, play a second role, by sending signals about the intentions of the follower. Depending on the number of patronage jobs that the follower distributes, the leader infers information about the follower's intention to challenge her leadership in the party.[7]

I analyse with a game theoretic model how this interdependent, but competitive, interaction between a leader and her follower in the party affects the particularistic distribution of public jobs to party members. Since the leader does not know the intentions of the follower, the interaction is modelled as an incomplete information game. The main result that I derive from this analysis is that the internal competition between party members who have a hierarchical relationship can constrain levels of particularism under two conditions: if the party (leader) support is important for politicians' re-election chances and if the party leader is not dominant in her own party. Under these conditions the follower limits the number of patronage jobs that he distributes in his administration in order to send a signal to the party leader that he does not have intentions to challenge her leadership in the party.

This finding about the impact of intra-party competition on patronage contributes to the discussion on how clientelism is related to political competition. As I have mentioned previously, most of the existing literature focuses on inter-party competition. However, there is no agreement on whether more competitive elections reduce or increase the level of patronage. While some (Grzymala-Busse 2007 and Geddes 1994) argue that political competition helps to depoliticise the state, others have argued that tight competition gives more incentives to politicians to distribute patronage benefits (Robinson and Verdier 2002; Remmer 2007). Yet, both groups of arguments miss the incentives that are created by characteristics of parties. A focus on internal party competition shows that when parties (either through party labels or financial resources) play a critical role in elections and when their leadership selection processes are more participatory and open, political competition within parties would help to reduce patronage.

Methodology of the empirical analysis

The literature on clientelism and patronage raises two important questions: Why was particularism not replaced by universalism in some countries as they developed economically and politically? And why does particularism cut across levels

---

7.   I refer to the follower as male and leader as female for convenience of exposition.

of socioeconomic development and major political institutions such as presidentialism/parliamentarism and federalism? These questions led me to choose for analysis two countries with similar levels of economic development and similar histories of political economy, but with contrasting cultural and political institutional contexts, Argentina and Turkey.

Even though prior to the 2001 economic crises, Argentina's per capita income was much higher than Turkey's (the corresponding figures in 2000 were US$ 7915 and US$ 3048 (World Development Indicators)) and there are important differences in the nature of economic production in each country (Argentina's exports rely less on manufacturing and agriculture formed a larger share of Turkey's GDP until very recently), they are both among upper-middle income countries. Also, they both experienced recurring economic crises and interruptions of democracy with military governments. In contrast, the institutional context in which the electoral competition takes place is considerably different. The three key dimensions along which they vary are: presidential/parliamentary system[8], federal/unitary structure and the fragmentation of the party system.[9]

Studying two countries that differ to a large extent in their cultural and political institutional contexts helps me in two ways: First, I discuss and try to introduce solutions to the problems of applying the hypotheses to different settings. I discuss this point in more detail below. Second, it helped me with developing the theoretical arguments. If I only focused on one case, I would have had more difficulties with observing the underlying pattern of intra-party competition that is relevant for the distribution of patronage jobs. For example, existing studies of intra-party politics in Latin America have mostly emphasised competition among well defined factions. If I had studied patronage only in Argentina, I could have concluded that competition among factions is related to the role of patronage within parties. Exploring the Turkish parties showed that the existence of well-defined factions is not necessary and that there is an underlying, broader dynamic of leadership competition that has an impact on the use of patronage jobs within parties.

Although most of the existing literature on clientelism, political parties, and politics in general in these two countries argue that particularism in state-citizen relationships is widespread in Argentina and Turkey, it is not possible to measure the aggregate levels of patronage jobs in these two countries and compare them along this dimension. Therefore, rather than analysing and comparing these two

8. As a result of a referendum carried out on October 21, 2007, the constitution was changed and the next president of Turkey will be directly elected by the people, which will turn the system into a mixed one. However, in the period of analysis in this book, Turkey had a parliamentary system.

9. Both countries, Argentina and Turkey, have recently been experiencing a transition in their party system. While the party system in Argentina, prior to the 2003 elections, is generally considered as a two party system (Jones 1997; Levitsky 2005), the party system in Turkey between 1983 and 2002 can be considered as a fragmented, multi-party system (Ozbudun 2000; Sayari 2002). The last decade, however, saw both countries moving towards a predominant party system (Anderson 2009; Carkoglu 2011).

countries through typical case studies, I conduct statistical and case study analyses separately within each country and see whether two factors that I hypothesise to have an effect on levels of particularism, have an impact on public employment across sub-national units.

A variable that can be used to measure levels of particularism in public employment within a country across administrative units is the size of public employment (measured either in numbers of employees or spending on personnel). Therefore, I use this measurement for statistical analysis in each country. Controlling for socioeconomic factors that would have an impact on the size of public employment, such as population, revenue, GDP, deficits and transfers from national government, I test whether two political factors, importance of party (leader) support for politicians' re-election and openness of party leadership competition, affect the size of public employment. As I mentioned previously, due to differences in the political institutional structure of these two countries, there are differences in the level of administration that is analysed and the ways I measure explanatory political factors.

In Argentina the statistical analysis is conducted across provinces that have independent public administrations and are controlled by elected governors. I use the number of temporary employees in each provincial administration as the dependent variable. I measure the importance of party (leader's) support by looking at the difference between the vote share of the governor and the party in that province (divided by the governor's vote share). The variable that I use to measure the openness of party leadership competition is the results of primary elections for the presidency. Alternatively, I limit the analysis to provinces that are controlled by governors from the president's party and use the provinces' financial dependence on the federal government and presidential approval rates as measurements of my explanatory variables. Turkey is not a federal system and the provincial administrations are decentralised branches of the national government. The head of the provincial administration, the governor (*vali*), is appointed by the ministry of interior and hence there is no elected public official directly responsible for the hiring decision at the provincial government. However, there are sixteen metropolitan cities whose municipalities control vast financial resources and have special legal status, which empowers the mayors of these municipalities. These mayors pose a serious threat to their party leaders' position in their parties. Therefore, I conduct a statistical analysis of spending on personnel across these sixteen metropolitan municipalities. As in Argentina, I use the difference between mayor's vote and the party's general election vote (divided by the mayor's vote) to measure the importance of party support and the internal party election results to measure the openness of party leadership competition.

In addition to these statistical analyses, I also examine in more detail the political competition, both among and within parties, at the provincial and municipal level. With these detailed case studies I illustrate the dynamics of vertical competition within the party and its effect on public employment at both levels in two provinces in each country. Deriving from the earlier literature on the impact of economic and social development on patronage, my initial intuition (even though not supported empirically) was that the role of party competition might be different in more populated and economically developed provinces compared to the less developed and smaller provinces. In order to check this intuition I chose two contrasting provinces on socioeconomic dimensions for detailed analysis. In Argentina these provinces are Buenos Aires and Chaco. In Turkey, I chose Istanbul and Bilecik.

Political competition and public jobs in two municipalities within each of these four provinces are discussed to illustrate how similar mechanisms work at the municipal level where now the competition is between the provincial level party leader and mayors. The municipalities are again chosen to reflect contrasting cases on the SES dimensions. In Buenos Aires, I chose La Matanza and Pilar and in Chaco, Resistencia and Fontana. In Istanbul, the two municipalities that I chose are Beşiktaş and Kartal and in Bilecik they are the municipality of the city Centre and Bozüyük.[10]

The Organisation of the Book

In Chapter Two, I provide a brief summary of the economic changes that Argentina and Turkey went through starting with the early 1980s. I analyse how these changes, mainly liberalisation and more specifically, privatisation, have had an impact on the demand and supply of patronage jobs. I also discuss regional variations in each country. The chapter ends with a review of the literature on vote buying. I argue that this type of a particularistic exchange works when the good that is exchanged is of low financial value to the politicians. In the case of public jobs, since, especially after the neo-liberal reforms, distributing these jobs has become more costly for politicians, politicians do not find vote buying through patronage jobs an efficient strategy.

Then the theoretical section on political competition follows. In Chapter Three I analyse Argentinean and Turkish parties and discuss why and how patronage jobs are used within parties. Chapter Four introduces the game theoretic analysis of intra-party competition between party members of hierarchical relationship and its effects on particularistic distribution of public jobs. The main argument that I derive from this analysis is that politicians that rely on their party (leader's) support and whose party leader is not dominant within the party, engage in these particularistic exchanges less in order not to appear as a challenger to the leader and to prevent the loss of support from the party (leader).

The next section is dedicated to the empirical analysis of the effect of these two political factors on public employment. The results in Chapter Five (on Argentina) and Chapter Six (on Turkey) show support for the expectation that internal party politics affect patronage in public employment. Each empirical chapter starts with detailed case study analyses. The discussion of the politics and municipal and

---

10.   The two municipalities that are examined in the case of Bilecik are the two most developed of the province due to data limitations.

provincial public employment in two provinces in each country illustrates the mechanisms of political competition, especially within political parties in different socioeconomic, institutional, and cultural contexts. The case studies are followed by the large-n statistical analyses across sub-national units.

Then, finally I conclude with a discussion of the implications of this research for our understanding of particularism in state-citizen relationships and internal party politics and with some suggestions on possibilities for future research.

chapter two | public employment reshaped: the impact of neo-liberal reforms on particularistic exchanges

In developing countries like Argentina and Turkey, public employment at different levels of state administration as well as in public enterprises is known to be manipulated by politicians (parties) to increase their political support. Two related channels are available for politicians to do so: they can expand the size of the public sector in order to create employment for citizens (their supporters) or they might distribute jobs in the public sector to some selected citizens in return for some type of political service. However, in the last two to three decades most developing countries, including the two countries analysed here, experienced major changes in their economic structure (neo-liberal reforms) that have shaped both the ability of politicians to provide new jobs in the public sector and the willingness of citizens to exchange political services for jobs. Even though some of these countries such as Argentina in the post-2007 period experienced some reversals in economic policies towards more state involvement, these countries are still faced with different conditions, in comparison with the earlier ISI period, that have transformed the particularistic distribution of public jobs by politicians. Even though citizens are still (or even more) dependent on public jobs for economic income, the number of jobs that politicians can create and allocate in a discretionary way is now very limited. As a consequence, politicians are forced to distribute the available jobs to a smaller group of supporters. Since the jobs now form a scarce and more valuable commodity, political services in return for the jobs are expected to go beyond just voting in elections. In addition to votes, the recipients of such jobs might be compelled to vote in internal party elections, contribute to electoral campaigns, and help with the daily party work. That is, as a result of the shrinking pool of resources, politicians now might prefer to give most public jobs only to active party members whose political service is safer (less risky) and more valuable than just one vote in general elections.

One crucial component of the neo-liberal reforms that has led to these new economic conditions with a limited number of available public jobs, was the privatisation of state owned enterprises and public services such as water, transportation, and electricity. Even though privatisation in Turkey has taken a much longer time compared to Argentina, in both countries the transfer of major public companies to private hands took away a significant quantity of jobs from politicians' control. Economic reforms have also influenced the supply of public jobs through trade and capital market openings. In this more competitive environment, governments face stronger pressure to establish and maintain macroeconomic stability, which is influenced by the government's fiscal situation. In order to attract more capital to their country and increase investments in production so that goods would be competitive in the international market, governments have to refrain from inflationary tendencies such as expanding the size of the public sector. As such, in the new economic context of both countries, it has become much more costly for politicians to manipulate public sector employment.

At the same time, in most developing countries the opening of the economies and reductions in the size of state, were accompanied by an effort to decentralise both the administration of the state and political decision-making. This potentially could have led to an opposite trend in the availability of public jobs at the decentralised level since sub-national governments, such as the provinces in Argentina or metropolitan municipalities in Turkey, could now control relatively more resources. However, as I will discuss later in this chapter, in the period of analysis, the sub-national governments' administrations did not expand much (even contracted in some cases) when controlled for increases in population.

On the other side of this exchange, that is from citizens' perspectives, public jobs that are distributed through political ties have also retained (if not increased in) their importance. Even though liberalisation efforts were expected to boost private sector production, and hence create employment, this expectation was not fulfilled. In Argentina after the introduction of the Convertibility Plan, growth rates in the economy were quite high until the recession of the late 1990s, but unemployment levels failed to decline, and starting with the second half of the 1990s, unemployment even started to increase to two digit levels (INDEC, 'Evolution de la Tasa de Desocupacion'). Instead of a steady increase in unemployment as in the case of Argentina, Turkey's unemployment rate ranged between 7 to 9 per cent throughout the late 1980s and 1990s until it increased to two digit levels after the economic crisis of 2001 (DPT, 'Yurtici Is Piyasasinda Gelismeler'). As can be seen from these figures, economic reforms in either case could not eliminate (or even decrease) unemployment, and citizens remained dependent on the economic resources that are provided by the state. However, this dependence showed considerable variation across regions and provinces.

Before analysing more deeply the effect of each aspect of neo-liberal reforms on the ability of politicians to allocate jobs in a particularistic manner and on the demands from citizens for these public jobs, I very briefly go over the existing arguments about the impact of economic structures and conditions on particularistic distribution of state resources by politicians. After discussing the privatisation process, trade and capital market liberalisation, decentralisation, and regional variations across each country, I conclude the chapter with a summary of how these economic changes are expected to transform particularistic exchanges of jobs for political support.

The effects of economic and political development on patronage

The socio-economic level of a society (Gellner 1977; Mouzelis 1978; Boissevain 1966, 1979; White 1980) or political development and modernisation (Huntington 2002; Boissevain 1966; Weingrod 1968; Gellner 1977) were the predominant explanatory factors in the earlier literature on patronage and clientelism. It was expected that with socio-economic or political development there would be a transition from a social and political system based on particularism (unequal exchanges between politicians and citizens) to a system where politicians appeal to voters on programmatic and policy grounds. However, these analyses have not dealt in detail with the economic and political-institutional factors that shape how these particularistic exchanges work. This is one of the reasons why their explanations fail to account for the variation across polities with similar levels of development.

Neither can these arguments explain why particularism persists in some societies in spite of changes in economic structure. Analyses of many societies have shown that, rather than disappearing, particularistic exchanges have altered their form in the face of changing socio-economic conditions. For instance, in some societies where agriculture is the dominant form of production, landlords distribute land to particular individuals for political loyalty. When the dominance of agriculture diminishes, particularism persists in some societies, but what is distributed and who distributes the benefits adjusts to the new socio-economic environment. In this new context, politicians and bureaucrats control valuable resources and they distribute these public benefits for political support (Gunes-Ayata 1994; Zuckerman 1979). Therefore, arguments that merely focus on socio-economic or political development fail to explain why this kind of transition occurs in some societies while, in others, particularism is replaced by universal criteria. In addition, these arguments contradict empirical observations of patronage in economically and politically developed countries such as Japan, Italy, and Austria (Kitschelt 2000) as well as the persistence of patronage in countries in which markets have expanded, the level of economic development in terms of production has increased, and the central government has penetrated the peripheral regions of the country, i.e. Argentina and Turkey.

Such empirical observations that falsify arguments concerning socio-economic and political development is consistent with the fact that most of these arguments were prevalent in early works on patronage and clientelism that preceded economic and political developments in most third-world countries. Recently, scholars, as a result of these new empirical observations, were forced to revisit earlier theories that expected an automatic transition with development to a merit-based universalistic system.

Yet, dismissing economic explanations completely is not easy, either. Even in the face of variation in terms of the level of particularism across countries with similar degrees of development, and the persistence of clientelistic relations in some countries that are relatively rich, countries with low levels of economic development (Wantchekon 2003; Gobel 2001; Kim 1999) and poorer regions within a country (Desposato 2003) tend to be disproportionately affected by the problem of particularism.

Noticeably, there seems to be a link between economic conditions and a tendency for particularism in politician-citizen linkages. Accounts of patron-client relationships by Auyero in *Poor People's Politics* (2001) very clearly portrays how political networks through which some citizens have access to public benefits are shaped by poor economic conditions in localities- widespread unemployment (sub-employment) and low income. In his analysis of the urban political machines in Chicago, Scott also considers the role of poverty in those machines' response to particularistic interests (2002: 221). His explanation focuses on the perceptions of the receivers of benefits that are provided by politicians and argues that poverty shortens people's time horizons (2002: 230).

This view that economic conditions affect citizens' calculations or their perceptions of exchanges (relationships) with politicians has been taken up by the recent work of political scientists that, in addition to economic factors, explicitly bring in political factors to the analysis (Calvo and Murillo 2004; Medina and Stokes 2002; Robinson and Verdier 2002; Brusco *et al.* 2007). All these cited works emphasise citizens' income levels and the dependence of voters on the public sector as important factors that affect voters' perceptions or calculations. The immediate logic behind the argument is that it is easier to buy citizens' votes if their income is low and if the private sector cannot offer alternatives to the public benefits that are provided by politicians.

Yet, arguments are more nuanced when this assumption is combined with political and other economic factors. For example, voters' income profiles were shown to affect the use and returns of clientelistic exchanges by different political parties (Calvo and Murillo 2004). The analysis of electoral results across Argentine provinces suggests that parties whose supporters have limited alternatives in the private labour market, and have lower levels of income, get higher returns in terms of votes in general elections than other parties (Calvo and Murillo 2004). Rather than supporting universal redistribution, some poor citizens might even vote against programmatic redistribution if they are targeted by particularistic benefits (Huber and Ting 2009; Dixit and Londregan 1996). In addition, the collective action problem that voters face when they are choosing between an opposition that proposes more desirable economic policies and an incumbent that promises them jobs in the public sector is affected by the economic conditions (Medina and Stokes 2002). In places with low economic development, a job in the public sector means a risk free activity for the receiver, increasing the stakes of losing the job, and making the collective action problem even more difficult to overcome (Medina and Stokes 2002).

Yet, economic conditions not only shape the perception of voters (citizens), but naturally also of the politicians who distribute benefits. Clientelism, which is partly a result of low productivity, provides relatively higher rents to politicians and hence politicians choose to shift resources from investments that could increase productivity to the creation of economic resources (such as public jobs) that can be distributed in a particularistic manner (Robinson and Verdier 2002). As these arguments suggest, it is crucial to analyse how the incentives of both sides of the exchange – citizens and politicians – are shaped by the changing economic conditions as well as political competition. Therefore, in the rest of this chapter I analyse the impact of neo-liberal reforms in Argentina and Turkey on citizens' and politicians' incentives, which subsequently shaped the use of the particularistic distribution of public jobs in the political competition between and within parties.

Voter-politician linkages in the aftermath of economic liberalisation

As the discussion in the previous section shows, works that combined economic and political factors have improved considerably our understanding of political-citizen linkages that are formed around the particularistic exchanges of public benefits. However, I would like to elaborate on two points that emerged out of these analyses. The first point is regarding the argument concerning productivity and private sector alternatives. The emphasis on the dependence of citizens on the public sector reminds us of previous work by Lemarchand (1988) who argued that there are more possibilities for political patronage when the public sector is large and the economy is protected from international competition as in import substitution industrialisation. For example, in Robinson and Verdier, they refer to works on Africa that emphasise the dominance of the state in the job market and the lack of a developed indigenous private sector (2002: 4). According to Robinson and Verdier, these two factors induce clientelism (2002: 4).[1]

Even though the argument that citizens' relationships with politicians tend to revolve around limited access to resources, when the alternatives in the private sector are scarce, is a logical conclusion that could be derived when economic factors are considered, I think it is important to explicitly state that the desired outcome of less particularism in citizen-politician (state) relationships might not be automatically achieved as a result of economic liberalisation. The two cases of Argentina and Turkey, which opened their markets to external competition and reduced their states' involvement in the economy, clearly demonstrate that particularism can persist even at the face of these changes in the economy. Indeed, a group of works on Latin America has claimed that liberalisation actually increased clientelism by providing immediate revenues to governments as a result of privatisation that could be channelled to financing other particularistic material benefits (Kessler 1998), by increasing dependence of citizens on state resources as a result of more limited universal welfare benefits (Roberts 1996), and an expansion of the poor population (Gibson 1997). An ethnographic study of a rural town in Turkey (Ozbudun 2005) shows how the liberalisation programs have increased demand for goods that are provided by patrons in the rural sector.

Rather than eliminating particularistic exchanges, neo-liberal reforms have thus modified the nature of the relationship between politicians and their supporters. I argue in this book that by making public jobs more valuable with regard to the perception of both sides, economic changes have led to a transition from particularistic exchanges between politicians and voters to those between politicians and active party members (militants). Even though the direction of the impact that economic liberalisation has on the level of particularistic relationships between the state and citizens is not clear and disputed in the literature, these changes in the economic system, without doubt, shape the perceptions and preferences of

---

1. Greene (2007) also discusses how economic liberalisation in Mexico deprived the PRI of the patronage resources that they had so skilfully employed to preserve their dominance.

the actors who are involved in particularistic exchanges of public benefits. In the following section, I discuss this effect that liberalisation has had on politicians' (patrons') and citizens' (clients') perceptions in Argentina and Turkey.

How economic liberalisation affects politicians' perceptions

Privatisation

Privatisation of public enterprises and public service provision has formed a major component of the neo-liberal reforms in Argentina and Turkey. Subsequent to the privatisation of state owned enterprises and the reduction in the size of the state administration, the number of public jobs under the control of politicians shrank, to a large extent, in both countries. Even though the first attempts to privatise in Argentina took place before Menem's coming to power in 1989, these earlier efforts had not been successful (Gerchunoff and Coloma 1993). After privatisations were integrated with major stabilisation efforts and state reform under Menem's rule, however, a large part of the transfer of these enterprises from public to private ownership came about just in four years between 1989 and 1993 (Gerchunoff and Coloma 1993). According to the Ministry of Economy, since 1980 sixty-seven state owned enterprises were privatised, liquidated or dissolved.[2]

These enterprises included Aerolíneas Argentinas (Argentina Airlines)[3] that before privatisation had more than 10,000 employees, part of ENTEL (National Enterprise of Telecommunications) that later became Telefónica S.A. and in November 1990 employed 21,770 people. According to Murillo (2001), ENTEL as a whole had 47,000 employees and EDESUR that was responsible for the electrical service to the Capital Federal and 12 departments of the province of Buenos Aires had 7,541 employees in September 1992.[4] Just these three examples clearly illustrate how large a resource these state owned enterprises had provided to politicians to use for particularistic exchanges prior to their privatisation.

As a result of this privatisation process, politicians lost a significant share of the public jobs that could be distributed for establishing and maintaining patronage networks. Even before the initiation of the actual privatisations of YPF (Fiscal

---

2. See the website of the Ministry of Economy (http://mepriv.mecon.gov.ar) for a list of these enterprises. The number is actually larger if different companies under some headings such as 'Gas del Estado' or 'YPF' are considered (see Murillo 2001:142 and INDEC 1996). Further information about the privatisation of these enterprises can be found on the Ministry of Economy's website or INDEC, Anuario Estadistico de la Republica Argentina 2000, 16: 495–498.

3. Aerolíneas Argentinas was later renationalised. It was the seventh nationalisation under Néstor and Cristina Kirchner's administrations (http://www.stratfor.com, July 21, 2008). The earlier nationalisations include AySA, the enterprise that provides water services for the City of Buenos Aires and seventeen departments of the province of Buenos Aires (http://www.aysa.com.ar). As of April 2012, the government was in the process of expropriating also the YPF. Rather than a complete reversal in economic policy, renationalisations can be seen as one component of a new political economic strategy that combines elements of populism with neoliberalism (Wylde 2011).

4. See the website of the Ministry of Economy (http://mepriv.mecon.gov.ar).

Oil Reserves) and ENTEL, their staff was reduced – in the case of YPF from 37,367 to 5,690 and by 6,000 in ENTEL – in order to enhance enterprise competitiveness (Murillo 2001). Moreover, the total number of employees in public enterprises diminished from 236,694 in 1990 to 41,102 in 1993 (excluding the banking system) (Etchemendy 2001: 8).[5]

In Turkey, privatisation has been proceeding much more gradually, but still has led to considerable reductions in public sector employment. Although the government passed Law No. 2983 that permits the sale of assets from public enterprises in February 1984 (Simga-Mugan and Yuce 2003), the first privatisation (of Teletas, manufacturer of telephone equipment) was carried out only in 1988 (Waterbury 1993). Starting from 1986, the state has sold its shares in 199 enterprises. 188 of these 199 enterprises have been totally privatised with no state shares remaining.[6] However, comparing the number of enterprises that are involved in the privatisation process in Argentina and Turkey does not give us any information about the extent of privatisation, because the size of these enterprises and the states' shares vary. In Turkey, most of the earlier privatisation involved small enterprises while the majority of the large enterprises were privatised between 2005 and 2008.

Just to illustrate by giving examples of two large sectors where the state was dominant in Argentina, the privatisation of Aerolíneas Argentinas earned the state 2,243,697.50 dollars and the sales of petrochemical industry, which was also largely privatised as of 1991, involved 186,398.56 dollars.[7] In contrast, in Turkey, the privatisation of both the national airlines and the petrochemical sector has been on the agenda for a long period, but it has only recently been carried out in the latter case and a sizeable share of the airlines still remains under state ownership. Even though the government decided to privatise THY (Turkish Airlines) in 1990 and Petkim (petrochemical enterprise) in 1987 (Simga-Mugan and Yuce 2003), the state still holds 49.12 per cent of THY's shares. The Petkim's privatisation was carried out in two stages: In April 2005 the government completed the public offering of 34.5 per cent of its shares. Fifty-one per cent of the remaining shares were privatised through a block sale on November 22, 2007. As these examples show, Turkey's privatisation process has not been as intense and rapid as Argentina's.[8] Yet, even in Turkey, employment in public enterprises has diminished in large quantities from 1,982,294 in the first quarter of 1994 to 975,483 in the first quarter of 2001 (DPB State Employment Department Publications).

If we look at examples at the industry or enterprise level, we can again see that these privatised state enterprises used to provide politicians with large quantities

5. A similar figure was provided by Fontdevila (1994): In three years between 1989 and 1992 there were about 180,000 workers that left public enterprises.

6. This data is taken from the website of the Prime Minister – Department of Privatisation on 14 October 2009 (http://www.oib.gov.tr/program/uygulamalar/1985–2003_gerceklesenler.htm).

7. See the website of the Ministry of Economy (http://mepriv.mecon.gov.ar).

8. Argentina was indeed acclaimed for the rapidity and intensity not only of its privatisation program, but its market reforms in general. (See Edwards 1995 and Etchemendy 2001 as examples of works on liberalisation in Argentina.)

of resources that they could use in particularistic exchanges with citizens. For example, in the cement industry in Turkey, the state used to own 24 firms in different localities. The total number of personnel that was employed by these 24 firms was 6,737 before privatisation.[9] The airport service industry which was divided into two enterprises as USAŞ and HAVAŞ employed at the time of their privatisation respectively 1,498 (in 1989) and 2,256 (in 1995) people. The public grocery store chain, GIMA's number of personnel, in turn, was 1,668 in 1992 – one year prior to its privatisation.

When we look again at the total number of personnel employed by the state owned enterprises in Turkey in the first quarter of 1994, we can see that employees with tenure (memur) comprised only 1.29 per cent of the total number of employees. In contrast, 12.3 per cent were contracted personnel and a vast 71 per cent were temporary workers (DPB State Employment Department Publications). These figures imply that it was relatively easy for politicians to influence the hiring decisions of personnel in state enterprises since turnover is easier when workers do not have tenure. In addition, in most of these public enterprises politicians had a major influence on administrative decisions. Although there were attempts by the military government to free the administration of public enterprises from political pressures, the democratically elected government of Özal in 1983 promulgated Decree 233 and ministers once again became directly involved in the management issues of public firms (Waterbury 1993).

Some existing academic works also support the argument that clientelistic ties were important for getting jobs in state enterprises. The analysis of letters written to Erdal Inonu, the leader of the RPP, between November 1991 and March 1993 illustrated that party members asked for jobs in public enterprises (Schuler 1999). Although Schuler does not provide information about what percentage of these letters involved requests for jobs in state owned enterprises, he includes a selective sample of the letters in his book and some of these letters show that, at least from the perspective of party members, hiring decisions in state enterprises were influenced by politicians.

In another work that analyses clientelism in a state owned enterprise (the name of the enterprise is kept confidential), Ozkul (1996) introduces a surprising database that was kept by the director of the enterprise. The director recorded all the requests related to the employees in a computer file. The names of the employees for whom requests were made, the (political) intermediaries who were communicating these requests to the director, and the outcomes of the requests were all included in the file. In the period of analysis, 1992–1995, there was a freeze on the hiring of new personnel because of the austerity program that was being implemented. Therefore, the requests do not involve new hirings. However, the analysis of the database shows that politicians – mostly parliamentarians, cabinet members, and

---

9.   The data on SOEs' personnel prior to privatisation are published on the website of the Prime Minister – Department of Privatisation (http://www.oib.gov.tr/program/uygulamalar/ok_faaliyet_bilgileri.htm, accessed 14 October 2011).

party officials at the district level – were used as intermediaries to put pressure on the enterprise administration to solve some problems of the employees in a selective manner. These requests mostly involved transfers and promotions.

These works and the data on the number of employees at the state enterprises in Argentina and Turkey show that state owned enterprises provided politicians with an extensive resource to be used in building political support in a selective manner. Their privatisation in both countries after the mid-1980s, in turn, clearly reduced these available resources. However, I argue and support with statistical and case study analyses that this cutback did not necessarily lead to the elimination of citizen-politician linkages that are formed around the particularistic exchange of public jobs. Rather, particularistic exchanges continue in the public administration. Yet, the forms through which these exchanges take place have been transformed. In the post-liberalisation era with less state resources that can be manipulated, politicians have to be more strategic in their decisions about patronage job recipients.

Especially when scarce resources are considered, together with the problems that politicians have with monitoring the voting behaviour of citizens, (Mainwaring 1999; Brusco, Nazareno and Stokes 2001), it is not hard to see that politicians would prefer to allocate these benefits to those whose political support they can better verify, such as party activists who work for them in election campaigns. Therefore, I argue that as economic conditions change and resources become scarcer, the networks that are formed around the distribution of material benefits include a narrower circle of supporters – such as party members (militants) rather than just voters – whose compliance with the exchanges' obligations the politicians can more easily monitor.[10]

Trade and capital account liberalisation

Privatisation is not the only way in which market reforms reduce the resources available to politicians for particularistic exchanges. As developing countries open their economies, they have to be more careful about their fiscal deficits. With the globalisation of capital markets, countries that open their capital accounts face a high degree of volatility in private capital accounts (Calvo and Mendoza 2000). When forming their decisions of where to invest, international investors update their information about possible returns to their investment in each country, which are clearly linked to macroeconomic performance (Jaspersen 1996). As the Russian and Brazilian currency crises of the 1990s show, large fiscal deficits can serve as a signal of problems with the economy and can build up to factors that lead to capital outflows (Calvo and Mendoza 2000). Therefore, as Jaspersen (1996) argues, states whose economy is linked to the global capital market have more incentives to improve the domestic investment climate in order to attract

---

10. As discussed by Gunes-Ayata (1992), parties, in the case of her study, the Republican People's Party in Turkey, used patronage jobs for party work even in the period prior to the neo-liberal reforms. However, the socio-economic changes are important in intensifying the pressures on parties and politicians for using these jobs effectively for political returns.

more foreign capital or to prevent major capital outflows.[11]

Keeping a healthy fiscal balance is definitely one major aspect that would help a country to be more attractive to investors. As such, after liberalising their economies, states in countries like Argentina and Turkey have found themselves under greater pressure to constrain state spending in order to prevent large fiscal deficits that would alarm foreign investors. In addition to the direct effects of fiscal deficits on investor confidence, fiscal policy was central for stabilisation efforts. In order to get inflation down, both countries abandoned free floating exchange rate systems. This, in turn, required the governments to tighten fiscal policy to avoid deficits. Clearly, in Argentina with the Convertibility Plan that set a one to one parity of the currency to the dollar, the pressures were even stronger. As the economic crises in both countries during the 1990s showed, such pressure did not necessarily lead to the desired outcome of no or low levels of fiscal deficits, but did make it more costly for politicians to manipulate state expenditures for their own political gain.

Decentralisation

In parallel with economic liberalisation efforts, both countries initiated a transfer of decision-making and spending responsibilities to lower levels of government. As in the case of privatisation, time wise Turkey lagged much behind, compared to Argentina. In addition, the federal character of Argentina, its long history of decentralisation (and recentralisation) attempts since the time of independence (Halperin-Donghi 1993; Eaton 2004), and the emphasis put on the unitary nature of the Turkish Republic since the fall of the Ottoman Empire (Yavuz 2002) made these countries start the decentralisation process from quite disparate initial points.

In Argentina, the increase in the provinces' responsibilities in health care and primary education took place starting with the military government (Eaton 2004: 145) even though the military also cut the level of revenue transfers from the federal government to the provinces. Four major changes occurred in the democratic period: First, in 1988 the new Coparticipation Law[12] gave provincial governments a larger share of the federal transfers. Second, this was partially overturned in 1992 and 1993 when the percentage was decreased (Daughters and Harper 2007), but a minimum floor guarantee[13] was established. Even though this meant that provincial governments would lose resources in the immediate aftermath of the 1992–3 Fiscal Pacts, the provinces stood to gain from the minimum floor arrangement starting with the economic downturn of the late 1990s (Eaton 2005). Third, the value of the mini-

---

11. See Fanelli and Machinea (1994) for a discussion on macroeconomic stability and capital movements in Argentina. Not only do open capital markets put additional pressures on countries for macroeconomic stability, but according to Bhagwati and Srinivasan (2002), countries that opt for freer trade have to maintain macroeconomic stability.

12. Co-Participation refers to the revenue sharing agreement that was reached between the two levels of government (federal and provincial) in 1934.

13. The *piso mínimo* (minimum floor) in 1992 referred to the transfer of U.S. $720 million every month to provinces. This was raised to $740 million in 1993 (Eaton 2005).

mum floor was negotiated several times until February 2002, when it was finally eliminated (Eaton 2005). Four, in contrast to the revenue transfers, the devolution of health care and education responsibilities saw a linear trend. The provinces acquired the sole responsibility for hospitals and secondary schools in 1991 (Daughters and Harper 2007). Overall, Argentina stands as a highly decentralised system with the sub-national expenditures constituting around 50 per cent of the national expenditure in 1996 and 2004 (Daughters and Harper 2007).

In Turkey, decentralisation is a much more recent phenomenon. It appeared in the public debate approximately around the time of the JDP's ascendancy to power in the 2002 elections, and materialised with the introduction of four new laws in 2004 and 2005 that regulate the provincial and local administrations, local municipalities and the metropolitan municipalities.[14] Although these new laws made some changes to the decision-making structure of the sub-national governments, in essence they mostly involved the devolution of expenditure responsibilities to local governments and the clarification of the assignment of these responsibilities among different administrative units.

From the perspective of our question, that is, the supply of patronage jobs by politicians, the decentralisation process in Argentina and Turkey (and more broadly in other developing countries) is relevant because it could have reversed the trend initiated by the neo-liberal reforms of making public jobs a scarce commodity in the sub-national administrations. While these economic reforms, especially privatisations, reduced the overall number of public employees that can be hired through patronage networks, this limitation on the governments can be offset at the sub-national level by increases in resources and transfer of personnel due to decentralisation.

In the case of Turkey, the lack of data for the period following the decentralisation reform prevents the empirical analysis of this possibility. The analysis of public employment figures in Argentina does not show an increasing trend uniformly for all provinces either with decentralisation or with time. Even though 210,000 personnel are estimated to be transferred to provincial jurisdiction as a result of administrative reform (Fontdevila 1994), as can be seen in Figure 2.1, the number of employees per one thousand people does show an increasing trend with time only in approximately one third of the provinces. A leap around the late 1980s can be observed in some provinces such as Jujuy, Neuquen, La Pampa, and Chubut, but the increase is relatively small in most provinces with the exception of Jujuy. In the rest, there is either no change or there are fluctuations with time that do not display a pattern that can be correlated with the decentralisation process. In a few cases there is even a linear decrease with time.

One limitation of this data is clearly the possibility of only observing changes in the aggregate. Some of the transfers in personnel might not appear in the aggregate data as increases because it might have been paralleled with decreases in employment that resulted from voluntary or early retirement programs (Author's

---

14. More information regarding these new laws can be found at http://www.yerelnet.org.tr/mevzuat/ makale_01.php and http://www.belgenet.com/hukuk.html.

interviews). However, regarding opportunities for patronage, decentralisation is even likely to have hurt the ability of the provincial politicians to hire new patronage workers, since some of the positions that opened up from the retirement programs were filled by transfers of personnel that used to be under the central government's jurisdiction.

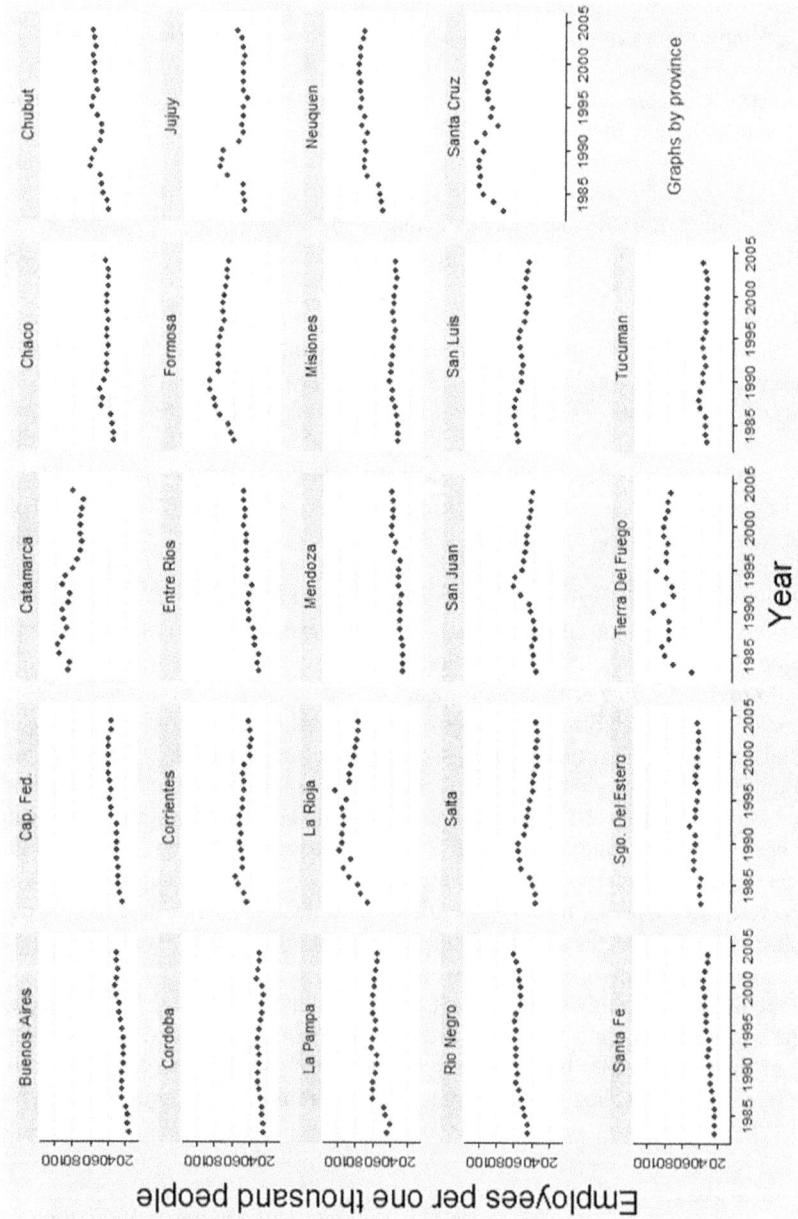

Figure 2.1: Decentralisation and the size of public employment in Argentina

Source: ProvInfo, Ministry of Interior.

Effects of economic liberalisation on citizens' perceptions

The preceding discussion illustrates how changing economic conditions affect the calculations or perceptions on the politicians' side by making it more costly for them to distribute patronage jobs. If we look at the exchange from the perspective of the receivers (demand side), we can again see that structural changes have had a strong impact. As the existing literature has very well described, voters' calculations or perceptions of the relationship with politicians and parties are influenced by private sector alternatives in the economy. When citizens are dependent on the state to fulfil their immediate needs, such as income (in the case of public employment), income supplements, education, and health-care, they are more inclined to prioritise particularistic exchanges with politicians to public goods and ideology. This suggests that, in places with low private sector productivity, a larger circle of citizens would demand to be included in politician-citizen linkages that are formed around the exchange of particularistic exchanges. Without doubt, private sector productivity is, in turn, affected by larger structural changes.

Unemployment

The outcome of the economic reform processes has been largely a disappointment for both countries of analysis in terms of job creation. While it was expected that economic reform would lead to growth which then would decrease unemployment, even when these countries saw high levels of growth, the decrease in unemployment was mostly slower, or in some periods non-existent. This is clearly evident in Figure 2.2 that displays the data on growth rates and unemployment for both countries. In relative terms, Argentina saw more fluctuations in the rate of unemployment compared to Turkey. Also, starting with 1997, the unemployment rate in Argentina rose to very high levels, reaching almost 20 per cent in 2002, while in Turkey the unemployment rate stayed in the 6.5 to 14 per cent range in the period after 1987, with the higher levels dominating the recent years after 2000. Even though there are important differences between the two countries, and Turkey has been more successful in keeping unemployment down until recently, the one common point is that joblessness remained as a major economic and social problem in both countries, especially so for Argentina. This means that for a considerable share of the population a job in the public administration still has a lot of value, keeping or even increasing the demand for jobs that can be accessed through clientelistic networks.

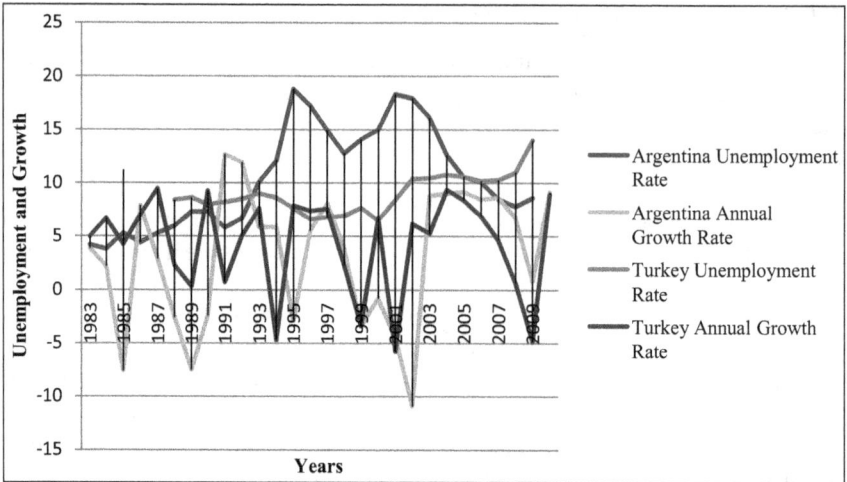

Figure 2.2: Unemployment and growth rate in Argentina and Turkey, 1983–2010
Source: World Development Indicators (World Bank).

Regional variations

One outstanding feature of the structural transformations in the Argentinean and Turkish economies over the last two-three decades has been provincial (regional) variation in private sector responses to these changes. As has been widely argued, opening the indigenous economy to international competition hurts those parts of the economy that were previously protected by the state.[15] Not only can this increase unemployment in general,[16] which makes citizens more dependent on state resources, it also brings about regional differences. In both countries, as a result of active state policy that promoted certain industries in some regions and other historical and geographical reasons,[17] regions differ with respect to the concentration of different types of industries and firm characteristics.

These initial characteristics of localities at the start of the liberalisation process, in turn, shape how a local economy responds to structural changes such as trade and capital account opening. These regional divergences are especially visible in job creation by the private sector. While the discussion of how opening an

---

15. See Lloyd-Sherlock (1997), Vacs and Renwick (1998), and Frenkel and Rozada (2001) as examples of country specific analysis for the Argentinean case and Nas and Odekon (1998) and Boratav, Yeldan, and Kose (2001) for the Turkish case.

16. The reductions in employment were especially high for full-time workers (Frenkel and Rozada 2001, Vacs and Renwick 1998).

17. See Keeling (1997) for an extensive discussion on regional variation in Argentina. The analysis covers government policies and geographical factors that have shaped these differences across regions and provinces.

economy to trade and capital flows affects the labour market is beyond the scope of this book,[18] it is important to note here that the availability of foreign capital and international competition have had diverse effects on local labour markets according to the concentration of industry in terms of its trade orientation (whether it is concentrated in the tradable sector, export sector or import-competing sector) and firm size (Levinsohn 1999). Since political units (provinces, municipalities) within the same country vary with respect to these aspects of their industry, labour markets in these different localities have adjusted to trade and capital account liberalisation in different ways. This, in turn, has affected citizens' alternatives in the private sector.

Variation across provinces in Argentina in terms of job creation by the private sector can be seen in Table 2.1. The data comes from national censuses that were conducted in the years 1980, 1991, and 2001. Since all these three years coincide with economic crises, we can expect that some overall downsizing might have occurred in employment figures. Still, the data is useful to illustrate some general trends across provinces over the years. The table presents percentage changes in private sector and total employment between the years 1980 and 1991 and between 1991 and 2001. The figures are controlled for population change. The second period between 1991 and 2001 can easily be associated with open markets both in terms of trade and capital accounts. The trade barriers were reduced very drastically in the beginning of the 1990s (Murillo 2001; Lloyd-Sherlock 1997; Fanelli and Machinea 1994) and important steps to open capital accounts were started in August 1989 with the Ley de Emergencia Economica (Law of Economic Emergency) that set equal terms for both domestic and international capital that would be used for production (Fanelli and Machinea 1994: 15).

However, such a clear-cut classification for the first period between 1980 and 1991 is not easy to make because of failed attempts to liberalise in the late 1970s. Even though full trade liberalisation was never attained through these reforms in the late 1970s, the capital market was opened to international flows (Fanelli and Machinea 1994). However, after large outflows of capital in 1981, these policies were completely reversed in 1982 (Fanelli and Machinea 1994). Therefore, the Argentinean economy in the decade between 1980 and 1990, can be characterised as a closed economy, but only with the caveat about the failed attempts to liberalise the economy in the late 1970s and early 1980s. Rather, the 1980s in Argentina can be easily associated with the deep economic crisis that preceded liberalisation efforts in the 1990s.

---

18. See Davis *et al.* (1996) for a survey of the literature on job creation and destruction and Roberts and Tybout (1996) for firm-level empirical analysis of how trade liberalisation affects employment in developing countries.

Table 2.1: Employment across regions in Argentina
Columns 1–6 include employment figures as proportions of the total population.
Columns 7–8 show percentage changes in private sector employment.

Province	1980 public	1980 private	1991 public	1991 private	2001 public	2001 private	1980–1991 private	1991–2001 private
Northwest								
La Rioja	0.11	0.09	0.15	0.09	0.13	0.11	2.79	12.88
Catamarca	0.10	0.08	0.13	0.08	0.11	0.09	-1.66	13.99
Jujuy	0.08	0.14	0.09	0.11	0.08	0.11	-24.08	1.30
Salta	0.07	0.13	0.08	0.11	0.06	0.11	-17.72	-1.92
Santiago del Estero	0.07	0.09	0.07	0.09	0.06	0.08	-6.36	-2.15
Tucuman	0.07	0.14	0.07	0.11	0.06	0.11	-23.24	1.01
Patagonia								
Chubut	0.11	0.17	0.10	0.15	0.09	0.15	-11.91	0.46
Neuquen	0.11	0.14	0.11	0.13	0.12	0.12	-6.49	-6.95
Rio Negro	0.08	0.17	0.08	0.15	0.08	0.14	-9.30	-6.30
Santa Cruz	0.17	0.19	0.19	0.12	0.16	0.14	-34.71	15.71
Tierra del Fuego	0.19	0.25	0.15	0.18	0.14	0.17	-28.84	-8.86
Pampaena								
Buenos Aires	0.07	0.19	0.06	0.17	0.06	0.15	-8.11	-10.08
Cap. Fed.	0.08	0.19	0.07	0.21	0.07	0.23	7.66	9.12
Cordoba	0.07	0.15	0.06	0.14	0.06	0.16	-8.41	13.96
Entre Rios	0.08	0.12	0.08	0.11	0.08	0.12	-3.48	3.65
La Pampa	0.08	0.15	0.09	0.14	0.10	0.14	-7.28	0.10
Santa Fe	0.07	0.15	0.06	0.14	0.06	0.14	-6.83	-0.62
Cuyo								
Mendoza	0.07	0.17	0.07	0.15	0.06	0.14	-12.76	-4.49
San Juan	0.07	0.14	0.08	0.13	0.07	0.13	-11.08	3.91
San Luis	0.11	0.12	0.09	0.16	0.08	0.14	32.97	-9.27
Northeast								
Chaco	0.06	0.12	0.07	0.12	0.07	0.09	0.96	-29.53
Corrientes	0.08	0.11	0.08	0.09	0.07	0.09	-12.22	2.60
Formosa	0.08	0.09	0.09	0.07	0.08	0.06	-19.27	-8.67
Misiones	0.06	0.13	0.06	0.11	0.05	0.10	-13.17	-13.01

Source: INDEC National Population Census.

With these major economic changes of the two decades in mind, it is useful to take a look at how employment patterns have changed through time and across provinces. Figures in Table 2.1 clearly support the argument that provinces among themselves vary with respect to how their labour markets have adjusted to the structural changes in the economy. If we concentrate on the second period between 1991 and 2001, percentage changes in the number of employees in the private sector range from the lowest of -29.3 per cent in Chaco to the highest of 15.7 per cent in Santa Cruz. However, these changes in the labour market across provinces, and two different periods do not necessarily match the arguments that interior provinces have been hurt more by recent structural transformations (Keeling 1997: xviii). Clearly, Chaco fits the expected pattern. Since Chaco is one of the poorest provinces in the northern interior with limited resources and infrastructure, it was expected that trade and capital account liberalisation would hurt the local private labour market and the data seems to support the expectations. While from 1980 to 1991, the private sector employment increased by 0.97 per cent, from 1991 to 2001 it decreased by -29.5 per cent.

However, other poor regions of the north, that were expected to show similar characteristics in their adjustment to the structural changes, do not necessarily follow the same pattern. For example, Catamarca and La Rioja seem to be following a totally distinct trajectory. In contrast to Chaco, the private sector employment in Catamarca decreased in the first period with -1.66 per cent. Then, it experienced a surge in job creation, and private sector jobs increased by 14 per cent from 1991 to 2001. A similar trend can also be observed for La Rioja. If we look at Table 2.1 where the provinces are categorised according to regions, such variation within regions is clearly observable. This variation can partly be explained by the effects of privatisation.[19] Even though there have been decreases in the total number of employees as a result of privatisation, there has been a net transfer in employees from the public to the private sector. Consequently, this leads to some artificial inflation in the number of private sector employees in the provinces that were affected most by privatisation, and it is not necessarily a sign that the private sector has been improving its capacity to generate new employment.

Unfortunately, quantified data on the provincial effects of privatisation do not exist. Therefore, it is not possible to systematically control for the effects of privatisation. However, we can look at examples of individual enterprise privatisation and the composition of production in each province to get a better understanding of these changes in private sector employment. The province of Santa Cruz with the largest percentage increase in private sector employment is an obvious example. With the privatisation of YPF and Gas del Estado the province experienced a major restructuring of its economy. Although these sectors have not necessarily performed well in generating new jobs (Schinelli and Vacca 1999: 47), their privatisation means that 4,709 employees working in that sector are now included in the private sector category (INDEC, Census 2001).

---

19. I thank Rebecca Weitz-Shapiro for drawing my attention to the effects of privatisation.

If we analyse the employment patterns of the Capital Federal and the 19 departments of the province of Buenos Aires, we see a similar shift from the public to the private sector.[20] According to the 1991 census (INDEC, *Censo Nacional de Poblacion y Vivienda*), 18,596 people in the 19 departments of Greater Buenos Aires were employed in the public sector under the following categories of activity – electricity, gas and water.[21] When we look at the figures from the 2001 census[22], there is a reverse trend. Under the same categories of activity- electricity, gas and water – 17,673 people are now employed in the private sector and only 1,507 in the public sector.[23] This means that the job creation capacity of the private sector in Greater Buenos Aires actually deteriorated even more than the figures in Table 2.1 show, since a part of the increase in private jobs is only a reflection of job transfers from the public to the private sector.

Due to the lack of systematic data on privatisation at the provincial level I cannot unfortunately analyse how much of these provincial and regional variations in job creation truly reflect how the local private labour markets responded to the economic transformations. One clear conclusion that we can derive from the analysis of provincial level employment at the private and public sectors, is that there is variation across provinces in terms of private sector alternatives in the labour market.[24] Even though we cannot say that these changes undoubtedly fit the expectation that, initially poorer regions would be hurt more by these structural transformations, it can be clearly observed that while in some provinces the private sector could generate more jobs and, in turn, could reduce the dependence of citizens on the state, other provinces lagged behind. Consequently, this is expected to lead to different patterns across Argentina's provinces in terms of citizens' propensities to engage in particularistic exchanges with politicians (due to varied needs for patronage jobs).

When we analyse the impact of economic restructuring on local labour markets in Turkey, we observe similar trends. Unfortunately, the data on employment in Turkey are even more limited. The only available information on the distribution of jobs across the public and private sectors exists for manufacturing and numbers of employees are reported only for those firms that employ more than

20. I am not able to present similar comparisons for the rest of the 22 provinces because I could get access to the data on the distribution of employees across activity types in 1991 for only the Capital Federal and the province of Buenos Aires.

21. State enterprises in all three sectors were privatised. The distribution across the three sectors was as follows: 12,176 in electricity, 4,289 in gas and 2,131 in the water sector.

22. The 2001 Census presents data for the 24 departments of Buenos Aires.

23. The corresponding figures for the Capital Federal are as follows: in 1991, of 8,677 employees (or workers) in the electricity, gas and water sector, 7,741 were in the public sector and 936 in the private sector. In 2001, the total number of employees under this category of activities was 6,958. 707 were employed in the public sector. 6,251 were employed in the private sector.

24. If we look at the data on percentage change in private sector employment (controlled for population), we can see that provincial variation is slightly smaller for the 1991–2001 period (10.00) when compared to the 1980–1991 period (13.07). See Table 2.1.

ten people.[25] Still, analysing these data might give us some idea about the private sector alternatives of citizens across provinces. Even though the information is available annually for the period between 1983 and 2001, for an easier comparison with Argentina here I present the percentage changes in the number of employees for two periods, 1983–1992 and 1992–2001.

Similar to Argentina, these periods coincide with significant structural changes in the Turkish economy. Yet, as I have already mentioned, the liberalisation process has been moving much more gradually in Turkey. Therefore, in contrast to Argentina where we can argue that the second period (1991–2001) reflects the effects of structural change more clearly than the first period, these two periods in Turkey coincide with continuous gradual change. In Turkey, earlier periods of these structural changes focused more on increasing the role of market forces in the economy through the elimination of price controls on state owned enterprises and the reductions of subsidies (Onis 1998). Even though the first steps of trade liberalisation were taken in the beginning of the eighties, especially with the removal of quotas for some imports and some adjustments of tariff rates in December 1983 (Onis 1998: 354–358), the process continued into the 1990s.

With respect to capital accounts, the climax occurred in August 1989 with the liberalisation of the stock market (Onis 1998; Henry 2003). Therefore, for Turkey we can say that the observed changes in public and private sector employment reflect how the labour market responded to a more gradual economic transformation that started in the beginning of the 1980s.[26] As in Argentina, in terms of its impact on citizen-politician linkages, what is important to observe when we look at the data on employment patterns across provinces (Table 2.2) is that in some provinces the dependence of citizens on public employment actually increased rather than decreased. Before any further discussion of the figures, it is important to remind ourselves of one critical shortcoming in the data, that it covers only the manufacturing sector. This is particularly a concern with respect to the service sector whose development in recent years has been a significant part of the recent economic transformation. Provinces with large urban centres have particularly benefited from the growth of the service sector. Therefore, negative growth patterns of provinces such as Istanbul and Izmir in Table 2.2 can partly be accounted for by the diminishing importance of the manufacturing sector relative to the service sector.

With these limitations in mind, we can still analyse general trends in the local private and public labour markets. As in Argentina, in both periods there is high variation across provinces. In the second period between 1992 and 2001, the percentage change ranges from -51.47 per cent in Rize to a high of 296 per cent

---

25. The data were collected by TÜİK (Turkish Institute of Statistics – formerly called as DIE, National Statistics Institute) through firm-level surveys and provided as "İmalat Sanayi İl Özet Tablosu (Provincial Summary Table on Manufacturing Sector)".

26. For a detailed econometric analysis of the effects of trade liberalisation on labour markets in Turkey with a focus on industry variation and labour demand elasticises, see Krishna, Mitra, and Chinoy (2001).

Table 2.2: Private and public sector employment across provinces in Turkey

Columns 1–6 include employment figures as percentages of total population
Columns 7–8 show percentage changes in private sector employment

Province	1983 public	1983 private	1992 public	1992 private	2001 public	2001 private	1983–1992 private	1992–2001 private
Adana	0.66	4.31	1.01	4.02	0.26	2.47	-6.85	-38.60
Adiyaman	0.72		0.59	0.24	0.12	0.11		-51.47
Afyon	1.26	0.44	0.99	1.18	0.57	0.79	168.74	-33.41
Agri	0.15	0.00	0.44	0.00	0.26	0.00		
Amasya	0.97	0.26	0.13	0.90	0.00	0.87	242.06	-3.66
Ankara	1.71	1.39	0.69	1.98	0.35	2.33	41.83	17.62
Antalya	0.62	0.83	0.32	0.63	0.08	0.51	-24.76	-18.17
Artvin	2.53	0.00	2.16	0.07	1.09	0.00		-100.00
Aydin	0.73	1.52	0.40	1.31	0.13	1.37	-13.99	4.93
Balikesir	1.06	0.97	0.88	1.39	0.52	1.94	42.77	39.48
Bilecik	0.92	5.04	0.62	9.53	0.15	9.57	89.22	0.43
Bingol			0.08	0.00	0.07	0.00		
Bitlis	0.46	0.00	0.34	0.00	0.16	0.00		
Bolu	0.73	1.62	0.61	3.02	0.15	4.42	86.58	46.33
Burdur	1.28	0.67	1.01	0.81	0.60	1.56	19.98	93.89
Bursa	1.19	5.79	0.74	8.12	0.17	9.26	40.08	14.09
Canakkale	0.06	2.36	0.16	2.29	0.13	1.58	-2.60	-31.07
Cankiri	0.19	0.03	0.49	0.26	0.30	0.75	700.27	186.87
Corum	0.13	0.51	0.26	1.10	0.17	1.28	118.07	15.83
Denizli	0.37	2.24	0.45	3.13	0.02	10.01	40.13	219.74
Diyarbakir	0.49	0.03	0.44	0.09	0.15	0.08	235.72	-12.41
Edirne	0.09	3.87	0.13	1.81	0.00	2.01	-53.13	10.78
Elazig	1.56	0.32	1.46	0.66	0.75	0.37	109.45	-43.93
Erzincan	1.43	0.36	1.35	0.17	0.60	0.20	-52.01	18.18
Erzurum	0.52	0.11	0.41	0.10	0.17	0.11	-4.79	6.65
Eskisehir	2.76	2.47	1.87	3.42	1.06	4.37	38.56	27.73
Gaziantep	0.31	1.52	0.18	2.50	0.04	3.45	64.01	38.28
Giresun	0.55	0.67	0.38	0.72	0.24	0.83	7.12	16.27
Gumushane	0.02	0.00	0.11	0.00	0.15	0.00		
Hakkari	0.03	0.00	0.11	0.00	0.20	0.00		
Hatay	3.43	0.63	2.39	0.64	0.80	0.62	0.27	-2.51
Isparta	0.86	1.10	0.50	1.10	0.06	1.68	0.18	52.60
Icel	0.07	2.81	0.24	1.44	0.10	1.64	-48.77	13.87
Istanbul	0.98	8.88	0.43	7.57	0.15	5.66	-14.76	-25.17
Izmir	1.73	5.55	1.35	5.25	0.57	4.61	-5.30	-12.20
Kars	0.25	0.02	0.43	0.07	0.41	0.12	298.40	81.53

Province	1983 public	1983 private	1992 public	1992 private	2001 public	2001 private	1983–1992 private	1992–2001 private
Kastamonu	0.59	0.22	1.03	0.47	0.67	1.08	116.85	132.07
Kayseri	1.21	2.28	0.79	3.00	0.11	4.27	31.70	42.61
Kirklareli	1.15	1.90	0.91	3.26	0.41	9.20	71.56	182.24
Kirsehir	0.03	0.24	0.61	0.40	0.21	0.35	69.05	-12.27
Kocaeli	4.13	11.36	1.59	8.23	0.59	9.74	-27.55	18.35
Konya	1.73	0.75	1.13	0.88	0.50	1.09	17.10	23.80
Kutahya	1.39	0.68	0.91	1.17	0.39	1.20	70.98	2.76
Malatya	1.85	0.21	1.45	0.47	0.57	1.15	126.61	144.07
Manias	0.37	1.85	0.23	3.01	0.11	3.47	62.29	15.42
K.maras	0.35	0.10	0.39	0.69	0.12	1.41	566.57	103.20
Mardin	0.01	0.00	0.03	0.19	0.04	0.17		-14.58
Mugla	0.95	0.30	0.60	0.13	0.01	0.30	-57.59	135.11
Mus	0.36	0.00	0.43	0.00	0.29	0.00		
Nevsehir			0.33	0.75	0.29	0.60		-20.93
Nigde	0.20	0.37	0.81	0.69	0.45	0.88	85.42	26.59
Ordu	0.14	0.61	0.07	0.69	0.02	0.92	13.16	33.31
Rize	7.61	0.04	6.39	1.03	4.06	0.50	2,774.32	-51.47
Sakarya	2.36	1.37	1.20	1.81	0.72	3.19	31.48	76.64
Samsun	2.57	0.52	1.66	0.65	0.51	0.60	25.38	-8.44
Siirt	1.47	0.00	0.28	0.00	0.00	0.00		
Sinop	0.71	1.08	0.89	0.36	0.00	0.22	-66.81	-37.36
Sivas	1.10	0.10	1.14	0.05	0.75	0.21	-46.89	296.95
Tekirdag	0.24	6.22	0.26	9.38	0.15	14.43	50.80	53.93
Tokat	0.85	0.31	0.89	0.56	0.62	0.40	79.77	-27.45
Trabzon	4.91	1.91	0.84	0.47	0.47	0.56	-75.30	18.55
Tunceli	0.01	0.00	0.12	0.00				
Sanliurfa	0.29	0.17	0.14	0.05	0.02	0.13	-72.52	173.19
Usak	0.75	1.31	0.77	2.52	0.45	2.97	92.14	17.97
Van	0.24	0.03	0.44	0.00	0.26	0.06	-100.00	
Yozgat	0.17	0.16	0.08	0.23	0.23	0.16	39.78	-30.13
Zonguldak	4.13	0.57	5.38	0.86	2.27	0.66	50.61	-22.91

Source: TÜİK

in Sivas. When we look at the first period between 1983 and 1992, we again see a wide range from the lowest of -75.3 per cent in Trabzon to the highest of 2,774 per cent in Rize.[27] As in the case of Argentina, these figures might be affected by employment shifts from the public to the private sector as a result of privatisation. Therefore, percentage changes in some provinces might be higher than the real job creation rates in the private manufacturing sector. However, compared to Argentina, I expect this effect to be less important since, as I have already pointed out, privatisation in Turkey was relatively slower until 2005.

More than privatisation, another aspect of the structural transformation was crucial for Turkey in this period: the export boom that took place after trade liberalisation (Onis 1998; Rodrik 1992). In line with the findings of the multiple-country analysis of trade's impact on employment (Krueger et al. 1983), time-series analysis of the trade flow's impact on employment in the manufacturing sector in Turkey, shows support that export-based employment has been dominant in the employment growth of the post-1980 period (Erlat 2000). Therefore, we would expect variation across provinces in terms of employment growth to be related to export-based production.

However, unfortunately, there are no studies that have analysed the regional or provincial impact of trade on Turkey.[28] Here, I present just the correlation between the percentage changes in private manufacturing sector employment from 1992 to 1997 and the changes in exports as a share of total production (see Table 2.3). The negative and low magnitude correlation (-0.12) clearly does not imply that there is no relation between export-based production and job creation, but it suggests that the relationship is complicated by other characteristics of the provincial economy, such as the initial as well as changing sector[29] and factor (capital, technology, and labour) allocations within industries and firms.

Another aspect of economic liberalisation that could affect provincial labour markets is foreign direct investment (FDI). The regional determinants of FDI in Turkey are analysed by Deichmann, Karidis, and Sayek (2003). They show that provinces that have deep local financial markets, human capital, and coastal access get higher levels of FDI. Therefore, following their analysis, we can look at the average proportion of private bank credit that was supplied in each province between the years 1992 and 1997 as one indicator of the provinces' propensity

---

27. The standard deviations of these variables are 390.89 and 74 consecutively for the two periods, 1983–1992 and 1992–2001. Clearly, variation across provinces in terms of job creation in the private sector is much higher for the first period.

28. The National Planning Organisation of Turkey has conducted some studies on regional development and inequalities. See its website (http://www.dpt.gov.tr/bgyu) for these studies. 'Illerin sosyo-ekonomik gelismislik siralamasi arastirmasi' (Research on Provincial Socio-economic Development Ranking) (1996) by Dinçer, Özaslan and Satilmis provides a good background on regional and provincial differences in Turkey.

29. Even though Krishna, Mitra and Chinoy's (2001) analysis of the impact of trade liberalisation on labour demand elasticises in the manufacturing sector of the greater Istanbul area shows no evidence for a relationship at the plant level, export-orientation, through its effect on investments, might lead to higher rates of job creation in local economies where labour intensive sectors are dominant.

to attract foreign investment. This, in turn, is expected to increase private sector employment in these provinces. When we look at Table 2.3, which includes the data on private bank credit, we can see that with the exception of Afyon, Antalya, Istanbul, and Adana, provinces with the highest proportion of private bank credit, and that are close to the coast, have indeed experienced high rates of increases in private sector employment. As these figures show, provinces that initially had more developed capital markets and occupy more advantageous geographical locations have benefited more from recent economic changes.

In both countries, the analysis of regional economic development throughout the 1980s and 1990s indicates major variations across provinces and regions. These distinct economic conditions, in turn, have made a higher share of citizens in some provinces dependent on state resources. Since this difference between provinces might have had an effect on the interaction between politicians and citizens, I carried out a qualitative in-depth analysis of the impact of political factors on particularistic exchanges of public jobs in two provinces in each country, that contrast with each other along these dimensions: Buenos Aires and Chaco in Argentina; and Istanbul and Bilecik in Turkey. In the statistical analyses of subnational administrations that are presented in Chapters Five and Six, I control for these socio-economic variations with only a rough measure of GDP per capita due to the lack of more detailed data. The purpose of the provincial case studies is to help the development of the theoretical arguments by exploring whether the nature of the politician-citizen linkages differs according to socio-economic dimensions. As I discuss in more detail in the empirical chapters, the distribution of patronage jobs in all cases involved the internal politics of parties rather than vote buying in general elections. This is largely due to the ineffectiveness of vote buying through patronage jobs, which I discuss in the following section.

Ineffectiveness of Vote Buying through Patronage Jobs

The first section of this chapter discusses how the economic liberalisation reforms in Argentina and Turkey have restricted the possibility of hiring new employees in the public administration. With the possibility of hiring only a small number of patronage workers and receiving votes in return, can the politicians and parties make a real difference in the election results? To illustrate the point, we can look at the changes in the total number of provincial personnel in Argentina between 1998 and 1999, the year when both national and provincial elections took place, and compare this change with the differences in the number of votes received by the two leading parties. It can be seen in Table 2.4 that in Tierra del Fuego, a new public job was created for almost every two votes. However, on the other extreme, in Santiago del Estero, while the difference in the votes was 84,672, only 182 new jobs were created. Across provinces, the average number of votes per every new job is 85.7. These figures suggest that even if we assume that all these new employees are hired through clientelistic ties, and take into account the possibility that the exchange of one job would also be accompanied by more than one vote, mostly by the family members of the new employee, we can see that on average

Table 2.3: Employment, exports and bank credits across provinces in Turkey, 1992–1997 Columns 1–4 include employment figures as percentages of total population. Column 5 shows the percentage change in private sector employment. Column 6 shows percentage changes in exports as a share of GDP. Column 7 presents each province's average credits as a share of total credits in the period between 1992 and 1997.

Provinces	1992 public emp.	1992 private emp.	1997 public emp.	1997 private emp.	1992–1997 private emp.	1992–1997 exports	1992–1997 credits
Adana	1.01	4.02	0.47	3.63	-0.095	0.344	9.00
Adiyaman	0.59	0.24	0.30	0.46	0.974	-	0.36
Afyon	0.99	1.18	0.21	0.38	-0.677	-	1.11
Agri	0.44	0.00	0.32	0.05	-	0.641	0.10
Amasya	0.13	0.90	0.00	1.11	0.229	-	0.68
Ankara	0.69	1.98	0.40	2.20	0.114	1.393	15.61
Antalya	0.32	0.63	0.15	0.62	-0.004	0.057	4.28
Artvin	2.16	0.07	2.75	0.00	-1.000	6.890	0.23
Aydin	0.40	1.31	0.24	1.69	0.293	-	1.47
Balikesir	0.88	1.39	0.61	1.72	0.236	-0.238	1.54
Bilecik	0.62	9.53	0.31	11.32	0.188	-	0.34
Bingol	0.08	0.00	0.09	0.00	-	-	0.12
Bitlis	0.34	0.00	0.16	0.00	-	-	0.13
Bolu	0.61	3.02	0.36	3.92	0.296	16.925	0.52
Burdur	1.01	0.81	0.79	1.45	0.797	-	0.46
Bursa	0.74	8.12	0.42	9.34	0.150	1.070	3.09
Canakkale	0.16	2.29	0.13	1.57	-0.318	0.007	0.81
Cankiri	0.49	0.26	0.29	0.68	1.608	-	0.35
Corum	0.26	1.10	0.15	1.55	0.401	-	0.87
Denizli	0.45	3.13	0.02	8.37	1.671	0.977	1.36
Diyarbakir	0.44	0.09	0.19	0.06	-0.389	0.554	0.42
Edirne	0.13	1.81	0.01	3.34	0.846	-0.658	3.42
Elazig	1.46	0.66	1.01	0.64	-0.033	-0.173	0.32
Erzincan	1.35	0.17	0.75	0.31	0.785	-	0.55
Erzurum	0.41	0.10	0.25	0.12	0.193	0.452	0.48
Eskisehir	1.87	3.42	1.22	4.59	0.340	1.965	0.93
Gaziantep	0.18	2.50	0.07	3.98	0.595	0.884	1.68
Giresun	0.38	0.72	0.31	1.15	0.604	3.116	6.67
Gumushane	0.11	0.00	0.17	0.00	-	-	0.10
Hakkari	0.11	0.00	0.52	0.00	-	-	0.02
Hatay	2.39	0.64	1.40	0.87	0.364	-0.090	0.88
Isparta	0.50	1.10	0.08	1.77	0.600	1.199	0.59

Provinces	1992 public emp.	1992 private emp.	1997 public emp.	1997 private emp.	1992–1997 private emp.	1992–1997 exports	1992–1997 credits
Icel	0.24	1.44	0.18	2.01	0.397	0.085	1.57
Istanbul	0.43	7.57	0.21	6.83	-0.097	0.300	7.85
Izmir	1.35	5.25	0.91	6.08	0.156	0.363	9.84
Kars	0.43	0.07	0.41	0.08	0.256	-0.537	0.48
Kastamonu	1.03	0.47	0.80	0.73	0.569	1.497	0.54
Kayseri	0.79	3.00	0.44	4.51	0.503	0.403	0.86
Kirklareli	0.91	3.26	0.41	0.00	-1.000	-	0.51
Kirsehir	0.61	0.40	0.86	0.47	0.168	-	0.43
Kocaeli	1.59	8.23	0.93	8.90	0.081	0.098	0.71
Konya	1.13	0.88	0.58	1.19	0.355	2.606	1.63
Kutahya	0.91	1.17	0.50	0.90	-0.229	-	0.51
Malatya	1.45	0.47	0.86	1.17	1.478	2.791	0.58
Manisa	0.23	3.01	0.15	3.08	0.025	0.649	1.93
K.maras	0.39	0.69	0.12	1.33	0.915	15.557	0.57
Mardin	0.03	0.19	0.05	0.06	-0.675	0.544	0.17
Mugla	0.60	0.13	0.31	0.26	1.083	0.207	1.18
Mus	0.43	0.00	0.36	0.00	-	-	0.13
Nevsehir	0.33	0.75	0.24	0.74	-0.019	-0.935	0.48
Nigde	0.81	0.69	0.39	0.73	0.056	-	0.40
Ordu	0.07	0.69	0.06	0.92	0.336	0.416	0.61
Rize	6.39	1.03	5.20	0.51	-0.505	23.799	0.20
Sakarya	1.20	1.81	0.92	2.71	0.498	28.119	0.58
Samsun	1.66	0.65	0.86	0.81	0.240	0.956	1.77
Siirt	0.28	0.00	0.17	0.00	-	-	0.05
Sinop	0.89	0.36	0.14	0.76	1.130	0.773	0.26
Sivas	1.14	0.05	1.12	0.16	1.951	-0.658	0.84
Tekirdag	0.26	9.38	0.16	15.84	0.689	-0.337	1.12
Tokat	0.89	0.56	0.75	0.59	0.065	-	0.87
Trabzon	0.84	0.47	0.55	0.67	0.423	13.772	0.62
Tunceli	0.12	0.00	0.07	0.00	-	-	0.16
Sanliurfa	0.14	0.05	0.04	0.07	0.478	-0.814	0.68
Usak	0.77	2.52	0.53	3.64	0.445	-	0.40
Van	0.44	0.00	0.40	0.03	-	2.579	0.22
Yozgat	0.08	0.23	0.10	0.17	-0.273	-	0.82
Zonguldak	5.38	0.86	2.35	0.73	-0.153	2.935	0.40

Sources: Employment and export information are provided by TÜİK. The data on bank credits is available at the Association of Turkish Banks' website.

the number of jobs that can be distributed to increase the share of votes in the elections is too limited to make a significant difference.

When I look at all gubernatorial elections, for which I have data, a similar picture emerges.[30] In the year preceding the elections, sixty-five incumbents out of one hundred and seven increased the size of personnel in their administrations.[31] However, only in nineteen out of these sixty-five, the ratio of the vote difference between the incumbent and the challenger to the increase in the number of employees was between -10 and 10. This means that in the rest of the gubernatorial elections, the use of patronage jobs for changing the election results was not an efficient strategy. It can be seen in Figure 2.3 that this conclusion does not depend on the arbitrary cut-off points of -10 and 10.

One can say that maybe the important figure is not the difference in the number of employees, but the aggregate number since politicians can expect to get the support of all their employees if they are the ones that hired these clients for these positions. However, as I will discuss in more detail in the empirical chapters, both countries, as most other middle income developing countries, have incorporated tenure in their civil service or public employment systems. This means that the aggregate figures reflect an accumulation of patronage workers, including those hired by previous governments.

Tenure creates an additional complication for politicians: Voters, if they are protected legally with tenure, might not have the incentive to alter their voting decisions with the threat of losing their jobs in the case of the incumbent not being re-elected. As one party official from Bilecik (Turkey) put it:

> We, during our incumbency, gave a man a position in the Telecom [state owned telecommunications company], population [institution], or for example, in the municipality, Tedas [a government enterprise]. The man does not recognise us anymore. It is not that we paid him ourselves. That's not it. We gave him an opportunity. Instead of someone else we put him there. There is loyalty. It is no longer left. He says: 'I already got the tenure'.[32]

In the case of jobs, this adds to the monitoring problem that is associated with vote buying. In addition to the politicians' (patrons') inability to verify the voting choice of the client due to the secret ballot, a repeated interaction between citizens and politicians, as analysed by Stokes (2005), does not work as an enforcement mechanism, either. When the job is protected by tenure, the continuation of the material benefit is not jeopardised by the politician's electoral failure and hence the client does not necessarily have an incentive to vote for his/her patron. Two ways that politicians and parties have managed to circumvent this problem

---

30. Unfortunately I cannot conduct a similar analysis on Turkey because data on the number of public employees across subnational units are not available.

31. These figures refer only to those provinces in which gubernatorial elections took place.

32. Author's interview (No. 39), January 2004. The explanations in parentheses are added by the author.

Table 2.4: Effectiveness of distributing jobs for votes (1999 elections)

Provinces	1998 number of employees	1999 number of employees	differences in votes of first two parties	differences in the number of employees	new jobs/ vote
Buenos Aires	365939	404655	284265	38716	7.34
Catamarca	22145	22963	12531	818	15.32
Chaco	40637	41776	147593	1139	129.58
Chubut	22349	22921	25444	572	44.48
Cap. Federal*	110847	114312	707122	3465	204.08
Cordoba	74369	72528	145854	-1841	-79.24
Corrientes*	42343	41401	62480	-942	-66.33
Entre Rios	49595	50283	10223	688	14.86
Formosa	32909	33440	97428	531	183.73
Jujuy	29133	28938	2936	-195	-15.06
La Pampa	17098	17178	29201	80	369.32
La Rioja	23253	23581	50753	328	154.74
Mendoza	54044	60347	47077	6303	7.47
Misiones	35577	35849	33029	272	121.43
Neuquen	34549	36177	15977	1628	9.81
Rio Negro	28430	28547	15716	117	134.02
Salta	38094	36238	80449	-1856	-43.35
San Juan	27866	29161	41633	1295	32.15
San Luis	16899	16652	14922	-247	-60.41
Santa Cruz	17728	17765	8872	37	239.78
Santa Fe	99792	101363	259640	1571	165.27
Sgo. Del Estero	34272	34454	84672	182	465.23
Tierra del Fuego	7010	7777	1380	767	1.80
Tucuman	46107	46306	4205	199	21.04
average					**85.71**

* For these cases I used the presidential election results because gubernatorial elections were not held.

Sources: The election results were obtained from Camara Nacional Electoral (National Electoral Chamber of Argentina). The data on public employees is provided by ProvInfo (Provincial Database of Ministry of Interior).

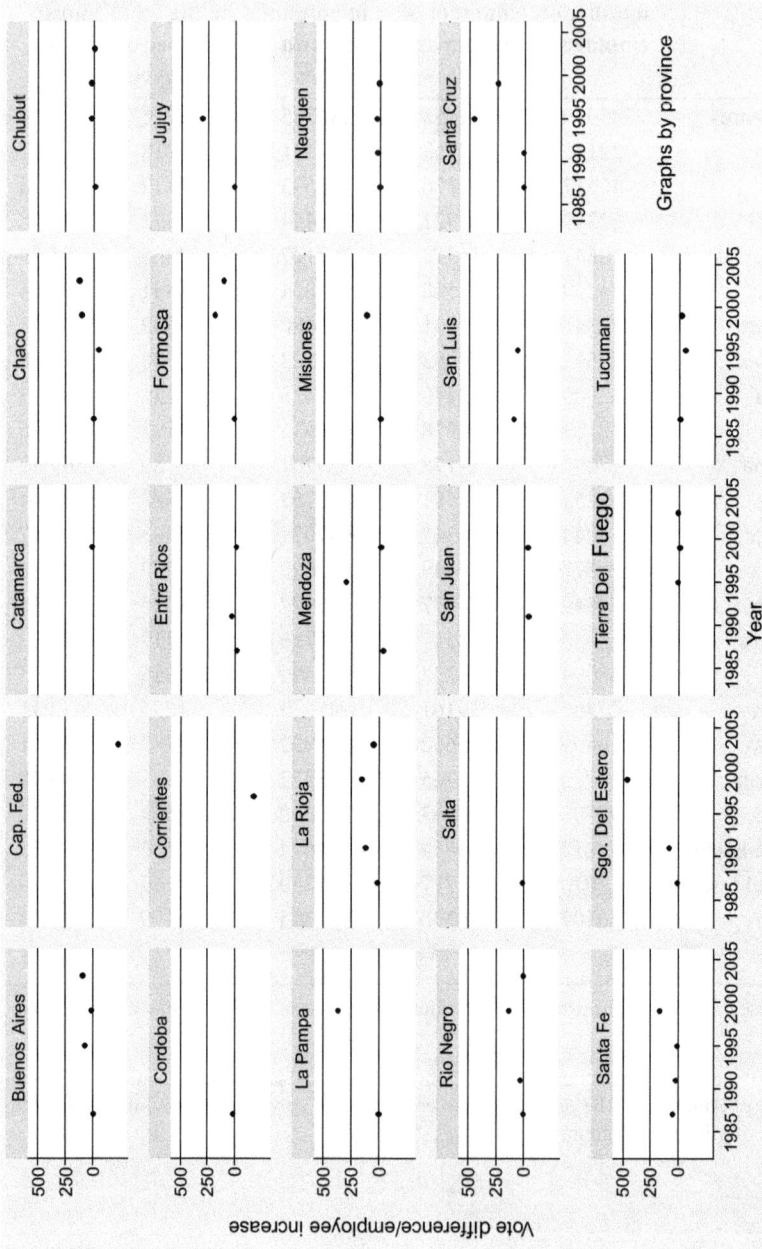

Figure 2.3: *Effectiveness of distributing jobs for votes (1987–2003 gubernatorial elections)*

Source: Election results were obtained from the website, Atlas Electoral de Andy Tow (http://www.towsa.com/andy/index.html). The data on public employees is provided by ProvInfo (Provincial Database of Ministry of Interior).

is through temporary contracts in both countries and hiring workers in contrast to civil servants in Turkey where the legal protection for workers is weaker compared to civil servants.[33]

However, due to budgetary and economic pressures that I have previously discussed in this chapter, increases in the number of employees have been limited in number. In turn, the scarcity of these jobs has made them more valuable for both politicians and citizens. As a result, politicians and parties want to make sure that they receive some type of political benefit in return when they give out these valuable and scarce patronage jobs. Rather than distributing jobs to citizens in return for their votes in general elections, which leads to monitoring problems and necessitates a larger number of jobs to make a difference in election results, politicians prefer to allocate these jobs in a direct and personal manner to active supporters in their parties.[34] Party members who participate in electoral campaigns, internal party elections, and daily party work receive the patronage jobs. We know, for example, of situations in which a party activist from the UCR found himself: 'I took 280 persons to vote. Next day, the guy from City Hall gave orders to give me a job there and the day after that I was at work' (Miguez 1995). Evidence from mass surveys also supports the idea that benefits of smaller material value, such as food baskets rather than jobs, are distributed in exchange for votes in general elections (Stokes 2005).

Even though, as I argue in Chapter Four, the nature of the electoral competition might be among the factors that influence the number of patronage jobs, or the extent of clientelism in public employment, in order to understand the mechanisms behind patronage jobs or the political factors that shape the relationships between elected office holders who distribute such jobs and their active supporters in the parties, we need to analyse the internal dynamics of political parties. This is what I do in the following chapter for Argentina and Turkey, in order to clarify why and how politicians and parties find it beneficial to hire their supporters in the public administration.

---

33. As I discuss in more detail in Chapter Three, there are also legal restrictions on the political party affiliation of civil servants in Turkey.

34. See Geddes and Neto (1992) for a discussion of the differences between ordinary citizens who have just votes to offer and other individuals who control more important political resources. A party activist who can devote his or her time to work for a politician or party's campaign would be an example of the latter.

chapter three | internal politics, organisation and role of patronage within argentinean and turkish parties

By clientelism you mean I hire you as personnel so that you work for me politically, right?

Author's interview with a Peronist provincial legislator (No. 60), May 2005.

As is true for all forms of patron-client relationships in democratic regimes, the formation and functioning of patronage networks in the context of public sector employment are affected by political competition. However, the literature has until now focused solely on one part of such competition – that between parties (candidates) in general elections (Kitschelt 2000; Brusco *et al.* 2001; Robinson and Verdier 2002; Medina and Stokes 2002; Wantchekon 2003; Chandra 2004; Calvo and Murillo 2004). Yet, for analytical purposes, we can distinguish between two separate stages of political competition in democracies: the general elections and the process of achieving candidacy.[1] Neither of these stages should be ignored if we are to understand the political and social factors that affect clientelism. Moreover, for understanding how clientelism works in the distribution of public jobs, analysing competition within parties is especially important in the aftermath of the political and socio-economic changes that these two countries experienced in the last two-three decades.[2]

Even though the kind of political support that politicians and parties expect from the recipients of public benefits might vary, the literature's focus on general elections has led to an emphasis on only one kind of political support: votes in general elections in return for the material benefits that are distributed. Yet, in the case of clientelism in public employment, allocating jobs to particular individuals in order to get their votes in a general election is not an efficient strategy. Limitations on the number of available jobs as a result of legislation introducing tenure,[3] privatisations, budget restrictions in large part resulting from broader eco-

---

1. As argued by Mayhew (1986), the party organisations are involved in both processes of electoral politics, nominating or general elections. See Benton (2007) for a discussion on the role of patronage as a first step in building political careers.

2. See Chapter Two for a review of these socioeconomic changes and their impact on particularistic exchanges between politicians and their supporters.

3. The 1949 constitution in Argentina introduced stability for all workers. According to the current national and provincial laws that regulate public employment, the permanent personnel have the right to stability. In Turkey, a detailed law on public employment was written in 1965. Although

nomic crises, and the consequent efforts to reduce the state, have made it difficult for politicians to distribute a sufficient number of jobs that would change election results.

Yet, as supported by interviews with politicians and public employees[4], we still observe political hirings at different levels of the public sector. If politicians cannot make an effective difference in the results of elections and if they cannot monitor the voting behaviour of the employees, why would they show any effort to allocate these public jobs to selected individuals who have close ties with the parties and politicians? I argue that the answer lies in how parties work in countries like Argentina and Turkey. The parties have a number of characteristics that shape the way in which electoral competition affects clientelism. These include the financing of parties, the role of party members and activists in campaigns for general and intra-party elections, and the rules for selecting candidates for public positions and party posts.

As the president of the electoral tribunal of the Radical party in Chaco described,[5] the party does not have the financial resources to hire the personnel to conduct the campaigns and do the daily work of the party in most provinces, cities, and smaller localities. As the president of the deliberative council of the locality, Pilar, in Buenos Aires argued,[6] only in some exceptional places like the Capital Federal[7] in Argentina do local politicians have the resources to conduct professional campaigns that use the media. In most other localities in Argentina, as well as in most areas of Turkey, house to house visits, face to face talks, coffee-house visits, *caminatas* (walks), and rallies constitute the major part of political campaigns.

Especially in places where unemployment is widespread and where the aver-

---

this law (Law No. 657) has gone through various modifications over the years, job security of the civil servants (memur) has remained intact.

4.   The interviewees for the research of this project included politicians from two main parties in Argentina, UCR and PJ, as well as some smaller national and provincial parties from three provinces, Buenos Aires, Chaco and Cordoba. In Turkey, the interviewees were selected from six parties that have participated in government in the period from 1983 to 2004: JDP (and its predecessors, WP and VP), RPP (and its predecessor, SPP), DLP, MP, TPP, and NAP (see list of Abbreviations). These politicians occupied positions either in the two provinces of Bilecik and Istanbul or in the national government and national party organisations with one exception. For both countries the selected politicians have occupied various public and party offices at the national, provincial, or municipal level. The interviewed public employees include three bureaucrats (from the federal government) in Argentina and various employees at the national and municipal level in Turkey. More than thirty interviews in each country have been conducted in the period between May 2002 and May 2005. When I quote the interviewees, I refer to their interview number. A comprehensive index with the public or political position of the interviewees, location and time of the interview can be found in Appendix D.

5.   Author's interview (No. 18), October 2003.

6.   Author's interview (No. 25), October 2003.

7.   Capital Federal refers to the City of Buenos Aires that hosts the federal government of Argentina. It has its own independent municipal government.

age income is low, as the ex-president of the Republican People's Party in the city of Çanakkale in Turkey, argued,[8] the people, the party members who participate in these activities are the ones who expect something in return and one of the most important type of benefits that they can receive is a job in the public sector. Not only do party campaigns depend on the voluntary work of the party activists and members, but also most of the party personnel who conduct the daily work of the party do not get any salaries. As the president of the electoral tribunal of the Radical party in Chaco stated, the personnel, including himself, work in other (mostly public) jobs in addition to their work in the party. Thus, exist concepts like *ñoquis*[9] in Argentina to refer to those public employees who show up at the work place only at the end of the month to get their salaries.

In this chapter, I provide a description of party financing, the role of party activists in electoral campaigns, and candidate nomination and party official selection processes of parties in Argentina and Turkey. I conclude with a discussion on how these three aspects of parties shape the context in which competition within parties takes place, where politicians distribute public jobs in a particularistic manner to party members and activists in order to build their independent power bases.

Party financing

In both countries, as in other developing democracies, how the political parties are financed is a widely debated political issue. However, detailed budgetary data from political parties and information about their campaign spending and resources are not easily accessible. Yet, in interviews with politicians, a recurring theme was the financial pressures on parties, especially at the provincial and local level. Decentralised organisations of the parties rarely have sufficient funds to conduct capital intensive campaigns before elections.

Turkey

National government support to political parties was introduced through a modification of the Political Parties Law (Law No. 2,820) in 1984 (Genckaya 2000). The specific amount was not written out in the legislation, but depended on the central government's annual budget. In the very limited information available about party budgets in Turkey, it can be seen that state help constitutes a significant share of their legally obtained resources. For example, in the six month period between January and June 2004, funds from the state constituted 87.3 per cent of the revenues of the JDP (the party that controlled the national government during that

---

8. Author's interview (No. 27), November 2003.

9. As Levitsky (2003: 69) explained, public employees who do not actually work, but get salaries from the state are referred to as *ñoquis* in Argentina. The name comes from the tradition in Argentina to eat *ñoquis* on the 29 of each month. Since these employees show up at the work place only at the end of the month to get their paychecks, they are called *ñoquis*.

time).[10] For the RPP, the party that received the second largest share of votes in the 2002 parliamentary elections, state support constituted 80 per cent of the revenues in the period between June 2001 and August 2003 (CHP Parti Meclisi Calisma Raporu- RPP Party Congress Report).

The law does not specify any conditions for how these resources can be used by parties. As a former local party official from TPP (Bakirkoy, Istanbul) stated,[11]

> Political parties never allocate the funds they get from the state to the lower levels in order to help with any campaign efforts, especially never in local elections. They only spend these funds centrally before legislative elections to get themselves re-elected.

In the interviews with politicians from various parties in Turkey, not only did party officials at the district level in Istanbul and Bilecik complain about the level of financial transfers from the central administration of the parties, but politicians who have occupied positions at the central administrations of the parties admitted that the resources that are distributed to the decentralised organs of the parties are very limited. As a legislator from Istanbul and former member of the RPP national congress stated,[12] 'There are no transfers of money from national organisations to the provincial organisations of the party. Therefore, candidates in provinces execute their campaigns with their own money.'

Again, when we look at the JDP's budget from 2004, transfers to the lower levels of party organisations constitute only 33 per cent of the total spending.[13] For the RPP in the period between 2001 and 2003, transfers constitute only 16 per cent of the total spending. As exemplified by these figures, decentralised organs of the parties in Turkey get only a minor share of the most significant funding source for political parties, state support. Interviews with party officials at the provincial and department level revealed that while the provincial level organisations get some support from the central administration, municipal level organisations are left almost totally on their own to generate resources. As a result, while the central party organisations can utilise professional campaign tools such as commercials on the radio, television and in newspapers, local organisations have to rely mostly on voluntary participants.

---

10. This information was retrieved from the JDP's website, www.akparti.org.tr (accessed August 2004).

11. Author's interview (No. 41), February 2004.

12. Author's interview (No. 29), January 2004.

13. This figure increased slightly to 36.7 per cent in 2007 (http://www.akparti.org.tr/gelir_gider/haziran.htm, accessed 11 May 2007). In the most recent budgetary information available (for the year of 2010), there was a major increase to 57.7 per cent, which might be a signal of the possible future changes in party organisations' financing in Turkey (http://www.akparti.org.tr/site/akparti/gelir-gider, accessed 21 October 2011).

Argentina

The Organic Law of Political Parties (Law No. 23,298) establishes a Permanent Party Fund, through which each party receives financial help from the federal government in accordance with the number of votes they got in the most recent election. In 1993 the amount was set to be 2.5 pesos per vote, then it was changed to 1 peso in the national budget legislation in 1997 and then through a decree in 2001, the decision on the amount of support was left to the Ministry of Interior. The 2007 changes in the legislation did not establish a specific amount, either (Law No. 26,215; 17 January 2007). A major difference between Argentina and Turkey is that according to the legislation, 80 per cent of the funds that come from the state have to be distributed to the district level organisations of the parties. Still, these resources are rarely spent on professional campaign workers.

Limited budgetary information on election campaigns exists for some cases in Argentina. The National Election Office of Argentina (Camara Electoral Nacional)[14] published on the internet the information provided by some parties in some provinces for the 2003 elections. Also, the non-governmental organisation, Poder Ciudadano[15] initiated a project to make campaign spending more transparent and asked candidates for local government office to present detailed information about their revenues and spending. Unfortunately, only a handful of candidates participated in the project, but some helpful information can be gathered from this data.

The most striking aspect of the spending data in terms of the main question of this book is that salaries for personnel are not included as part of any of the campaign budgets. For example, when we look at the information that was provided by the candidate for the mayor of Moron, Buenos Aires, from Agrupacion Nuevo Moron, Martin Sabbatella, we can see that there was no explicit reference to spending on personnel. Of the $47,841 spent in total, only $5,000 is designated as having been spent on the placement of posters, which might have involved payments to some workers, and $2,500 on public transportation, which could have again involved some payments to drivers. However, the large part of the spending seemed to have gone to printing and phone expenses. When we analyse the budgetary data of the PJ's provincial organisation in Buenos Aires, the only reference to spending on staff are professionals of publicity agencies, $193,600, and on legal professionals, $4,700, out of a total budget of $3,040,260. The corresponding figures for UCR are: $7,501 on professional advisors out of the total spending, $337,226. These illustrations of campaign spending by provincial and local level organisations of Argentine political parties support the information that was provided by the interviews with politicians that most of the labour participation in the electoral campaigns is voluntary, at least in the formal sense.

---

14. The information was published on the website of National Election Office of Argentina, www.pjn. gov.ar/cne (accessed 7 August 2004).

15. The data on campaign spending was made available on Poder Ciudadano's website, www.poder-ciudadano.org.ar (accessed 6 June 2004).

Party Activists and Party Members

Both in general elections and in internal party elections, participation of party activists in the campaigns is fundamental. Its significance increases as party organisations' financial resources to hire professional labour for their campaigns decrease. As the discussion in the previous section illustrates, the local and district level party organisations in Argentina and Turkey rely mainly on the voluntary participation of activists for their campaigns due to financial limitations. According to interviews and newspaper coverage of the campaigns, typical methods that are employed by politicians to appeal to their electorate, either in general or internal elections, include village, house to house, association and coffee house (in Turkey) visits, walks, and rallies.

According to the interviewees, such face to face interactions are very effective in appealing to the electorate and for communicating their message, but they are also very labour intensive. As one of the council members from PJ in La Matanza said,[16]

> We use all methods. House to house visits have turned out very well [...] [Party] militants are fundamental. All the people that voluntarily want to help the party. Walking, visiting needs a lot of people. House to house [visits] need a lot of people.

As another council member from PJ in La Matanza, said,[17] 'The campaigns, they are conducted house to house. We go to four hundred thousand houses in La Matanza. About ten thousand militants (activists)'.

Direct communication between party activists and voters is not only popular in Argentina, but also in Turkey. There is still (if not increasing) participation of party members in campaigns where party activists carry out visits to apartments, coffee houses, and work places. As a party official from MP[18] in Istanbul, emphasised, this type of campaign strategy necessitates the participation of a high number of party activists:

> In campaigns there is a lot of participation by party members. There will be even more. Today, in an apartment building there are at least fifteen apartments. [...] You have to go through the building, talk with each for one-two minutes. We need even more people now.

Another method that is used in both countries is large public rallies where the party leaders make speeches. However, the effectiveness of these rallies was disputed by the politicians that were interviewed. For example, a former governor of the province of Chaco argued that these large rallies were very important in the

---

16. Author's interview (No. 23), October 2003.

17. Author's interview (No. 24), October 2003.

18. Author's interview (No. 44), February 2004.

past, but that they are losing significance as the use of mass media replaces them.[19] Still, whenever these rallies take place, the number of people who participated in these events seems to be of utmost importance, especially as a signal of parties' or candidates' strength. Again, as one of the council members from PJ in La Matanza emphasised,[20]

> In La Matanza, at a gathering by the Peronists, very easily you get 30,000 people. In the last gathering at the central market there were more than fifty thousand. They are party affiliates and those that support the mayor.

Another example can be given from the year 1995, where in one of the Peronist gatherings that Eduardo Duhalde (gubernatorial candidate) participated in the Gregorio de Lafferrere Station, La Matanza, an estimated 60,000 people participated.[21] These examples show how important the involvement of party activists is for these rallies, not only due to their actual participation, but also because of their role as mobilisers of other supporters. (See Auyero 2001 for a meticulous analysis of such events and the role of party activists.)

Even though the participation of these party activists is sometimes truly voluntary, the use of selective material incentives by politicians to motivate activists to work in electoral and party activities is widely recognised by the literature on political parties. (See Ware 1992, 1996 and Lawson 1980 on parties in industrialised democracies; Epstein 1986; Mayhew 1986; Wolfinger 1972; Steed 1998 and James 2005 on parties in the US; Chubb 1982 and Zuckerman 1979 on Italian Christian Democrats; Coppedge 1994 on parties in Venezuela and Levitsky 2003 on the PJ, as few examples.) The works by Ware (1996), Epstein (1986) and Steed (1998) emphasise the decreasing role[22] of material incentives to get political activists to work for European and North American political parties. Although there is not any systematic work on the recruitment of party activists in Turkey, interviews with party officials and politicians who have occupied public office suggest that material incentives still play a significant role. In addition to the information that was provided by the interviews for the case of Argentina, some systematic analysis is conducted by Levitsky (2003). According to a survey of Peronist base units (neighbourhood organisations of the PJ, *unidades basicas*), the role of selective material incentives to foster activist participation actually increased in the case of the PJ (Levitsky 2003: 209). Given that political parties lack financial resources, especially at the provincial and local level, politicians resort to public benefits, such as jobs in the public sector, when they are able to do so to encourage activist

---

19. Author's interview (No. 19), October 2003.
20. Author's interview (No. 24), October 2003.
21. *La Nación*, 19 November 1995.
22. An opposing view is introduced by Rommele, Farrell and Ignazi (2005) who argue that European parties increasingly rely on linkages by rewards.

participation. As one party member from the PJ, Chaco, said:[23]

> Yes, in a campaign there is great participation of militants. Voluntary, yes. Some people have some salary from the legislature, or some contracted jobs in the nation, or some substitute from Plan Trabajar.[24] However, there are also some people who voluntarily dedicate hours by their own means. At least in Peronism. I think in Radicalism, no. Because they are in government. They manage all contracts, all positions. As such, they can pay their militants. Public employment works for the party.

Candidate and party authority selection

The discussion in the previous two sections gives examples of cases where particularistic distribution of public jobs is utilised by parties in Argentina and Turkey to motivate activist participation in campaigns for general and internal elections. Still, there is variation across and within countries in the degree to which parties and politicians make use of particularism to run the party machine and in the way they utilise particularistic exchanges. The main critical factor that affects how and to what extent politicians distribute public jobs to party activists is the internal competition for party and public positions. Even though politicians within the same party share some common goals (whether these goals are electoral, programmatic, or ideological), they also compete with each other to control the party and to win nominations for elected public positions. As such, the internal politics of parties are shaped by the formal and informal rules of candidate and party official selection. This, in turn, leads to variations in the strategies that politicians use to further their career goals, including the distribution of material benefits.

Therefore, in order to understand how politicians within the same party interact, one needs to know the party's candidate and party authority selection methods. Rahat and Hazan (2001) point out four dimensions of the candidate selection process: the qualifications required of the candidates, the profile of the selectors, the geographic units of selection, and voting or appointment systems. The same dimensions are also relevant to analyse the selection of party officials. There are important variations in these dimensions across parties in Argentina and in Turkey.

Turkey

The law of political parties (Law No. 2,820) specifies in detail how parties should be organised and how they should select their party authorities. However, it leaves the decision of candidate nomination methods to the parties. According to the law of political parties, party delegates are selected at the neighborhood (*mahalle*),

---

23. Author's interview (No. 20), October 2003.

24. Plan Trabajar is a targeted social assistance program.

municipal (*ilce*) and provincial (*il*) levels for the higher level. Municipal and provincial organisations choose the authorities for their respective level. The national convention, where the delegates chosen at the provincial convention participate, is of utmost importance because that is where the national party authorities, including the party leader, are selected.[25] Since Turkey has had a parliamentary system, the party leader that is elected at the national convention is most likely to become prime minister in the event the party wins the general elections.

The party law authorises the parties to choose their own nomination methods. In none of the parties do the statutes define a specific nomination method, but leave it to the national party authorities to choose among various methods – elite decision at the national level, elite decision at the provincial or local level, indirect assemblies where the delegates vote, and direct primaries where party members vote. Therefore, the national convention where the national party authorities are chosen, gains even more importance. When we look at the period after 1983, the method that is employed most frequently is elite decision at the national level. The RPP (and its predecessor, SPP) in the 1980s and in the first half of 1990s used indirect assemblies for choosing their candidates for general and local elections in some provinces. During this period, two centre-right parties, the TPP and the Motherland Party, also used indirect assemblies to choose their candidates in some provinces. In the period after 1983, direct primaries were employed only once and it was by the SPP in the 1987 general elections. Only party members could vote in these primaries. However, recently the dominant method in all parties to select their national and local candidates has become an elite decision at the national level and on some occasions an elite decision at the local level for local candidates.[26]

As a result, although the party leaders are elected at national conventions, they are rarely replaced because of their control over candidate nominations and financial resources (party and public when they are in government).[27] Indeed, in the period between 1983 and 2005, the leader of a party that was in government was defeated only once, when Yildirim Akbulut of the Motherland Party was defeated at a national convention by his challenger, Mesut Yilmaz, in 1991. According to the interviews, party leaders either directly contact the delegates and use public resources to influence their decisions or use intermediaries (local party bosses), most of the time the provincial president of the party or the legislators from that province, to preserve their leadership.

---

25. The Law of Political Parties originally had a term limit of five consecutive times for the party leader, but this restriction was later removed in 1990. (*Milliyet* 8 May 1990)

26. One exception was the use of primaries in 29 selected provinces by the RPP prior to the 2011 general elections. (*Radikal* 4 April 2011)

27. In the RPP, an additional rule that puts further limits on party leadership competition is the requirement that 20 per cent of the convention delegates give signatures in support of a candidate for the party leadership position at any level. (See the party by-laws at http://www.chp.org.tr/wp-content/uploads/CHPTuzukNISAN2010.pdf, accessed 21 October 2011.) This process forces the opponents of the party leader to reveal their identities and those who fear the loss of leadership support refrain from openly supporting another candidate.

Argentina

Until December 2009, according to the Organic Law of Political Parties (Law No. 23,298), the party statutes defined whether and how to conduct internal elections, though this decision might have been subject to limitations of the electoral legislation at the sub-national level. Prior to the presidential elections and national legislative elections in 2003, the law was modified (Law No. 25,611) to introduce simultaneous and open primaries for choosing presidential and national legislative candidates. However, especially due to internal competition within the PJ, the decision was contested politically and was modified by various decrees. Although legislation was passed to suspend the initial modification that introduced open, simultaneous and mandatory primaries (Law No. 26,191; 20 December 2006), the decision was again reversed in 2009 (Law No. 26,571; 14 December 2009). Currently the Article 29 of the Law dictates simultaneous, open and obligatory primaries for national elected offices.

Selection methods for provincial level offices are established by provincial statutes or provincial legislation when relevant.[28] Even though most provincial level party organisations have selected primaries[29] as the nomination method, in some provinces and municipalities, where the party has a dominant leader, an alternative list does not compete (Levistky 2005a). For example, in Chaco, after Ángel Rozas won the internal elections against León's internal line in 1995, the Radical party reached an agreement on a consensus list for all the provincial level nominations during Rozas' two terms as governor.

Even though the organisational structure of two major parties in Argentina is similar to the organisation of parties in Turkey in that they are organised at the municipal, provincial and national level, one crucial difference is that in two major parties, the PJ and the UCR, the delegates for the national convention are chosen through direct elections at the provincial level. Although according to Levitsky (2003), the national authorities of the UCR have more power compared to those of the PJ, provincial actors in all Argentine parties, especially governors, are more independent vis a vis national party figures than their counterparts in Turkey. Direct elections for national convention delegates, the selection of provincial candidates at the provincial level and more financial resources at the provincial level make provincial organisations of Argentine parties very powerful. (See Jones *et al.* 2001, Eaton 2005 and De Luca *et al.*2002 on the role of governors in Argentinean political parties and the political system in general.)

---

28. For example, the province of Buenos Aires implemented open, simultaneous, and mandatory primaries (Law No. 12,195, 31 July 2002), but this law was later repealed and the decision to hold primaries was left to the party statutes. (Law No. 13,640. 8 February 2007)

29. The participation of the independents varies across periods and provinces. See De Luca *et al.* (2002) for further information on the use of primaries for selecting national legislative candidates and De Luca *et al.* (2008) for selecting governors in Argentina.

Internal elections and material benefits

As a result of these differences across the two countries, parties, and provinces in terms of candidate and party official selection, the critical actors that are involved in the internal party competition and the nature of the competition vary. In some provinces and parties, internal elections are held for selecting candidates for public office as well as party authorities. In others, they are used only to elect party authorities. In these internal elections, whether they are held by the participation of delegates, party members, or independents, public jobs might be distributed in order to influence the voting decisions of the selectors. As it was mentioned in many interviews with politicians in Turkey, when the number of selectors is low, such as in the case of indirect assemblies with delegates, the exchange of material benefits might be more efficient from the perspective of competitors.

In those cases where party members as well as independents can vote, as a former Argentine cabinet minister said, 'The primaries are like general elections.'[30] However, one main difference is that the turnout in Argentine primaries has, in general, been very low. Even though it is hard to get systematic data on turnout in primaries, some information is available for the 1999 Radical primaries for municipal offices in Chaco, [31] and some information on turnout in municipal level primaries for Peronist candidates at the province of Buenos Aires in 1991 was published in the Argentine newspaper, *La Nación*.[32] When we look at this data, we can see that the turnout for Radical primaries for municipal office in Chaco in 1999 ranged from the lowest of 23 per cent to the highest of 57 per cent with an average of 34 per cent. In the province of Buenos Aires, the available figures for the Peronist primaries in 1991 had a range of 25 to 50 per cent.

These examples show that candidates can actually affect the primary results by mobilising their supporters. Therefore, in addition to their participation in campaigns, party activists are critical for mobilisation on the day of internal elections. Party machines that are maintained via patronage (De Luca *et al.* 2002) play an important role in Argentine primaries. This gives an additional incentive to candidates within parties to distribute material benefits like public jobs to activists to work for them in internal elections as well as in general elections. Since both participation in electoral campaigns and in mobilisation efforts are observable services, monitoring problems that make the exchange of material benefits for political support less efficient from the perspective of the provider are also solved.

---

30. Author's interview (No. 49), May 2004.

31. The data on turnout and results of Radical primaries for selecting candidates for municipal offices on April 24 1999 was made available by the director of ECOMCHACO.

32. *La Nación, suplemento*, 30 July 1991.

Conclusion

The discussions in the preceding sections of this chapter show that politicians have various purposes for distributing material benefits in exchange for political support. In return for distributing benefits, politicians might be expecting votes in general elections, votes in direct primaries and indirect assemblies, as well as participation in electoral campaigns and in mobilisation efforts. All politicians need to form a network of supporters to be able to win public office, and in some cases, particularistic distribution of material benefits is a useful tool to build political loyalties.

However, from the point of observers, the purpose of the politician for engaging in particularistic networks with citizens by distributing jobs is not clear. The politician might be allocating these public jobs just to mobilise activists and increase his party's vote shares in the general elections, but he might also be seeking to build an independent power base for himself in order to move up in the party hierarchy. As a consequence, politicians who are occupying positions high in the party hierarchy, and are uncertain about the lower level politician's ambitions, might be alarmed by the level of clientelistic networks formed in the lower level politician's electoral district. In this interaction between the politicians of the party hierarchy, the number of patronage jobs that are distributed in the public administration of the lower level politicians' electoral districts, that is, the effort they put into building political support, serves as a useful signal to the higher level politicians about the lower level politicians' ambitions. I analyse, in the following chapter, with the aid of a game theoretic model the factors that lead to variations in the interaction between politicians of the same party and hence variations in the formation of these networks of supporters through particularistic distribution of public jobs.

chapter four	a game theoretic analysis of internal party competition and particularistic exchanges within parties

[In all modern parties] there is a continual latent struggle. [...] Every oligarchy is full of suspicion towards those who aspire to enter its ranks, regarding them not simply as eventual heirs but as successors who are ready to supplant them without waiting for a natural death.

Robert Michels, *Political Parties*,(1962 [1915]): 176

In this chapter I introduce a general model that analyses the interaction of two actors who compete within the same party and the role of patronage jobs in this interaction. One of the players (Leader) is a politician with a higher, more valued position in the party. This position can either be an elected public office or a party position. The player can be an individual or a collective actor (such as a faction or the national council) that dominates the party organisation. The second player (Follower) is another politician from the same party with a lower, less valued position. Again, this can be an elected public office or a party position.

The model can be applied to the analysis of various empirical cases. For example, the follower might be a mayor whose next step in his political career might be a provincial level position like the governor. In that case, the two relevant actors would be the mayor and the governor. In the following chapters, I analyse subnational public employment in Argentina and Turkey, where the model is applied to the political relationship between governors and their national party leaders in the case of Argentina, and the relationship between mayors of metropolitan municipalities and their national party leaders in the case of Turkey.[1]

The key assumption of the model is that there is a potential rivalry between these two politicians for the leadership position in their own party. The politician with the lower level position might want to replace the politician with the higher (more valued) position, or form an opposition movement with others in the party to challenge the current party leadership. All leaders maintain their power in the party by forming alliances with other party members who have strong positions within the party and with the general public (Panebianco 1988; Benton

---

1   A second level of analysis is the municipal administration where in Argentina the relevant political interaction is between mayors and the governors, and in Turkey between mayors and important legislators as well as the mayors of metropolitan municipalities, if applicable. The next two chapters also include case study analyses at this level.

2007). However, these alliances last only as long as those, who are not the leaders, are insufficiently independent to challenge the leaders. One politician expressed this point many others alluded to: 'In politics, today's friends are tomorrow's enemies.'[2] Thus, the tension in the interaction between these two players derives from the fact that the higher level politician prefers the other politician to have sufficient public support to benefit the party as a whole, but not so much that he can challenge the leader's own position. Whether the lower level politician successfully takes over his superior's position depends, in turn, on his ambitions and the level of support he has in the party and with the general public, which can be improved by distributing patronage jobs.

Since the leader does not know for certain whether the follower aspires to challenge her leadership, I model the interaction as an incomplete information game. At the same time, the leader has means to infer information about the follower's intention and the number of patronage jobs that are distributed in the follower's district is one of them. (The availability of other cues such as raising money for campaigns is discussed in the Chapter Seven.) Therefore, the situation is suitable to be modelled as a typical signalling game where the number of patronage jobs is the signal that is sent by the follower. Even though patronage jobs help the follower to build political support among his clientele, increasing the number of these jobs is costly for the follower in two ways. First, the politician has to exert some effort to establish these clientelistic networks. Second, and more importantly, the financial resources that are allocated to pay the salaries of these public employees who do not provide any efficient economic returns hamper the economic performance, especially when the number of patronage jobs is very high. This, in turn, is likely to hurt the electoral chances of the follower. Therefore, distribution of patronage jobs is a costly signal of the follower's leadership ambition (his type). If we consider good economic performance as a public good, the follower has to choose the optimal number of patronage jobs that is not too high to prevent the provision of this public good (Magaloni *et al.* 2007).

In response to the follower's action, that is, the new information provided by the number of patronage jobs about the follower's ambition, the leader decides whether to support the follower. Support can take different forms: financial or symbolic. According to the information provided by interviews, financial support can include campaign contributions and if the leader is holding public office, public investments such as building infrastructure like roads and bridges, as well as public credit to the administrative unit of the follower. If the leader is also the President, she has vast resources at her disposal to distribute to the various governors. Many federal government transfers to the provinces in Argentina are written into a tax sharing agreement (*co-participación*) and the President has little discretion in the distribution of these funds (Tommasi 2002; Gordin 2006). Yet, as a former minister of economy and production says:[3] 'Although the federal government cannot arbitrarily shift money from one province to another, it can help a

---

2. Author's interview (No. 22), October 2003.

3. Author's interview (No. 49), May 2004.

province borrow money.' For example, in Córdoba, according to this interviewee,[4] 'Once he [De La Sota – governor of Córdoba at the time] was elected, he needed support to run the province. It was in bad shape.' Not only does the President approve loans to the provinces, he makes the final decision on large public works, which are mostly funded by the federal government. For example, Menem's 1991 promise to Chaco to finish the Barranqueras- Resistencia dam and fix the roads gave the gubernatorial candidate credibility with both his fellow party members and the general public.[5] Most of the interviewees claimed that symbolic support in the form of joint participation in rallies or on posters is also valuable if the leader has name recognition and is popular.

Turkish party leaders, like their Argentine counterparts, show their support by contributing to the campaigns,[6] providing public investment and government loans for their provinces if they control national office, and lending symbolic support. As a JDP legislator stated,[7] '[During our campaign] the leader [Tayyip Erdoğan] visited the provinces. It is important to see the party leader with the candidates and pre-candidates in the provinces and towns and at the rallies.' Moreover, Turkish party leaders (who hold public office) have more freedom to provide financial support than their Argentine counterparts. Even though the Turkish Prime Minister, like the Argentine President, has limited discretion to shift resources to the municipalities and provincial administrations,[8] she has the power to transfer national government funds to decentralised organisations of the national government in the provinces. The party leader (prime minister) can increase the popularity of the candidates at the sub-national level and enhance the candidates' chances of re-election by sending more money to selected provinces. In Turkey, party leaders can also directly nominate politicians as candidates for public, elected office. Since primary elections are very rare, support can take its maximum value in contexts where the possibility for the politician (follower) to switch to another party is very low.

---

4. Author's interview (No. 49), May 2004.

5. *Diario Norte*, 9 July 1991: 2.

6. As the interviews suggest and a survey conducted by Genckaya (2000) with legislators corroborates, the national party organisation very rarely contributes financially to provincial campaigns. However, if the party leader does decide to channel party resources to the provincial politicians' campaigns, these resources are expected to have a significant impact on the election results.

7. Author's interview (No. 28), December 2003.

8. In the period of analysis, Law No. 2380 regulated the transfer of resources from the national government. According to this legislation, the national government transferred 6 per cent of its total tax revenues to the municipalities and 1.12 per cent to the provincial administrations (*il ozel idareleri*). (The shares were higher, with 9.25 per cent to the municipalities and 1.70 per cent to the provincial administrations between 1987 and 2001.) The total amount was first transferred to the Bank of Provinces (Iller Bankasi) and then allocated between municipalities and provinces according to the administrative units' population shares in the most recent Census (Article No. 1). The metropolitan municipalities got a share of the general tax revenues that were collected within their boundaries. The exact amount has varied over the years. In July 2008 changes to the local governments' resources were introduced by Law No. 5779.

As can be seen from the discussion in the previous two paragraphs, even though the electoral chances of the follower and his potential to replace the leader are influenced by this support from the leader, the value of the support depends on many exogenous factors, such as the party's popularity in the follower's electoral district, the financial resources that are available to the leader and the formal rules of leadership or candidate selection in the party. Therefore, the *effectiveness* (value) of the leader's support (for general and internal competition) is taken as an exogenous variable in the model.

Since the leader wants the follower to be successful in the general election, because his re-election will benefit the party, the leader has an incentive to support the follower. However, if the follower has adequate political backing in the party, and if his intention is to challenge the leader's power, the leader risks her own position in the party by giving out this support to the follower. This is where the party leader uses the information, revealed by the number of patronage jobs, about the follower's intentions. If the number of patronage jobs (that is, the efforts to build a strong machine) signals that the follower has ambitions to take over leadership, the leader might withdraw her support. Knowing this, the follower makes his strategic choice about the number of jobs, which could potentially make him lose the leader's support. Thus, the level of patronage in the public sector is an outcome of the strategic interaction between politicians from the same party who simultaneously compete with and rely on each other.

Basic structure

The setup of the game is as follows. Nature moves first and determines the follower (P_F)'s type $t \in \{0, 1\}$ where $t = 1$ denotes challenger type and $t = 0$ denotes the ally type. Let p denote the probability of P_F being type 1. Then, knowing his own type, P_F chooses the extent of patronage in his provincial administration (x). On the extreme, the follower (P_F) can use all his budget to establish clientelistic exchanges and x would equal 1. Or the politician does not hire anyone through clientelistic exchanges, and then x would be equal to 0. Therefore, x is a continuous variable that ranges between 0 and 1 ($x \in [0, 1]$). P_F pays a cost for these clientelistic hirings in the public sector, $c(x)$. Since the financial costs of expanding the public sector increase with the number of employees and the inefficiency that patronage jobs create is higher when the number of patronage jobs is high, $c(x)$ is a function that increases with x at an increasing rate. That is, the first order partial derivative, $c_x > 0$ and second order partial derivative $c_{xx} > 0$.

Observing the level of jobs, but lacking information about the type of the lower level politician (P_F), the leader (P_L) decides whether to support P_F. That is, P_L chooses $s \in S = \{0, 1\}$ where $s = 1$ denotes supporting and $s = 0$ denotes not supporting. The number of jobs that are distributed (x) and whether the higher level politician supports the lower level politician (s) affect both the probability that the lower level politician will win the general election and the probability that the lower level politician will replace the higher level politician. Let $\pi(s, x)$ be the probability of P_F successfully replacing P_L, $\tau(s, x)$ be the probability of P_F winning the elections and $\theta(s, x)$ be the party's vote share in the follower's district.

Table 4.1: Summary of exogenous parameters

σ_1	effectiveness of leader's support (s) for follower's re-election
σ_2	effectiveness of distributing jobs (x) for follower's re-election
α_1	effectiveness of leader's support (s) for replacing the leader
α_2	effectiveness of distributing jobs (x) for replacing the leader
β_1	effectiveness of leader's support (s) for vote shares
β_2	effectiveness of distributing jobs (x) for vote shares
v	the rate of cost (c) from distributing jobs
M	the value of re-election for the follower
R	the value of leadership for the follower
G	the value of vote share for the leader
Q	the value of maintaining the leadership for the leader

The payoffs of the players are defined as follows: The follower gets utility M if he is re-elected to his lower level position. If he is a challenger type, he wants to replace the leader and get the higher level position. Let the utility that a challenger type gets from taking over the leadership be R. The leader (P_L) wants to keep her higher level position and gets utility Q if she keeps it. P_L also wants to increase the party's vote share in the follower's district and gets utility G from the party's electoral results in the district.

To simplify the analysis, I assume linear functional forms for $\tau(s,x)$, $\pi(s,x)$, and $\theta(s,x)$: $\pi(s,x) = \alpha_1 s + \alpha_2 x$ where $\alpha_1 s + \alpha_2 x \leq 1$; $\tau(s,x) = \sigma_1 s + \sigma_2 x$ where $\sigma_1 s + \sigma_2 x \leq 1$; $\theta(s,x) = \beta_1 s + \beta_2 x$ where $\beta_1 s + \beta_2 x \leq 1$. I also assume the following function for the costs from patronage: $c(x) = vx^2$. As such, the vote share of the party in the district and the probabilities of re-election and leadership replacement increase with support from the leader (s) and the level of jobs (x). The relative rate of their effect depends on, $\beta_{1,2}$, $\sigma_{1,2}$, and $\alpha_{1,2}$. Therefore, we get the following utility functions:

$$U'_{P_F} = (\sigma_1 s + \sigma_2 x)M + (\alpha_1 s + \alpha_2 x)Rt - vx^2$$
$$U_{P_L} = (\beta_1 s + \beta_2 x)G + [1 - (\alpha_1 s + \alpha_2 x)t]Q$$

Equilibria

Without any interactions with P_L, the follower in the party would choose to provide the level of x that maximises his utility function. Let x_t^* be the value of x that maximises P_F's utility function, $x_t^* = \arg\max U_{P_F}^t$. Then, we get the following lemma.

Lemma 1. $x_1^* = \frac{\sigma_2 M + \alpha_2 R}{2v}$ and $x_0^* = \frac{\sigma_2 M}{2v}$ where $0 < \sigma_2 M$,
$\sigma_2 M + \alpha_2 R < 2v, \sigma_2^2 M + \alpha_2 \sigma_2 R < 2v(1 - \sigma_1 s)$.

Proof. See Appendix A.

As expected, given the utility function of the follower, without any interactions with the party leader the challenger politician would choose to provide higher numbers of jobs to build support in the party and public. This is true because the challenger type follower gets additional utility from taking over the leadership and the number of jobs that he distributes, x, increases his probability of leadership take-over. The critical question is whether the interaction with the party leader can induce the challenger to behave in another way.

Before analysing the game under incomplete information I will present the solutions for the complete information game where P_L knows whether P_F is a challenger type or not. This analysis will show us that if the leader knows the follower's ambitions about leadership, she would not be able to credibly condition her support to the follower based on the level of patronage in the follower's district and hence the interaction between two politicians would not be able to induce lower levels of particularism in public employment.

Under complete information version of the model we can use backwards induction to find the equilibria:

Lemma 2. P_L's best response strategy to P_F is:

$$s_{P_L}^*(x) = 1 \quad \forall t \in \{1,0\} \text{ when } \frac{G}{Q} \geq \frac{\alpha_1}{\beta_1}$$

$$\text{and } s_{P_L}^*(x) = \begin{cases} 0 \text{ if } t = 1 \\ 1 \text{ if } t = 0 \end{cases} \text{ when } \frac{G}{Q} < \frac{\alpha_1}{\beta_1}.$$

Proof. See Appendix A1.

From Lemma 2 we see that, if the effectiveness of leader's support for leadership takeover (α_1) is sufficiently large, then the leader withdraws her support from the follower. Given the best response of the leader, P_F chooses the value of x that maximises his utility:

Proposition 1: P_F's best response action at the first stage is

$$x^* = \begin{cases} \frac{\sigma_2 M + \alpha_2 R}{2v} \text{ if } t = 1 \\ \frac{\sigma_2 M}{2v} \text{ if } t = 0 \end{cases} \text{ where } \sigma_2 M + \alpha_2 R < 2v.$$

Proof. Lemma 2 implies that P_L's best response strategy to P_F when P_F is of the challenger type depends on condition, $\frac{G}{Q} \geq \frac{\alpha_1}{\beta_1}$. Since the level of x does not have an impact on P_L's best response strategy, P_F chooses the level of x that maximises his utility function, which gives the same equilibrium value of x_t^* as in P_F's maximisation of his utility without any interactions with P_L. (see Appendix A for the solution of this optimisation problem).

Therefore, under complete information, the follower's choice of x (the number of patronage jobs) is the same as it would be without any interaction with the party leader. When the follower is a challenger type the leader would benefit from P_F distributing fewer jobs when $\beta_2 G < \alpha_2 Q$. However, the leader cannot credibly threaten to cut down on support to force the follower (P_F) to distribute fewer jobs. When the follower is of the ally type, the leader's utility is maximised when $x = \frac{\sigma_2 M}{2v}$, that is at the value of x that maximises the follower's utility. Therefore, the analysis of the complete information game shows that when the leader knows the follower's type, the interaction with the leader has no impact on the follower's choice of x, the number of patronage jobs that he distributes in his electoral district.

In the incomplete information version of the game, the leader does not know the follower's type, but can infer information about it through the follower's signal, the number of patronage jobs. All the possible equilibria of the model are derived formally in Appendix A.2. Here I first explain the logic of why we get pooling on a low level of jobs under some conditions in the incomplete version of the game, and then present a summary of how two variables – the importance of the leader's support for leadership competition and the importance of the leader's support for general elections – lead to different outcomes in the number of patronage jobs in different equilibria.

Let x' be the level of x that is chosen by the challenger and ally type follower. By definition of pooling equilibria, the leader does not infer any additional information about the type of the follower from observing x. Therefore, the updated beliefs are $\mu^*(t = 1; x = x') = p$ and $\mu^*(t = 0; x = x') = 1 - p$. Let q be P_L's belief that $t = 1 \mid x > x'$.

Lemma 3. Given the updated beliefs, the leader's best response to $z^*(x' \mid t) = 1, \forall t$ is:

when $\frac{G}{Q} > \frac{q\alpha_1}{\beta_1}$, $r^*(s = 1 \mid x) = 1 \ \forall x \in X$.

when $\frac{p\alpha_1}{\beta_1} < \frac{G}{Q} < \frac{q\alpha_1}{\beta_1}, r^* = \begin{cases} s = 0 \text{ if } x > x' \\ s = 1 \text{ if } x \leq x' \end{cases} = 1$
and

when $\frac{p\alpha_1}{\beta_1} > \frac{G}{Q}$, $r^*(s = 0 \mid x) = 1 \ \forall x \in X$

Proof. See Appendix A2.

From Lemma 3 we can see that if the condition, $\frac{p\alpha_1}{\beta_1} < \frac{G}{Q} < \frac{q\alpha_1}{\beta_1}$, is met, the leader's decision to support the follower depends on the level of x. This means that in the incomplete version of the game, the leader can credibly threaten to cut down on her support to the follower if $x > x'$ and $\frac{p\alpha_1}{\beta_1} < \frac{G}{Q} < \frac{q\alpha_1}{\beta_1}$.

Proposition 2. Pooling equilibria exist where

$$\frac{p\alpha_1}{\beta_1} < \frac{G}{Q} < \frac{q\alpha_1}{\beta_1} \quad \text{and} \quad \sigma_1 M - \frac{\alpha_2^2 R^2}{4v} + \alpha_1 R \geq 0$$

$$r^* = \begin{cases} s = 0 \text{ if } x > x' \\ s = 1 \text{ if } x \leq x' \end{cases} = 1$$

$$z^*(\forall t \in \{0,1\}, x = \frac{\sigma_2 M}{2v}, r^*(x)) = 1$$

and

$$\mu^*(t = 1 \,|\, x = \frac{\sigma_2 M}{2v}) = p$$

Proof. See Appendix A2.

The existence of a pooling equilibrium where both types choose $x = \frac{\sigma_2 M}{2v}$ implies that under the two conditions specified in Proposition 2, the follower of challenger type chooses a level of x that is lower than the number of jobs he would have distributed without any interactions with the leader and with competition under complete information. This is the most critical implication of the game theoretic analysis, because it suggests that under some conditions the competition between the leader and her follower within the party leads to lower expected levels of patronage in public sector employment, if the leader does not have complete information about the follower's ambitions for leadership.

We know from *Lemmas 2* and *3* that under some condition that relates how much the leader values the party's vote shares in the district and her own leadership, to the impact that her support has on vote shares and leadership takeover (the conditions are $\frac{G}{Q} < \frac{\alpha_1}{\beta_1}$ and $\frac{p\alpha_1}{\beta_1} < \frac{G}{Q} < \frac{q\alpha_1}{\beta_1}$ respectively for the complete information game and pooling equilibria), the leader is better off supporting only the ally type. Since under complete information the leader knows the follower's type, the leader's best response action does not depend on the follower's action, the number of patronage jobs. Hence, the leader cannot credibly threaten to withdraw her support from the follower and the follower has no incentives to cut down on patronage in order to get the support of the leader.

However, under incomplete information, if $\frac{p\alpha_1}{\beta_1} < \frac{G}{Q} < \frac{q\alpha_1}{\beta_1}$, the leader can credibly condition her support on the level of patronage jobs (the follower's signal). Then, the challenger type follower can make the leader support her by reducing the level of patronage jobs in his district to ally type's level, that is by pooling on the ally type's actions. Yet, a second condition, $\sigma_1 M - \frac{\alpha_2^2 R^2}{4v} + \alpha_1 R \geq 0$, must be fulfilled in order for the follower to have the incentive to reduce the number of jobs in order to get the support of the leader.

The different equilibria of the model are summarised in Figure 4.1.[9] What

---

9. Please see Appendix A2 for the parameter values that make the P_L indifferent between $s = 1$ and $s = 0$.

we can see from this Figure is that when $\frac{G}{Q} > \frac{\alpha_1}{\beta_1}$ the leader would not be able to credibly threaten to withdraw her support from the follower. This condition would be more easily met when her support has low levels of impact on leadership takeover (that is, for small values of α_1) because then the leader would always prefer to support the follower in order to increase the vote share of the party in the follower's district without the fear of losing her leadership position. In response, the follower would have no incentive to cut down on the distribution of jobs in order to change the leader's action. This would lead to the outcome of high expected levels of patronage if we assume that the challenger type followers exist with some positive probability.

	$\sigma_1 M - \frac{\alpha_2^2 R^2}{4v} + \alpha_1 R \leq 0$	$\sigma_1 M - \frac{\alpha_2^2 R^2}{4v} + \alpha_1 R \geq 0$
$\frac{G}{Q} > \frac{\alpha_1}{\beta_1}$	$t = 1 \quad x = \frac{\sigma_2 M + \alpha_2 R}{2v}$ $t = 0, \ x = \frac{\sigma_2 M}{2v}$ **H**	$t = 1, \quad x = \frac{\sigma_2 M + \alpha_2 R}{2v}$ $t = 0, \quad x = \frac{\sigma_2 M}{2v}$ **H**
$\frac{q\alpha_1}{\beta_1} < \frac{G}{Q} < \frac{\alpha_1}{\beta_1}$	$t = 1, \ x = \frac{\sigma_2 M + \alpha_2 R}{2v}$ $t = 0, \ x = \frac{\sigma_2 M}{2v}$ **H**	hybrid equilibria **M**
$\frac{p\alpha_1}{\beta_1} < \frac{G}{Q} < \frac{q\alpha_1}{\beta_1}$	$t = 1, \ x = \frac{\sigma_2 M + \alpha_2 R}{2v}$ $t = 0, \ x = \frac{\sigma_2 M}{2v}$ **H**	$t = 1, \ x = \frac{\sigma_2 M}{2v}$ $t = 0, \ x = \frac{\sigma_2 M}{2v}$ **L**
$\frac{G}{Q} < \frac{p\alpha_1}{\beta_1}$	$t = 1, \ x = \frac{\sigma_2 M + \alpha_2 R}{2v}$ $t = 0, \ x = \frac{\sigma_2 M}{2v}$ **H**	hybrid equilibria **M**

H indicating high expected levels of patronage.

M indicating medium expected levels of patronage.

L indicating low expected levels of patronage.

Figure 4.1: Outcomes in different equilibria of the model

In the pooling and semi-separating (hybrid) equilibria, lower levels of patronage jobs are distributed because either the challenger type follower pools on the action of the ally type and chooses low level of patronage jobs or mixes between two pure strategies. For the challenger type follower to do this, the second condition, $\sigma_1 M - \frac{\alpha_2^2 R^2}{4v} + \alpha_1 R \geq 0$, should be met. That is, the follower should be willing to trade-off jobs for the leader's support. From the analysis of this condition, we can see that when the leader's support is important for the follower's re-election chances (that is, when σ_1 is sufficiently high) the follower would distribute fewer patronage jobs in order to signal to the party leader that he has no ambitions for taking over her leadership, so that the leader would then decide to support the follower.

As this discussion shows, two clear predictions about the number of patronage jobs can be made from the analysis of the conditions for the existence of different equilibria:

Hypothesis 1. Expected levels of patronage jobs in the follower's district decrease when

    (a)   the leader's support has some effect on internal party competition (for high values of α_1); and

    (b)   the party (leader's) support is important for the follower's re-election (for high values of σ_1).[10]

Hypothesis 2. When the leader's support has no effect on internal party competition (small values of α_1), expected levels of patronage jobs in the follower's district are not influenced by the importance of the party (leader's) support for the follower's re-election (σ_1).

Conclusion

One way of building networks of supporters for politicians and parties is to form particularistic relationships with citizens through the exchange of public material benefits. This strategy usually turns out to be costly for society because of the economic inefficiencies it creates, the inequalities it leads to in the short-term allocation of resources, as well as in the long-term possibilities of citizens making programmatic demands from the state, and their consequent questioning of the political system's legitimacy.

In order to understand why such a socially costly form of politician-citizen relationship persists, the literature has focused on the role of elections in democratic systems and the availability of public and private economic resources. One conclusion that can be taken from these earlier analyses is that the mechanisms behind these particularistic exchanges vary according to the nature of the benefit that is exchanged. When we focus on one of the most cited type of benefits in the

---

10. If $\alpha_2^2 R + 2\alpha_2(\sigma_2 M) \leq 4v$ and $\alpha_2^2 R^2 + 2\sigma_2^2 M^2 \leq 4Mv$ are satisfied, the conditions of the pooling equilibria meet the following probability restrictions, $\alpha_1 s + \alpha_2 x \leq 1$ and $\sigma_1 s + \sigma_2 x \leq 1$.

literature, public jobs, we can see that internal competition in addition to competition between parties in general elections, is a factor that cannot be ignored if we are to understand the mechanisms of how politicians exchange public jobs in a particularistic manner to build political support in developing democracies like Argentina and Turkey.

As discussed in Chapter Two, economic changes that these countries have been experiencing, have reduced the public resources that are available for politicians to use in these particularistic exchanges. Manipulating public sector employment is particularly costly due to the large public deficits that form one of the major factors leading to economic crises. Higher economic costs of expanding the public sector and reductions in available jobs with neo-liberal reforms, force the politicians to be more strategic about who the recipients are and what the politicians expect from them in return.

Chapter Three has illustrated that beyond voting for the party (politician) in general elections, which is not easily verifiable, the services that are expected from those who receive public jobs include participation in electoral campaigns, mobilising supporters for elections and voting in favour of the patron in the indirect or low turn-out internal elections. The dependence of parties on voluntary participation of party activists in local campaigns and daily party activities, due to financial limitations and methods of candidate and party authority selection that are not truly participatory, give incentives to politicians to make use of public resources such as employment in the public sector to motivate party members to participate in party activities.

What this chapter showed is that the final outcome of the number of jobs to be distributed in order to build support, is a result of the intersection of the factors that are related both to competition between parties and competition within parties. The dependence of the party actors on each other for electoral success and internal party competition provide the possibility for the existence of incentives by individual politicians to restrict their use of public jobs to build political support. In the competition for the leadership of the party, the uncertainty concerning politicians' intentions to compete for the leadership and ambiguity with respect to motivations behind the distribution of jobs to build support, whether it is to build support for internal competition or for parties' electoral success, allow possibilities to develop for restricting the level of patronage jobs.

The politician who needs the support of the leader for his re-election has incentives to hold back on the efforts to build individual loyalties in order to signal to the leader that he is not a potential challenger. Since exchanging jobs for support is an easily observable activity that might trigger suspicion from the perspective of the leader, politicians who need the backing of the leader might, under some conditions, have the incentive to cut down on patronage. According to the results of the model, such incentives exist when the support of the party leader is important for the politicians' electoral chances and when the impact of the leader's support on internal competition is high. The latter would likely happen if the party leader is not dominant within the party.

From a broader perspective, these results imply that internal party competition has the potential to contain the proliferation of patronage in public sector employment. However, some conditions are necessary for this desired outcome to be reached: The party should have a significant effect on the electoral chances of individual politicians and the leadership in the party should be a contestable position. Leaders' support would have an impact on leadership turn-over only when there is real competition in the party, that is, when the leader is not dominant in the party. As a result, we would expect politicians to have the incentive to reduce their patronage networks when parties have an important role in the electoral competition and when leadership is open to competition.

chapter five | provincial and municipal public employment in argentina

Political patronage has long been a feature of public employment in Argentina. Politics played a role in the appointment decisions during different historical periods: when the dominant party (PAN – Partido Autonomista Nacional) ruled; when the Radicals challenged the PAN between 1912 and 1944 (Rock 1975; Garcia-Zamor 1968), and when the Radicals and the Peronists competed after 1946. Up until 1983, frequent military coups had configured different administrative landscapes than those brought about by regularly scheduled democratic elections. Whether civilian or military, once the 1949 Constitution introduced tenure for public employees,[1] new governments had trouble replacing public employees with their supporters. Aside from encouraging early retirement to open up positions for political hirings, public sector expansion has been the favoured strategy for placing political supporters.

The most significant regulatory changes for public sector employees since the 1949 introduction of tenure were the reforms implemented during President Menem's administration in the 1990s. 'Forced retirement' cut the total number of public employees, whole agencies were closed, and Menem's government created a new National Civil Service System (Sistema Nacional de la Profesión Administrativa – SINAPA).[2]

Although attempts were made to increase transparency and curtail the role of politics in hiring and promotion decisions, standardised entrance exams were not introduced for public sector employment. The new system covered only some federal employees but left the status of state and municipal employees unchanged. No independent agency oversees and coordinates hiring and promotion decisions in the public sector. As a result, the relative ease with which politicians and parties can appoint their followers to public jobs contributes to the widely held belief in public, academic, and administrative circles that political patron – client relationships and particularism are widespread in the Argentine civil service.

In this chapter I introduce a systematic analysis of the impact of political factors on patronage in public sector employment. The three previous chapters introduced theoretical arguments specific to the analysis of particularism in public sector employment. This chapter uses 1984–2001 employment statistics in the provinces to analyse those arguments. The analysis uses total number of temporary employees (per ten thousand people) as the dependent variable. Although this

---

1. Although the military government that was formed after the 1955 coup abolished the 1949 reforms, the Constitutional Convention incorporated stability for the public employees in the new Constitution. (Unamuno and Bortnik 1986: 35).

2. SINAPA was created by decree (Decree-Law No. 993/ 1991). For more information on administrative reform in Argentina during Menem's presidency, see Rinne (2003).

variable clearly does not directly measure whether political factors influence hiring decisions, controlling for economic and social factors that affect the number of personnel allows me to separate out the effect of political factors on the numbers of state employees.

In this chapter, I first illustrate with different empirical cases, how the theoretical model that is introduced in the previous chapter is applied to the analysis of provincial and municipal level patronage in Argentina. Then, I discuss why the statistical analysis focuses on provincial level public employment. This is followed by an explanation of how dependent and independent variables are measured. Finally, I present the results of the analysis, which support the arguments introduced in the previous chapter. I observe a smaller number of temporary employees when the party (leader's) support is important for the electoral chances of politicians and when the party leader is not dominant in the party so that leadership is open to competition.

Intra-party competition and patronage jobs at the sub-national level

The hypotheses that are derived from the game theoretic model in Chapter Four examine leadership competition between two politicians in the same party. One actor is the party leader and the other, who distributes jobs, is a rival. The national party leader (or the President, if the party is in government) and provincial governors, are two actors whose interaction can easily be characterised in the model. Governors in Argentina[3] oversee a significant part of the budget and manipulate these financial resources to build their political power (Jones *et al*. 2001; Eaton 2005; Calvo and Murillo 2004). As Levitsky (2003) notes, governors have become major figures, particularly in the PJ, since union leaders have largely lost their influence in the party. Generally speaking, governors are more powerful than the members of the official national party organisations, who are actually relatively powerless. So governors are considered potential rivals for the party leadership. Since 1983, all but one of the Peronist pre-candidates have previously been governors, and one-third of Radical pre-candidates were governors before they were candidates.[4] As Menem (PJ, President from 1989–1999) once said, 'Every governor, every powerful politician, is a potential presidential candidate'.[5]

In this section, I first discuss the examples of two provinces, Buenos Aires and Chaco, to illustrate how this potential rivalry between governors and their party leaders has an impact on patronage jobs.

---

3. See De Luca (2008: 191 and references within) for a discussion on the important role of governors.

4. De la Rúa (UCR, the president between 1999 and December 2001) has not been a governor, but he was the former elected mayor of the Capital Federal, which puts him in an equivalent position. Before his first attempt to be a candidate in 1983, he had not held such a position, so I count that case as an example of a pre-candidate who had not been a governor.

5. *La Nación*, 20 November 1995: 1.

Two provinces: Buenos Aires and Chaco

These two provinces have had distinct electoral environments in terms of the competition between parties as well as different socio-economic characteristics. According to previous literature, the level and structure of economic production, the dependence of citizens on the state, and the density of the population can have a major impact on the nature and extent of patronage. (See Appendix B for more information on these socio-economic dimensions in these two provinces.) As discussed in more detail in Appendix B, even though Buenos Aires and Chaco show major differences between themselves, both have a considerable share of their citizenry dependent on the state due to high levels of unemployment and slow (or negative) job creation in the private sector, creating a demand for patronage jobs from the population. As the president of the electoral tribune of UCR in the province of Buenos Aires said,[6]

> In reality, as a consequence of the contraction of the labour market, they or we as political parties use public employment to find jobs for the people because there are no jobs, that is, factories are not opened. [...] As political parties, we commit the error of using the state as a form of financing our parties.

However, we also need to see whether similar dynamics of intra-party competition influence the supply of patronage jobs by politicians in contrasting socio-economic conditions. Therefore, I conducted interviews and more detailed qualitative research in these two provinces that differ to a large extent on relevant socio-economic dimensions. Here, I use brief examples from Buenos Aires and Chaco to illustrate the mechanisms of internal party competition and its impact on public employment.

Buenos Aires

In the period after the democratic transition in 1983, the province of Buenos Aires constituted approximately 35 per cent of the electorate in general elections. Such a high potential influence in elections, added to its economic power, has made the province critical for the success of any politician with national career goals in Argentina. In terms of my theoretical analysis with respect to patronage jobs, particularistic networks that governors and party leaders have formed in such an influential district have been crucial in two forms. First, the mobilisation efforts that were enhanced through particularistic exchanges of public benefits have played a significant role in the parties' success in presidential elections. Second, they helped provincial party leaders (governors) to build a support base independent from national party leaders so that they have become important challengers to the national leadership. Indeed, since 1983, two governors of Buenos Aires (both Peronists), Antonio F. Cafiero (1987–1991) and Eduardo Duhalde (1991–1999), either ran as pre-candidates in the internal elections for presidential candidate or became national presidents.

---

6. Author's interview (No. 68), May 2005.

The governorship of Eduardo Duhalde is an illustrative case of how a politician's interaction with his party leader has an impact on patronage jobs. After losing the Peronist primary in 1988 to Carlos Menem, Antonio F. Cafiero did not re-run for the gubernatorial post. Instead, Menem's vice-president, Eduardo Duhalde, who had been the mayor of the municipality of Lomas de Zamora (in the province of Buenos Aires) from 1974–1976 and then again from 1983–1987, stepped away from the vice-presidential post and ran in the Peronist internal elections as the pre-candidate for governor against Carlos Brown. Brown was the mayor of another municipality in the province, General San Martin, and was supported by the (then Menemist) trade union leader, Barrionuevo. On July 28, 1991, when the Peronist party in the province of Buenos Aires chose their provincial candidates for the first time via direct vote by party members, Duhalde won an easy victory in the elections, of 80.53 per cent against 19.28 per cent for Brown.[7]

Although Menem's consolidation of power in the party and the public, in general, took off when his economic program of neo-liberal reforms started to bear fruit as inflation went down and economic growth resumed in the beginning of the 1990s, he did not yet have a dominant position in the party. Menem had won the presidential primary with only 53 per cent of the vote and it took him some time to build up his power in the party after he assumed the presidency. Therefore, in Duhalde's first years as governor, he could have still been seen by Menem as a valuable, but dangerous ally in the province of Buenos Aires. As a consequence of the large share of votes that the province contributed to national elections, it was important to keep Duhalde as an ally, but he would still be considered as a potential rival for party leadership. Therefore, a very strong effort from Duhalde to build a strong and independent power base in the province would be seen as a quite threatening signal for Menem's leadership.

From Duhalde's point of view, it was important to get the support of Menem, especially for financial reasons. In the Co-Participation agreement between the provinces and the federal government, Buenos Aires had lost 6–7 points in the index that would determine the amount of transfers from the federal government.[8] However, Duhalde managed to recover some of this loss in resources as a result of support from Menem in the form of a discretionary fund provided by the federal government (El fondo de reparación histórica del conurbano bonaerense- The fund for the historical reparation of the Buenos Aires Urban Belt), which amounted to approximately $700,000. Therefore, right after his election as governor, Duhalde was dependent on Menem for these financial resources, yet Menem, who was still vulnerable as the leader of the Peronist Party, could also see Duhalde as a potential rival.

Signs of such rivalry or challenge would have an impact on Menem's decision to support Buenos Aires financially. Although governors sometimes declare

---

7. *La Nación*, 29 July 1991.

8. Author's interview with a Peronist provincial legislator from the province of Buenos Aires (No. 60), May 2005.

their challenge explicitly, for example, by announcing their intention to run as presidential candidates in the party's primary, these declarations are not necessarily reliable. Like Reutemann (governor of Santa Fe) before the 2003 elections, potential candidates might keep their word and not run, after announcing they are not going to be pre-candidates. Or like Menem, who declared he was not going to run again, they might change their mind and try to run as candidates.[9] In addition to public declarations, politicians can signal their intention to challenge their leaders. As one politician said[10], 'It is like a marriage. There are no explicit guarantees, just subtle messages. People don't usually say what they mean in politics'. Besides cost-free signals of their intention, challengers might make costly attempts to build an independent power base. For example, having a strong machine in the province through patronage jobs and other clientelistic and non-clientelistic means is one prerequisite of independent political power. Attempts to build a personal following through the distribution of public sector jobs tells the party leader a lot about governors' intentions, especially since governors make the final decision about the number of public employees in the provincial government and their appointments.

In the period of analysis, when Duhalde needed Menem's financial support and Menem was not dominant in the Peronist Party, Duhalde had the incentive to send such a credible and costly signal, that is, a small number of patronage jobs in the provincial administration, to Menem to show that he was not a challenger to the latter's leadership. This is exactly what we see if we look at the employment data. As can be seen in Table 5.1, the number of both total and temporary employees per capita are low in the earlier years of Duhalde's incumbency, and it remains at these low levels until 1995 when Menem consolidated his dominance in the party.

By 1995, Menem had managed to implement sweeping economic reforms, reduce inflation, and pass a broad constitutional reform. For the 1995 elections, without any challenge from other Peronists, he received the nomination for another term as the president of the nation and his popularity levels among the public were high. His dominance in the party was so strong that Bordón, the Peronist governor of Mendoza, quit the party and opted to run for the presidency outside the party.[11] As such, efforts by Duhalde to build his political machine in the province would not pose a threat for Menem's leadership in the party for the time period. This new context opened the way for Duhalde to increase the number of patronage jobs in his administration (see Table 5.1).

Duhalde had no reservations about sending signs to Menem about his power base in the province of Buenos Aires. For example, the newspaper *La Nación* reported a large political gathering that was organised by the provincial Peronist organisation in November in La Matanza as Duhalde's intention of showing his

---

9. *La Nación*, 20 November 1995: 1. Menem was President when he announced, not a governor.

10. Author's interview (No. 23), October 2003.

11. Author's interview with a cabinet minister in Menem's government (No. 57), May 2005, Novaro and Palermo (1998).

Table 5.1: Employment per capita in two provinces, Buenos Aires and Chaco

year	Buenos Aires		Chaco	
	Temporary employees	Total number of employees	Temporary employees	Total number of employees
1984	0.22	1.65	0.12	3.57
1985	0.26	1.66	0.12	3.70
1986	0.22	1.84	0.11	3.83
1987	0.32	2.30	0.20	4.90
1988	0.30	2.31	0.21	4.79
1989	0.24	2.30	0.21	5.14
1990	0.23	2.29	0.21	4.59
1991	0.23	2.24	0.20	4.24
1992	0.23	2.25	0.18	4.32
1993	0.23	2.24	0.19	4.37
1994	0.23	2.22	0.17	4.21
1995	0.27	2.45	0.45	4.38
1996	0.27	2.45	0.11	4.33
1997	0.26	2.62	0.09	4.22
1998	0.27	2.72	0.09	4.33
1999	0.27	2.98	0.08	4.38
2000	0.26	3.13	0.09	4.35

Sources: Provinfo on total number of employees. Provincial budgetary legislations on temporary employees.

influence in the district and power to mobilise people. According to the same newspaper article, 3,000 buses were used to mobilise the party activists[12] and clearly the political machine that Duhalde had built partly through the distribution of public jobs and other public benefits helped his mobilisation efforts in the province.

In the 1995 elections, Duhalde actually started to distance himself from Menem[13] and his policies. Although Duhalde's candidacy for the gubernatorial position was not disputed, his internal group, the Federal League (Liga Federal) competed at the local and provincial level with candidates that got support from Menem and his close ally in the province, Alberto Pierri, who was known to have a strong political power base in the province's largest municipality, La Matanza.[14] By 1997, Duhalde even explicitly attempted to build an opposing coalition against

---

12. *La Nación*, 19 November 1995.

13. *La Nación*, 13 February 1995.

14. *La Nación*, 5 March 1995.

Menem: a national faction called the Federal Union (Levitsky 2003: 176).

The power balance in the PJ in fact started to change in 1997. The constitution had a two time term limit for the presidency. Although Menem later challenged this article by claiming that he could rerun for the presidency because he was elected the first time under the old constitution, ambiguity about his ability to re-run weakened his position in the party. In addition, in the legislative elections, the Peronist party experienced a decline in their vote share from 43 per cent in 1995 to 36.33 per cent. In hindsight we know that Duhalde had the intention to challenge Menem's candidacy for presidency (he ran a campaign in the party against Menem's intent to get re-elected for the third time) and his leadership in the party. At the same time, Duhalde did not need the support of the party to get re-elected because he had already built a strong political base in the province. Therefore, he again in this period had no incentive to send a signal to Menem by cutting down on patronage jobs. As expected, we see an increase in the size of public employment in these years (see Table 5.1).

Chaco

Even though Chaco contributes a much smaller share of the country's electorate (3 per cent in the 2003 elections) when compared to the province of Buenos Aires, important national political figures have emerged from this province as well. In the first elections after the democratic transition the provincial Peronist leader, Deolindo Bittel, ran as the vice-presidential candidate, and Ángel Rozas (two-time governor from the Radical party) has served as the president of the UCR between 2001 and 2005. The politics in the province have, for a long time, been dominated by the Peronists until they lost power in 1991 to the provincial party AC (Acción Chaqueña, Action of Chaco). Then, with an unexpected victory in 1995 by the Radicals, the province became a stronghold of the UCR.[15]

The provincial politics of Chaco experienced a major change in 1995 when Ángel Rozas (the president of the Radicals in the provincial legislature and Luis León's partner as the lieutenant-gubernatorial candidate in 1987) won the Radical primaries to become the gubernatorial candidate. The senator Luis León had domi-nated the Radical party politics in Chaco for a long period until in 1995 Rozas broke away from León's internal group, MAY, and his new group, Convergencia, won the primaries against León's candidate, Federico Kaenel. Before the prima-ries on March 19, 1995, both León and Rozas made strong mobilisation efforts throughout the province,[16] but Rozas managed to come out as the winner with 66.8 per cent of the vote against Kaenel's 33.2 per cent in the primaries, in which

---

15. In 2007, the Radicals lost it back to the Peronists with a small margin of 0.23 per cent. The Peronist incumbent governor, Jorge Capitanich, then built his political base in the province and came out as the winner in the 2011 elections with 66.6 per cent of the votes against his Radical rival's 30.3 per cent.

16. *Diario Norte*, various issues in February–March 1995.

85,000 Radical party members voted.[17] Even though Rozas came out behind the Peronist candidate, Florencio Tenev, in the first round of elections, he secured victory in the second round.

Furthermore, he managed to build a strong political base in the province and emerged as a national figure starting with his second gubernatorial term due to the power vacancy that was left in the Radical party with de la Rúa's precipitous decline in 2001. Rozas served as the formal president of the party for two terms (2001–2003, 2003–2005) and had also started to challenge the de facto leadership of the former president, Alfonsín, in the party[18]. Therefore, in hindsight we know that Rozas had ambitions for national leadership.

Although it is not clear exactly at what point Rozas started to form these national ambitions, we would expect him to have had intentions to build a strong power base in his party that would allow him to compete for national leadership. However, the nature of competition within the Radical party and with other parties in the general elections also provided him with reasons to constrain his efforts to form an extended patronage network by distributing public jobs. During the time period when Rozas controlled the provincial administration, the Radical party did not have a dominant national party leader. In 1995, there was close competition for the presidential candidacy between Horacio Massaccesi, the governor of Rio Negro, and Federico Storani. In the primaries Rozas sided with Storani and even though Storani lost with 35 per cent of votes to Massaccesi's 65 per cent nationwide, Storani won the primaries in Chaco with a small margin of 3.3 per cent.[19]

Massaccesi and the Radical party performed very badly and managed to get only 16.8 per cent of the votes in the presidential elections. If we consider Massaccesi and his supporters in the party as the national party leaders in the immediate aftermath of the presidential elections, they clearly did not have a dominant position in the party. The party leadership was open to competition. In addition, the fact that Rozas supported Storani in the primaries definitely made Rozas a threat to the national leadership. As such, any efforts by Rozas to expand his patronage networks in the province would make it too risky for the national party leadership to support him. At the same time, Rozas had just become the governor and his support in the province was not yet established. Therefore, support from the party would have been helpful, especially in the second part of Rozas' first term as the popularity of the Radical party started to increase and the Radicals started to approach the leading opposition coalition, FREPASO, to form a larger coalition, Allianza, before the 1999 elections (Ollier 2001).

In the second half of Rozas' term, a new national leader started to emerge

---

17. *Diario Norte*, 20 March 1995.

18. Author's interview with four Radical politicians in May 2005 (Former Secretary of Economic Planning (No. 56), secretary of the Radical Block in the Senate (No. 58), a provincial legislator from the province of Buenos Aires (No. 59), and the president of the Electoral Commission in the province of Buenos Aires (No. 68).

19. *Diario Norte*, 28 November 1994.

within the Radical Party: the mayor of the City of Buenos Aires (Federal Capital), Fernando de la Rúa. Even though de la Rúa had much more popularity among the public in general compared to the preceding national party leader, and was eventually elected president of the nation in 1999, he still lacked a dominant position within the party (Ollier 2001: 86). Therefore, throughout Rozas' first term as governor and in the first year of his second term[20] for which we have data on public employment, we would expect Rozas to constrain his efforts to distribute public jobs in a particularistic manner because he had incentives to send a signal of a non-challenger type to the national leadership of the party. The figures on public employment in Table 5.1 support this expectation. During most of Rozas' government, the number of public employees remained stable at a lower level than the period between 1987 and 1989, the time period for which we would expect high levels of patronage due to the internal politics within the Peronist party.

This internal competition within the Radical party opened ways to hold back the expansion of the state in Chaco further through patronage hirings, even if it did not completely eliminate inefficiency in the administration. As the president of the provincial legislature in Chaco said, 'The state, in addition to its huge size, is inefficient. It is overloaded with people that in reality do not fulfil their responsibilities.'[21] However, as the experience in Chaco shows, if the government is controlled by a party where the leadership position is contested and if the party's support is critical for the governor's political career, an opportunity might arise to contain the expansion of the provincial government's size and inefficiency.

Patronage in four municipal governments

In Chapters Three and Four, I have argued that the number of patronage jobs is mainly affected by internal party competition and this competition was analysed with a game theoretic model. The same model can also help us to understand some mechanisms behind patronage at the municipal level. In the case of the local (municipal) public administration, the political actor who has the final decision on the distribution of public jobs, is the mayor. Since an important step up in a mayor's political career would be to become the provincial party leader, and mayors and provincial party leaders (governor, if the party is holding this post) are interdependent for their party's electoral success, I expect the interaction between a mayor and his provincial party leader to have a crucial impact on the level of clientelistic exchanges between the mayor and his supporters in a district, that is, on the number of public employees in the municipal administration.

I again illustrate the political dynamics by using two examples (municipalities) that contrast in terms of their socio-economic characteristics: La Matanza and Pilar in the province of Buenos Aires, and Resistencia and Fontana in Chaco. See Appendix B for more information on their socio-economic characteristics.)

---

20. Rozas could be reelected as the governor because there was a constitutional reform that allowed a second term.

21. Author's interview (No. 16), October 2003.

The province of Buenos Aires

La Matanza

Since La Matanza retains a large share of the voters in the province,[22] the interaction between the local politicians and the provincial politicians within the same party is of outmost importance. Provincial leaders of parties (governor if the party is holding this position) know that their party's performance in the province, and hence their own political career, is influenced significantly by the party's support in La Matanza. In addition to the general elections, support from La Matanza can be helpful in internal competition between provincial leaders of the same party.

The political situation prior to the 2007 elections is a case in point. The year 2005 was witness to a major confrontation for the control of the province between the two time ex-governor of Buenos Aires and former president, Duhalde, and the then-governor of the province, Felipe Solá.[23] In addition to the two separate internal groups that they have formed, two concrete examples of this division between these two provincial leaders are the difficulties that the provincial legislature was suffering in passing the annual budget[24] and the highly vocal discussions about the nominees for the national legislature.[25] In this internal competition between the two leaders, Solá and Duhalde, the mayor of La Matanza, Alberto Balestrini, sided with Solá. This alliance between Balestrini and Solá (who also at that time had the support of the president, Kirchner) was critical for Solá's success in his struggle for power in the province. As the president of the municipal council put it, 'The electoral power that the mayor [Balestrini] has and the Peronist movement in La Matanza has is important. The governor and the president want the mayor to support them.'[26]

However, as a provincial legislator from La Matanza stated, '...the support can be bottom up or top down'[27] and this is what we observe in the interaction between Solá and Balestrini. As a consequence of the alliance with Solá, Balestrini's municipality received valuable economic resources from the provincial government. Even though Solá had initiated a provincial level Co-Participation agreement between the provincial government and the municipal governments[28], and hence, could not arbitrarily increase transfers to some municipalities, La Matanza had been receiving a disproportionate share of direct investments for public works

---

22. In the 2003 elections, the number of citizens eligible to vote in La Matanza comprised approximately 12 per cent of the province. (Author's interview with the president of the municipal council (No. 24) in La Matanza, May 2005).

23. *Clarín*, 4 March 2005.

24. *La Nación*, 23 February 2005.

25. *Clarín*, 30 June 2005.

26. Author's interview (No. 24), May 2005.

27. Author's interview (No. 60), May 2005.

28. Author's interview with a provincial legislator from La Matanza (No. 60 May, 2005).

or resources from the provincial government to spend on certain specific public works. Just to name a few, the enlargement of provincial roads that pass through the municipality, such as key routes 21 and 17, construction of a bridge over the San Justo Circle, and a hospital, have been executed with resources that originated from the provincial government.

Since all these works have high levels of visibility among the electorate, the municipal government of Balestrini has benefitted politically from this financial support from the provincial party leader. In order to increase the impact on Balestrini's popularity and the political support in La Matanza for both Balestrini and Solá, the alliance with Solá and the consequent flow of resources to La Matanza from the provincial government have been emphasised by Balestrini in his appeals to the public and party members in the municipality. An example of this strategy occurred in a public gathering of the Peronist Party in the Club Huracán of San Justo in which Balestrini and Solá participated together. Balestrini spent a large part of his speech going over the public works that have been initiated with the support of the provincial government of Solá in the past year.[29] Even though the alliance between Balestrini and Solá was beneficial for both in that period, it also carried risks for Solá's future power in the province. Since Solá was barred constitutionally from getting re-elected as governor, he had to leave his position to another popular politician in the province and Balestrini seemed to have a strong potential

Table 5.2: Public sector employment in two municipalities in the province of Buenos Aires

La Matanza	Personnel spending	Total revenue	Share
1995	100,688,097	150,454,087	0.67
1996	88,392,605	165,326,196	0.53
1997	86,940,826	183,813,285	0.47
1998	87,692,323	177,805,352	0.49
1999	90,882,863	187,248,965	0.49
Pilar	**Personnel spending**	**Total revenue**	**Share**
1995	11,540,054	23,730,992	0.49
1996	12,978,680	28,679,972	0.45
1997	14,197,271	33,606,332	0.42
1998	16,731,100	38,546,361	0.43
1999	19,456,789	35,867,517	0.54

Source: Recursos y Gastos Municipales 1995–1999.

---

29. Author's own observation, 5 May 2005.

for taking over this position.[30] As such, although Balestrini was a valuable ally in the political environment of the period, he was also a strong future rival to Solá's political power in Buenos Aires.

As this brief overview of the political interaction between Balestrini and the two provincial leaders illustrates, the internal competition between the mayor of La Matanza and the provincial leader of the party fits well with the theoretical model that I introduced in Chapter Four and analyses the impact of intra-party competition on particularistic distribution of jobs in the public sector. Now, I turn to the examination of data on public sector employment in La Matanza for the period between 1995 and 1999[31] in order to see how the interaction between the mayor and the governor, in this time period, influenced the size of the municipal administration. I use the municipal governments' revenues to control for the impact of socio-economic changes across the five year time period and analyse personnel spending as a percentage of municipal revenues. (The figures are presented in Table 5.2).

In 1995, the Peronist party in La Matanza went to elections with the contemporary mayor, Hector Cozzi, as their candidate. Cozzi (who was then the secretary of public works in the municipality) had won the primaries in 1991 against Ricardo Rolleri, who was supported by Federico Pedro Russo (the mayor of La Matanza at that time), and approximately 20 other candidates. Both Cozzi and Rolleri at the provincial level had allied with Duhalde, but Cozzi came out as the winner with almost 60 per cent of the votes cast in the primary.[32] Four years later, Cozzi was directly confronted in the primaries by the former mayor, F. Russo. In the internal elections in which 214,000 party members voted, Cozzi won with more than 70 per cent of the votes against Russo. While Russo was supported by Duhalde in these elections, Cozzi allied with the competing provincial leader, Alberto Pierri. This choice by Cozzi to form an alliance with Pierri seems to indicate that Cozzi did not think that he needed the support of Duhalde in his efforts to get re-elected as mayor. Since Cozzi did not have any incentive to send a signal to Duhalde that he was not a rival for Duhalde's control of the province, we would not expect intra-party competition to lead to lower levels of patronage. When we compare personnel spending in the year 1995 with the following years for which data is available, the highest figure is indeed observed in this year.

In Cozzi's first year of his second term, we see a slight drop in the levels of personnel spending. This decrease can be linked to the fact that the general elections and primaries were held the previous year and provided incentives to increase the distribution of public jobs for mobilisation efforts. In the following

---

30. In the following 2007 elections this candidacy instead went to the then vice-president of the nation, Daniel Scioli. Balestrini accompanied Scioli as the candidate for the lieutenant-governor on the Peronist ticket. Solá's alliance with Kirchner broke down and Solá joined the dissident Peronists.

31. This time period is chosen due to data availability.

32. *La Nación*, The Supplement, 30 July 1991.

three years the spending on personnel composed even a smaller percentage of the municipal revenues. This decline can mostly be explained by the changing nature of the relationship between Cozzi and Duhalde. Both Cozzi's and Duhalde's positions in the party, respectively at the municipal and provincial level, started to change with 1997. The decline in Cozzi's popularity culminated with his loss in the primaries against Balestrini in 1999. Faced with waning political support, we would expect Cozzi to pursue some support from the provincial party leader and governor Duhalde and, according to one of his former rivals, in the 1999 primaries 'Cozzi was with Duhalde'.[33] In addition to Cozzi's need for Duhalde's support, Duhalde's emerging struggle with Menem for the national party leadership had started to weaken Duhalde. Both of these factors are expected to give Cozzi incentives to constrain his efforts in building patronage networks in his municipality through the distribution of public jobs. Since sending signals of a challenger type through high levels of patronage networks might have risked Duhalde's support, and since Cozzi needed this support for his career goals, he traded-off patronage jobs for support.

Pilar

Even though the municipality of Pilar plays a much less important role politically and economically in the province, we would expect the competition between the mayor and his provincial party leader to still have an impact on the efforts to establish patronage networks in the municipality. In 1995 the municipality of Pilar was governed by the Peronist Mayor, Alberto Alberini. The winner of the 1991 municipal election was, however, Jorge Perez. Perez had won the Peronist primaries on the 1 August 1991, where 7,646 party members voted, against four other candidates. Perez' votes equalled 3,211 against the runner up, Humberto Zuccaro's, 2,385 votes.[34] However, in the beginning of 1993 Perez resigned from his post[35] and Alberini took over the municipal government. Alberini ran for re-election in 1995 and won the primaries with a wide margin of 62.3 per cent of the votes against the leading candidate's 14 per cent.[36]

As in La Matanza, the municipality of Pilar spent a large share of its revenue on personnel in the year 1995 when compared to the following three years. Similar to the case of Cozzi in La Matanza, Alberini won the primaries with ease against his rivals in the municipality. Therefore, in terms of getting the nomination from the Peronist party, he did not really need Duhalde's support. In addition, in that period Duhalde's leadership in the province was quite strong. Therefore, intra-party politics did not provide any incentives for Alberini to constrain levels of patronage in his municipal administration.

---

33. Author's interview (No. 23), October 2005.

34. *Resumen*, 2 August 1991.

35. Perez was then elected as a National Deputy.

36. *Resumen*, 8 March 1995.

In the following year, the size of public employment was considerably smaller. As in the case of La Matanza, this decline can again be accounted for by the fact that 1995 was an election year and Alberini might have used patronage networks to mobilise party members and voters for the internal and general elections. The political context and the interaction between the mayor of Pilar and the governor, Duhalde, was again similar to the situation in La Matanza in the years 1997 and 1998. Alberini, similarly to Cozzi, was losing popularity and ended up barely winning the primaries against Sergio Bivort before the 1999 elections. Alberini could achieve only 48 per cent of the votes while Bivort achieved 37 per cent.[37] In hindsight we can see that Duhalde's support was more valuable for Alberini in these latter years of his second term. As I have already discussed in the case of La Matanza, Duhalde was confronting Menem nationally and this struggle was weakening the latter. Therefore, the internal politics of the Peronists provided the ideal context to limit patronage exchanges in the municipal administration.

Yet, a major difference between La Matanza and Pilar took place in 1999. In the case of La Matanza, the size of personnel spending remained more or less stable at low levels between 1997 and 1999. However, in Pilar, personnel spending increased significantly in 1999 after being much lower in 1997 and 1998. When we consider internal party politics, we can see that the change cannot be a consequence of the interaction between Alberini and Duhalde, because the critical political factors related to their relationship remained the same. One explanation can be derived from the analysis of general elections. The competition between candidates in the general elections of 1999 in Pilar was an exceptional case because the loser of the Peronist primaries, Bivort, ran in the elections as an outside candidate and won an unexpected victory.[38] Even though Alberini formed an alliance with Duhalde at the provincial level[39] the tight competition in the general elections at the municipal level might have led Alberini to risk foregoing Duhalde's support by increasing the number of patronage jobs in his province.

Chaco

As in the case of the Province of Buenos Aires, my analysis in Chaco focuses on two municipalities that vary along key socio-economic dimensions. However, data limitations caused major difficulties with the analysis. First of all, in Chaco the administrative units that are used in data collection do not match with municipalities. Therefore, exact statistical data on municipalities is not available. Second, the data on public employment at the municipal level is available only for three years, 1992, 1997, and 2002, and they are not comparable across years within the same municipality. Due to lack of data on municipal revenues in 1992, I cannot even control for any socio-economic factors across municipalities within the same

---

37. *Resumen*, 11 May 1999.

38. *La Nación*, 27 October 1999.

39. *Resumen*, 8 May 1999.

year. Therefore, I removed 1992 from the analysis. Since the data from 1997 is on personnel spending and the data from 2002 is on the number of employees, I cannot compare the two years across the same municipalities. As such, I examined the impact of internal political competition on levels of patronage by looking at where the two municipalities stand when compared to the rest of the municipalities in the province.

Resistencia

In terms of political competition between parties, both municipalities were more competitive when compared to the two municipalities that I analysed in the Province of Buenos Aires. In 1997, the Peronists controlled the government in Resistencia. In the primaries before the 1995 elections Rafael Gonzalez had formed an alliance with Florencio Tenev who ran as the pre-candidate for the gubernatorial position.[40] Their group, the Peronist Groups' Front (FAP), won the primaries where 161,206 party members and 265,000 independents were eligible to vote. Gonzalez got 4,720 votes against the leading candidate's 2,751.[41] These primary results suggest that in the couple of years that followed the internal elections, Gonzalez' position in the party was quite strong and that he did not necessarily need the support of his party's provincial leader. Even though during this period the Peronists did not have a dominant party leader in the province, which opened ways to curtail patronage jobs in the municipality, we would not expect Gonzalez to have the incentive to trade off the distribution of patronage jobs in return for support from the provincial leader because the leader's support was not crucial. In addition, the results of both the 1995 and 1997 elections showed that the Peronists were losing popularity among the broader public in the province. Therefore, any support from the provincial party leader or organisation did not seem to be very helpful and we would expect to observe high levels of spending on personnel. Table 5.3 presents the personnel spending as a percentage of municipal revenues across municipalities in the province. There, we can see that Resistencia's level of spending (as a share of revenues) was indeed larger than the average.

---

40. *Diario Norte*, 3 May 1995.

41. *Diario Norte*, 13 March 1995.

Table 5.3: Municipalities in Chaco, 1997 and 2002

Municipality	Personnel spending	Total revenue	Per cent
Barranqueras	6,254,245	7,113,788	87.92
G.San Martin	2,281,449	3,578,639	63.75
Las Breñas	2,359,729	2,589,180	91.14
Saenz Peña	10,930,422	15,071,723	72.52
Quitilipi	2,516,467	3,443,073	73.09
Resistencia	**47,720,853**	**60,501,886**	**78.87**
Villa Angela	4,735,741	6,347,069	74.61
Avia Terai	441,885	800,775	55.18
Campo Largo	777,706	1,067,667	72.84
C.Du Graty	866,160	1,343,406	64.47
Corzuela	933,065	1,289,114	72.38
Fontana	**1,229,793**	**2,020,642**	**60.86**
Gral. Pinedo	1,154,221	1,418,326	81.38
H. Campo	955,777	990,297	96.51
J. J. Castelli	2,323,231	2,862,664	81.16
La Escondida	530,933	724,008	73.33
Machagai	1,525,943	2,511,765	60.75
Makalle	211,805	742,321	28.53
P. del Indio	696,120	825,665	84.31
P.de la Plaza	894,972	1,338,624	66.86
Pto. Tirol	919,312	1,294,488	71.02
Pto. Vilelas	1,916,222	2,744,601	69.82
Santa Sylvina	1,156,702	1,174,914	98.45
Taco Pozo	390,390	748,506	52.16
Tres Isletas	1,730,353	2,682,075	64.52
Capitán Solari	350,890	641,836	54.67
Ciervo Petiso	152,252	313,933	48.50
Colonia Elisa	404,582	771,094	52.47
Col. Popular	183,844	572,673	32.10
Col.Unidas	290,290	390,946	74.25
Cote Lai	174,861	359,934	48.58
Charadai	294,866	457,368	64.47
Enrique Urien	187,328	193,699	96.71
F. Esperanza	347,210	569,319	60.99

Municipality	Personnel spending	Total revenue	Per cent
Gancedo	234,497	482,709	48.58
G. Capdevila	86,345	349,394	24.71
G. Vedia	190,958	279,494	68.32
I. del Cerrito	323,115	632,979	51.05
La Clotilde	291,202	643,530	45.25
La Verde	418,045	660,450	63.30
L. Blanca	195,068	347,521	56.13
Lapachito	230,855	425,665	54.23
Las Garcitas	252,348	619,348	40.74
M. Belén	495,772	661,714	74.92
Miraflores	275,987	629,948	43.81
Napenay	230,395	692,123	33.29
P. Almiron	251,510	431,900	58.23
P. Roca	284,989	612,894	46.50
P. Bermejo	230,548	523,262	44.06
P. E. Perón	150,508	309,242	48.67
V. R. Bermejito	371,237	773,706	47.98
average			**62.33**

Source: Sub-secretary of Municipal Affairs, Province of Chaco.

Municipalities in Chaco, 2002

Municipality	Total revenue	Number of Employees	Per cent
Barranqueras	371,368	528	0.14
Charata	189,069	283	0.15
G. San Martin	169,028	247	0.15
Las Breñas	126,538	241	0.19
Saenz Peña	595,697	1,240	0.21
Quitilipi	152,394	220	0.14
Resistencia	**3,127,550**	**3,860**	**0.12**
Villa Angela	284,130	447	0.16
Avia Terai	42,773	71	0.17
Campo Largo	42,955	81	0.19
C. del Bermejo	32,661	60	0.18
C. Du Graty	54,589	96	0.18
Corzuela	58,790	82	0.14

Municipality	Total revenue	Number of Employees	Per cent
Fontana	**114,689**	**170**	**0.15**
Gral. Pinedo	68,095	110	0.16
H. Campo	47,927	73	0.15
Juan J. Castelli	142,009	248	0.17
La Escondida	46,566	54	0.12
La Leonesa	71,449	117	0.16
Las Palmas	57,733	88	0.15
Machagai	99,774	178	0.18
Makalle	25,128	45	0.18
P. del Indio	36,958	60	0.16
P. del Infierno	45,304	74	0.16
P. de la Plaza	58,095	102	0.18
Pto. Tirol	60,218	146	0.24
Pto. Vilelas	120,323	211	0.18
San Bernardo	54,673	63	0.12
Santa Sylvina	53,247	106	0.20
Taco Pozo	35,788	126	0.35
Tres Isletas	109,614	214	0.20
Villa Berthet	48,003	83	0.17
Basail	18,696	29	0.16
Capitán Solari	29,763	50	0.17
Ciervo Petiso	16,473	28	0.17
Col. Benitez	26,508	90	0.34
Colonia Elisa	21,176	32	0.15
Col. Popular	15,905	21	0.13
Col. Unidas	29,202	92	0.32
Cote Lai	12,636	27	0.21
Charadai	19,547	35	0.18
Chorotis	17,406	48	0.28
El Sauzalito	28,350	111	0.39
Enrique Urien	18,057	21	0.12
F. Esperanza	28,262	64	0.23
Gancedo	23,432	39	0.17
G. Capdevila	10,825	13	0.12
G. Vedia	20,623	46	0.22

Municipality	Total revenue	Number of Employees	Per cent
Isla del Cerrito	31,790	86	0.27
La Clotilde	27,319	31	0.11
La Eduvigis	18,045	29	0.16
La Tigra	26,631	31	0.12
La Verde	22,732	30	0.13
Laguna Blanca	12,775	26	0.20
Laguna Limpia	18,386	31	0.17
Lapachito	9,795	16	0.16
Las Garcitas	26,621	46	0.17
Los Frentones	27,307	54	0.20
M. Belén	31,405	48	0.15
M. N. Pompeya	28,695	77	0.27
Miraflores	23,386	40	0.17
Napenay	19,880	33	0.17
P. Almiron	18,488	19	0.10
P. Roca	33,271	56	0.17
P. Bermejo	20,173	47	0.23
P. E. Perón	15,792	39	0.25
Samuhú	46,498	133	0.29
V. R. Bermejito	21,532	38	0.18
average			**0.18**

Source: Sub-secretary of Municipal Affairs, Province of Chaco.

In 2002, the municipality was controlled by the Radicals. Before the 1999 elections, internal elections for the position of mayor in Resistencia were not held and a consensus was reached on the candidacy of Benicio Szymula. In the 2003 elections as well, only in very few municipalities was there internal competition for candidacy.[42] Therefore during this period, support from Rozas, the governor and the provincial leader of the Radicals, was essential for being nominated for any public position by the Radical party. Even though Szymula later did not run again for the position of mayor, Rozas' support was also critical for the general elections. As the then president of the municipal council, who in 2003 ran as the Radical candidate for the mayor's position in Resistencia, stated,

---

42. Author's interview with the president of the Electoral Commission in the Radical party (No. 18), October 2003.

> For the campaign, it is of course [important to have the support of Rozas.] [...] The figure of Rozas and his help influence a lot. Especially, in the posters. I have a poster where I was with Rozas, the gubernatorial and lieutenant-gubernatorial candidates. It was strong.[43]

Even though at this period it was important for local and provincial politicians to get Rozas' support, a second condition had to be met in order for Szymula to trade-off jobs for Rozas' support. Rozas needed to see other politicians as threats to his leadership in the province. Although Rozas was very strong in the province, we can argue that this condition was met because he was going to lose his formal power as the governor in the following year. Since Rozas had already served two terms as governor he was approaching the end of his formal control over the provincial administration. This loss in formal power would be expected to make potential rivals threatening to his leadership. As such, Szymula might have had incentives to trade off jobs for Rozas' support because the support was very valuable and could be conditioned on the signal that Szymula sent through the distribution of patronage jobs. When we compare the number of public employees as a percentage of the municipal revenues in Resistencia with the rest of the province, we can indeed see that the amount of public employees was lower than the average.

Fontana

Fontana's mayor, the Peronist Augusto Rey, ran in 1995 for his fifth term as mayor. However, as at the provincial level, the Peronists lost the election to the Radicals. The 1995 Radical primaries saw fierce competition between two internal groups – those led by Luis León and Ángel Rozas. In Fontana, León's group came out as the winner with 179 votes against 127 for Rozas'. The elected mayor was Pedron Gallardo. However, in 1996 the province intervened in the municipal government and Victor Zimmerman, who was the secretary of the economy in Rozas' provincial government, became the intervening mayor. Therefore, in 1997 the municipality of Fontana was controlled by Zimmerman. If we analyse the interaction between Zimmerman and Rozas at this period, we can say that Zimmerman was very likely to find Rozas' support helpful for his re-election as the mayor of Fontana. Since he was not the winner of the 1995 primaries, he did not have the full support of the party in Fontana. As a former mayor of Fontana put it,

> When you have a leader like Rozas for example, it is important that you appear on a poster with him, that he talks about you, and that publicly he keeps his support for you.[44]

In 1995 Rozas had won a surprising victory against the provincial party leader,

---

43. Author's interview (No. 17), October 2003.

44. Author's interview (No. 15), October 2005.

Senator León. In 1997 Rozas was still in the process of establishing his power in the party. Therefore, we would expect Zimmerman to have the incentive to send a signal to Rozas that he was not a rival for his power by constraining the level of patronage jobs that he distributed. The figures in Table 5.3 support this expectation. The spending on personnel as a percentage of municipal revenues was slightly below the average in Chaco.

In 1999, Zimmerman ran for re-election as the mayor. As in most other municipalities, internal elections were not held and according to the consensus list Zimmerman ran as the Radical candidate. However, in 2001 he became the Subsecretary of Social Development in the Province and left the position of mayor. Therefore, again Fontana had a mayor whose support in the party was not ratified by a victory in the general election. In addition, by 2002 it was well-known that lists were made not through primaries, but through consensus. Therefore, support from Rozas was important for almost all politicians that aspired to be candidates from the Radical party. In addition, as I have already discussed in the case of Resistencia, Rozas, by 2002, was already in his second and last term as governor, which somewhat weakened his power within the party. Even though Rozas was still very popular among the public and party, his rivals knew that Rozas was not going to be formally in control of the provincial administration after 2003. Hence, these two factors, that Rozas' support was valuable, but could be conditioned on the signal sent by mayors, opened ways to contain patronage efforts in Fontana and as we can see in the Table 5.3, the number of public employees as a percentage of the municipal revenues, was lower than the average in Chaco.

Statistical analysis of provincial employment [45]

Even though the examples in the previous section illustrate how the interaction between a politician and his party leader can have an impact on patronage jobs in both municipal and provincial administrations, large-n data that would allow a statistical test, exists only for the provincial level. In this section, I provide a statistical analysis of this data, where the dependent variable is the number of temporary employees (per 10,000 people) hired by a provincial administration in a year.

There are two types of employees in Argentina: permanent employees (planta permanente) that have tenure and the temporary employees (transitorios or contratados). It is more difficult for politicians and parties to manipulate permanent jobs for political purposes because provincial governments cannot replace tenured employees hired by previous governments. They can place their supporters in these permanent jobs by creating more positions, but this is not an easy strategy given the financial pressures in recent years.

My interviews reveal that even though politicians hire supporters for both types of position, patronage is more prevalent among the temporary jobs since politicians can condition the clientelistic good on the provision of political support. Although in theory these positions should be temporary, created in special cases

---

45. See Appendix C for sources of data.

when a particular job is beyond the scope of the permanent workforce, in practice temporary contracts are renewed as often as necessary, and temporary contractors actually conduct the day-to-day business of the provincial government. As one PJ party member in Chaco said,[46]

> There is also the so-called contract system. [...] The ruling political party has the power, which it frequently uses in Chaco, to hire personnel with temporary contracts who actually end up doing the political work.

Therefore, the analysis of temporary jobs should be able to reflect patronage dynamics more closely than an analysis of the whole public labour or the permanent positions. As such, I use the number of temporary employees as the measurement of patronage jobs.

Explanatory variables

According to the hypotheses derived from the model, a governor has less incentive to distribute patronage jobs when he needs the party (leader's) support in order to get re-elected, and when the support has some effect on internal leadership competition, that is, when the leadership position is open to competition. Since the game theoretic analysis implies that both of these conditions must be present to have an impact on the number of patronage jobs, I use an interactive term to test my argument. However, before explaining how I analyse the interaction effect, I first discuss the operationalisation of these two variables.

A very good indicator for the importance of the party leader's support for the politician, is the difference between the governors' vote share and the party's vote share in presidential and legislative elections. Since the party and the presidential candidate are stronger and more popular in these provinces, we should expect the national leader's support to help governor's electoral chances. I expect this difference to be less important when the governor already has a high percentage of votes. Therefore, I divide this difference between the party's and governor's vote shares by the governor's vote share. For each year I use the most temporarily proximate of the past, simultaneous or future election results. When presidential and legislative elections are held simultaneously, I use the presidential election results. When the party's (presidential candidate's) vote share increases relative to the governor's vote share, I expect that the governor needs the party leader's support to be re-elected.

To measure the effectiveness of the leader's support for leadership competition, I look at the strength of the current party leader. If the leader is in a dominant position and the leadership position is not open to competition, she would be able to maintain her leadership even if she gives support to the challenger followers. Therefore, her support would have no effect on leadership turnover. In order to measure the strength of the party leader, I use the presidential primary election

---

46. Author's interview (No. 20), October 2003.

results.[47] They serve as good indicators of the leader's strength because when the party holds the presidency, the President can be considered the party leader who may face internal competition from governors in her own party, since the presidential candidacy is the position that governors would like to contest in upcoming elections. For parties that do not control the presidency I assume that the politician with the most power usually aspires to this position and will become a pre-candidate for the presidency. Good examples would be Alfonsín as one of the UCR pre-candidates for the presidency in 1983 (and then the elected President between 1983 and 1989); de la Rúa in the UCR (Alianza) as the candidate in the 1999 elections (then the elected President between 1999 and December 2001); and Menem in the PJ after the1989 internal elections. The pre-candidate's vote share in the primaries then indicates her strength in the party.

Yet the actual party leaders do not always run as pre-candidates. In elections where the party is weak, the leader might calculate that running as a presidential candidate and then losing, will cost her prestige and hurt her political career. Or in some cases where other positions might allow them to control significant resources (such as the leadership of a trade union) these politicians might prefer to stay in the background. Therefore, although they might be the most powerful actors in the party, the leaders might make a strategic decision not to run for the presidency. For example, the real party leader of the PJ prior to the 1983 elections was not the presidential candidate. Although union leaders, especially Lorenzo Miguel, had the real power in the PJ, they did not run as candidates (Levitsky 2003; McGuire 1997; Manzetti 1993). However, these leaders, especially Miguel, influenced the selection of the presidential and vice-presidential candidates, Ítalo Luder and Deolindo Felipe Bittel respectively (Levitsky 2003: 52 and McGuire 1997: 182). Therefore, the vote shares received by the actual candidates in the primaries can be used as proxies for the strength of the actual leader's power in the party. If a pre-candidate who has the backing of the actual leader cannot succeed in the internal party elections, the leader must not be particularly strong. As a result, in these cases I again use the presidential primary results, considering the highest vote share as the indicator of the leader's strength and hence the openness of party leadership competition.[48]

---

47. In 1988 the PJ and the UCR, in 1994 and 1999 the UCR used primaries to select their presidential candidates. Here I treat indirect party conventions such as those held by the UCR in 1983 as primaries for practical purposes. In 1995 the Peronist president Menem's candidacy was not contested, so it was coded as 100. I discuss the two exceptional cases of the Peronist nomination in 1983 and 1999 in a later footnote.

48. Before the 1983 elections, Peronists were supposed to select their candidate in the national convention. However, the leaders reached a consensus before the national convention. In this case, I use the election results from the province of Buenos Aires, where the delegates to the national convention were chosen. Two groups, one led by Herminio Iglesias and the other by Antonio Cafiero competed in these elections. Since Iglesias had the support of Miguel (Romero 2002: 252), I use Iglesias' vote share as a proxy for the strength of Luder, the presidential candidate who had Miguel's backing. (*cont.*)

Since the results of the game theoretic analysis predict that the number of jobs will decrease when these two conditions – open party leadership competition and important party support – are present, I include a multiplicative term of these variables. I expect that the number of jobs will decrease when the vote share of the party, relative to the governor's vote share, increases if the governor's party leader did not dominate the primaries. The equilibria of the model also predicts that when the leadership is not open to competition (measured by primary results), the number of patronage jobs will be high compared to the case where there is competition for leadership, but the importance of the party (leader's) support will have no effect on patronage jobs. See Figure 5.1 for a representation of the game theoretic results with the measurements that are used in this empirical analysis.

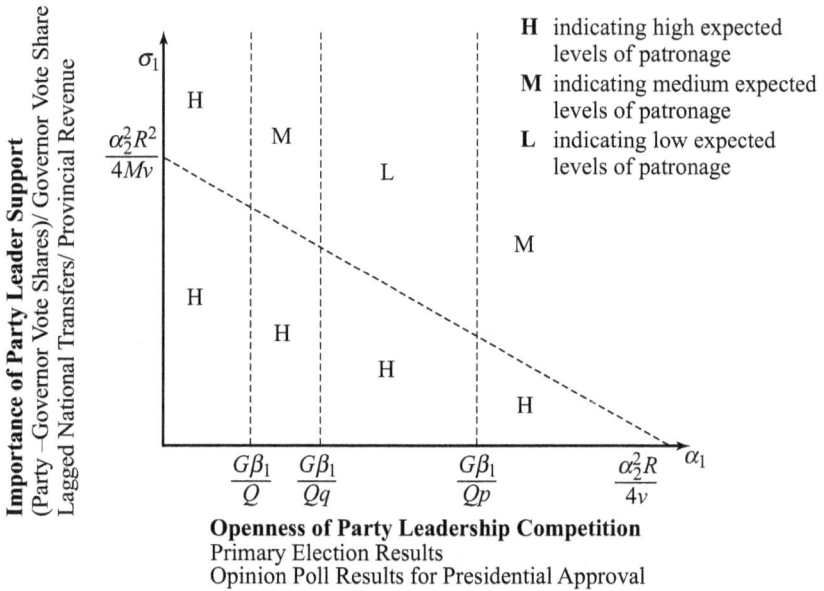

Figure 5.1: Impact of two factors on the expected number of patronage jobs

(*48. cont.*) Before the 1999 elections, Duhalde was unopposed in the presidential primaries that were scheduled for July 4 after Adolfo Rodríguez Saá withdrew on June 7. However, the real competition that is not reflected in the primary results is the one between then-President Menem, and Duhalde. Although Menem was not supposed to run again since the Constitution has a two-term limit, Menem wanted the Supreme Court to interpret the Constitution to say that his first term did not count, since he was elected before the constitutional reform incorporated the term limit (Helmke 2003). Meanwhile, Duhalde was challenging Menem's leadership of the party. For the years 1999, 2000, and 2001, I use the results of the voting that took place in the July 1998 national party congress. Of the 788 delegates, 415 voted to allow the party authorities to appeal to the Court to bar President Menem from running in the 1999 elections (*La Nación*, 19 July 1998). I use this result as a proxy for Duhalde's strength in the party. (I would like to thank Steven Levitsky for his suggestion to look at the national party congress of 1998.)

Since party leaders that are also Presidents tend to be more powerful politically, especially because they control important financial resources from the central government, the mechanisms that are analysed in the game theoretic model would be expected to fit the intra-party politics of presidential parties even more closely. The president's support would be crucial for governors who are either politically weak or who have administrations that depend on the central government economically. Therefore, I conduct the statistical analysis also for this subset of data, that is, for presidential parties. For these presidential parties, I alternatively measure the dependence of governors by the lagged national transfers as a share of provincial revenue, in order to get at financial dependence. When the party leader is also the national president, her strength can alternatively be measured by public approval of the presidents in the opinion polls.[49] I expect governors from presidential parties to hire fewer temporary employees as the importance of party leader's support (share of transfers) increases when the president's popularity and strength are not so high to prevent competition for the party's leadership.

Then, I control for the variables suggested by previous literature. Jones *et al.* (2000) and Remmer and Wibbels (2000) argue that governors who belong to the same party as the President tend to constrain their levels of public spending either because the President, who is held accountable for the national economic performance, influences the governors' decisions (Jones *et al.* 2000) or because the governors from non-presidential parties tend to be from one-party dominant states where they are insulated from electoral competition, and hence, accountability (Remmer and Wibbels 2000). In order to control for this effect in the analysis that includes provinces that are controlled by presidential and non-presidential parties alike, I include an indicator variable that takes on the value of one when the governor is from the President's party. In addition, I control for the timing of presidential elections with an indicator variable that takes on the value of one, if presidential elections were held in that year.

Calvo and Murillo (2004, 2008) demonstrate how partisanship and patronage interact in the case of Argentina. Therefore, I control for the effect of party identity by including an indicator variable that takes on the value of one when the Radicals (or an alliance of Radicals) has the gubernatorial position. Since I exclude those cases where the ruling party is a provincial party, the variable captures whether the Radicals or the Peronists hire more temporary employees at the provincial level. I expect the Peronist governments to hire more employees.

Since politicians in instrumental short-term exchanges promise to distribute these jobs when they come to power after elections, I expect public employment to increase just after gubernatorial elections (Remmer 2007). If the politician or party is already in power, and there are repeated long-term interactions between politi-

---

49. Calvo (2007) shows that presidential approval also correlates with presidents' ability to pass their legislative bills, which is another indicator of their strength within their party. I, therefore, also created an ordinal variable that is derived from Calvo's (2007) analysis. The results are similar and are available from the author upon request.

cians and their supporters, the candidate may need to distribute some jobs before the elections to make her promises credible. Therefore, I also include a variable for the gubernatorial electoral cycle. I count the number of days between the date of the most recent gubernatorial elections and the last day of each year. I include this variable and the quadratic term of this variable in the analysis because I expect the number of employees to increase right before and after the elections. Another variable related to the use of patronage for the purpose of increasing vote shares in general elections is the competitiveness of elections, which I measure by the absolute value of the difference between the governor's and his closest competitor's vote share. We would expect the distribution of particularistic goods to increase in competitive (marginal) districts (Dahlberg and Johansson 2002; Denemark 2000).

Since I am looking at the aggregate data on public employment, I have to control for the relevant socio-economic variables that impact the public sector. We should expect economic development and resources available to provincial governments to influence the number of public employees. Due to some problems with standardising the GDP at the provincial level across years, I use the percentage of total GDP for each province. Since the impact of increases in economic development is expected to be smaller when the level of economic development is already high, I use the logged values for the GDP shares per capita. For the economic resources, I include the logged revenues of provincial government per capita. Since the country experienced major economic restructuring beginning in late 1989 (Acuña, Galiani and Tommasi 2004), which included decentralisation and transfer of some responsibilities to the provincial governments, I include an indicator variable that takes on the value of one in the period between 1990 and 2001 to control for these changes. Since the ability of the provincial government to spend might also be affected by previous deficits, a lagged value of the provincial deficit as a share of total revenues is also included. Governors that have been in power for a long time could have switched some of their loyal supporters to permanent positions in their administrations. In order to control for the effect of a transition to a new governor, I also include the number of permanent employees (per 10,000 people) as a control variable.

Analysis and results

Since most of the political explanatory variables are related to internal party competition, the units with non-elected provincial governments (Federal Capital had an appointed mayor prior to 1996, and the federal government intervened in some provinces), and whose government was controlled by a provincial party, were dropped from the analysis. The number of observations in the dataset is eighty-two and number of provinces (groups) is nine.[50] The cross-sectional time-series

---

50. Neuquén and Corrientes, which have had provincial parties and experienced federal interventions throughout this period, are not included. As explained in the Appendix C, other provinces and years are missing due to data availability problems. This exact small sample was used to analyse

nature of the data makes the model specification challenging. I use an OLS model and include fixed effects for groups (an indicator variable for each province)[51] and lagged dependent variable in order to take care of serial correlation (Beck and Katz 2001).[52] I estimate panel-corrected standard errors (PCSEs Beck and Katz 1995) to correct for contemporaneous correlation of errors and panel heteroskedasticity.[53]

Table 5.4 shows that the first hypothesis related to effects of internal party competition on patronage jobs is supported by the analysis of temporary employees across provinces. As expected, governors seem to distribute fewer temporary jobs to their supporters when they belong to a party where leadership is open to competition, and when the party (leader) support is important for the governors' re-election. Figures 5.2–5.4, which are produced with the code provided by Brambor *et al.* (2006), are helpful to understand the results regarding multiplicative terms. The figures display the estimated coefficients for the variables that measure the importance of leader support at different values of the variables that measure the openness of leadership competition. The dashed lines show the confidence intervals at 95 per cent.

As can be seen in Figure 5.2, when the primary result is less than or equal to 63 per cent, that is when the party leader is not dominant in the party, increases in the vote share of the party relative to the governor leads to a smaller number of patronage jobs. As such, the empirical analysis supports the argument that governors trade-off patronage jobs in order to get the backing of the party (leader) when they need this support to be re-elected and when they know that their party leaders' backing would be conditional on the level of jobs that they distribute.[54] The latter

---

the data on total number of personnel to check the possibility of any bias. No major differences are observed between the analysis of the small sample and the analysis that includes a larger set of provinces and years except the findings on permanent employees and lagged deficit. The results are presented in Table 5.5.

51. The Chi-square test that rejects the hypothesis that the coefficients for provincial indicators equal zero also supports the decision to include fixed effects in the analysis.

52. The analysis of data revealed serial correlation. The simulations that are run by Kristensen and Wawro (2004) show that even though OLS estimation with both fixed effects and a lagged dependent variable leads to some bias, it might be worse to ignore the heterogeneity in the data. Keele and Kelly (2004) show that the bias caused by the lagged dependent variable is trivial when the residual serial correlation is small.

53. For six of the nine provinces, the number of observations in the dataset is equal to or larger than nine.

54. If the interactive term is not included in the model, the coefficient of the difference between party and governor vote shares divided by governor vote share is not statistically significant. Therefore, we should not be concerned about an endogeneity problem where patronage decreases the difference between the vote share of the party and the governor. Neither should we be concerned that presidential strength decreases with patronage. I use results from primaries that elected the leader of each particular year and hence primaries occur prior to the decision on patronage. When the interactive term is not included, the relationship is actually positive. The results are available from the author upon request.

Table 5.4: OLS parameter estimates for models predicting provincial patronage (1984–2001)

		(1)	(2)	(3)	(4)
Intra-party	Primary Results	0.157***	0.217***		0.771***
		(0.053)	(0.057)		(0.292)
	Party-Governor Vote/ Governor Vote	-30.677*	-77.142***		-202.679**
		(16.414)	(21.459)		(98.784)
	Primaries* Party-Governor Vote/ Governor Vote	0.368	0.903***		3.038**
		(0.251)	(0.286)		(1.437)
	Presidential Approval			-0.814**	
				(0.330)	
	Lagged Transfers			-84.379***	
				(22.794)	
	Approval* Transfers			1.053**	
				(0.505)	
	President's Party	-10.151***			
		(2.973)			
Inter-party	Competitiveness	-0.093	-0.175*	-0.063	
		(0.089)	(0.091)	(0.084)	
	Gubernatorial Elections	-0.034***	-0.021**	-0.006	
		(0.008)	(0.009)	(0.007)	
	Gubernatorial Elections Squared	0.000025***	0.000014***	0.000006	
		(5.62×10^{-6})	(5.42×10^{-6})	(5.13×10^{-6})	
	Presidential Elections	-2.359	-4.438*	1.768	
		(2.191)	(2.654)	(2.217)	
	UCR	2.041	3.074	2.217	
		(2.592)	(4.644)	(3.976)	
Socio-economic Controls	Reform	3.823	7.344	-3.257	
		(3.948)	(6.845)	(6.383)	
	Logged GDP Per capita	7.809	0.634	-11.431	
		(9.784)	(15.586)	(14.508)	
	Logged Revenue Per capita	3.594	1.512	-8.377	
		(4.212)	(3.580)	(5.544)	
	Permanent Employees	-0.133***	-0.129***	-0.073**	
		(0.043)	(0.036)	(0.037)	
	Lagged Deficit Over revenue	-4.229	5.380	-5.752	
		(10.917)	(9.845)	(9.241)	
	Lagged Dependent Variable	0.452***	0.337***	0.253*	
		(0.145)	(0.124)	(0.142)	
	Constant	145.182	37.887	-66.699	-7.909
		(125.305)	(198.187)	(185.759)	(20.716)
	Provincial Indicators	Yes	Yes	Yes	No
	Observations	82	58	58	107
	Number of prov	9	9	9	15

Standard errors in parentheses *** p<0.01, ** p<0.05, * p<0.1

would happen only when the party leader is not strong. If we look at an example of such a case when the party leader's vote share in the primaries is 53 per cent, we see that an increase in the party's vote shares from 30 to 33 per cent when the governor has 30 per cent of the votes leads to a decrease of approximately one job for every 10,000 people. The mean number of temporary jobs per 10,000 people in the dataset is 43 (see Table 5.6).

As expected from hypothesis 2, party (leader) support does not have an impact on patronage jobs when the party leader is strong in the party. It can be seen in Figure 5.2 that when the vote share in primaries is larger than or equal to 64 per cent, the coefficient of the variable that measures the difference between the party's and governor's vote shares (divided by the governor's vote share) is not statistically significant.

For the analysis of presidential parties only, as expected, we find a larger substantive effect of the importance of party support on the number of temporary employees. The values of the coefficient for importance of party support when the primary result is less than 73 per cent are negative and larger than the ones estimated from the model that analyses all parties. This time, when the primary result is 53 per cent, an increase in the party's vote shares from 30 to 33 per cent when the governor has 30 per cent of the votes, leads to a decrease of approximately three jobs for every 10,000 people (see Figure 5.3). The range for which the interactive term is statistically significant at 95 per cent is less than 73 per cent, which is also larger than in the model that analyses all parties.

The theoretical expectations are also supported by the model (Column 3, Table

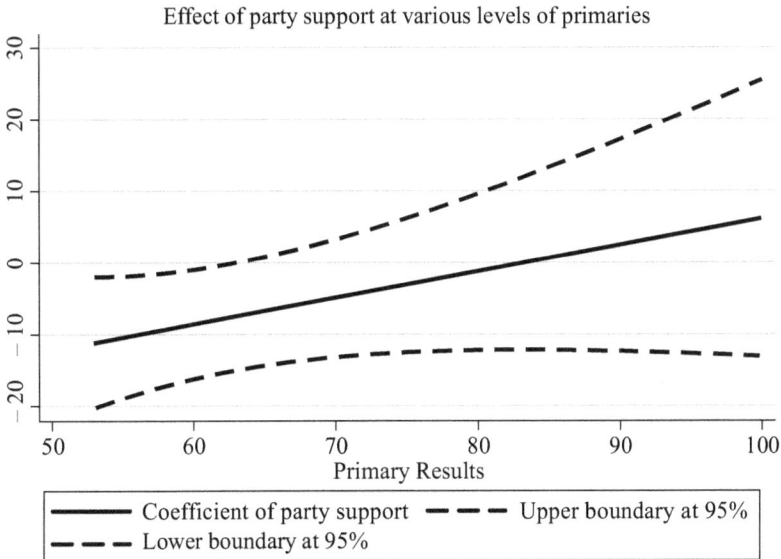

Effect of party support at various levels of primaries

Primary Results

— Coefficient of party support   — — — Upper boundary at 95%
— — — Lower boundary at 95%

From Model 1 (Column 1) of Table 5.4

Figure 5.2: The results for the interactive term

Table 5.5: Bias check: replication of Model 1 in Table 5.4 with total number of employees (as opposed to temporary employees)

		(1) Larger Dataset	(2) Limited Dataset
Intra-party	Primary Results	0.26 (0.192)	0.06 (0.244)
	Party-Governor Vote/ Governor Vote	59.79 (61.064)	69.22 (77.180)
	Primaries* Party-Governor Vote/ Governor Vote	-0.67 (0.913)	-1.07 (1.067)
	President's Party	-13.71** (6.428)	-12.87 (8.436)
Inter-party	Competitiveness	-0.07 (0.316)	0.21 (0.381)
	Gubernatorial Elections	-0.05* (0.028)	-0.09** (0.035)
	Gubernatorial Elections Squared	0.00* (0.000)	0.00** (0.000)
	Presidential Elections	-6.54 (7.643)	-10.94 (9.939)
	UCR	-8.57 (6.661)	-8.36 (9.561)
Socio-economic Controls	Reform	-30.12*** (9.203)	-25.75 (15.808)
	Logged GDP Per capita	26.59 (20.830)	-6.25 (22.652)
	Logged Revenue Per capita	25.88* (13.456)	60.81*** (18.966)
	Permanent Employees	0.02 (0.019)	0.59*** (0.221)
	Lagged Deficit Over revenue	62.00** (25.307)	-27.34 (34.289)
	Lagged Dependent Variable	0.77*** (0.079)	0.42*** (0.135)
	Constant	453.92* (263.892)	42.12 (288.566)
	Provincial Indicators	Yes	Yes
	Observations	175	82
	Number of prov	20	9

Standard errors in parentheses*** p<0.01, ** p<0.05, * p<0.1

Effect of party support at various levels of primaries

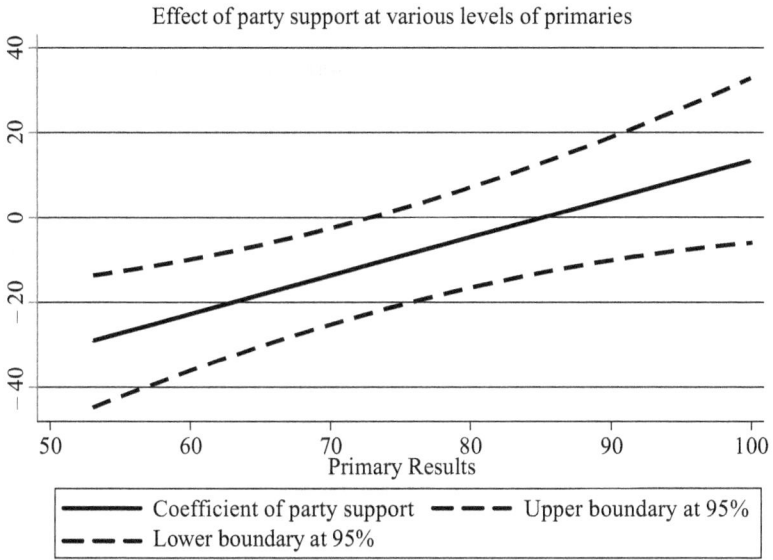

From Model 2 (Column 2) of Table 5.4

Figure 5.3: The results for the interactive term

Effect of financial support at various levels of presidential approval

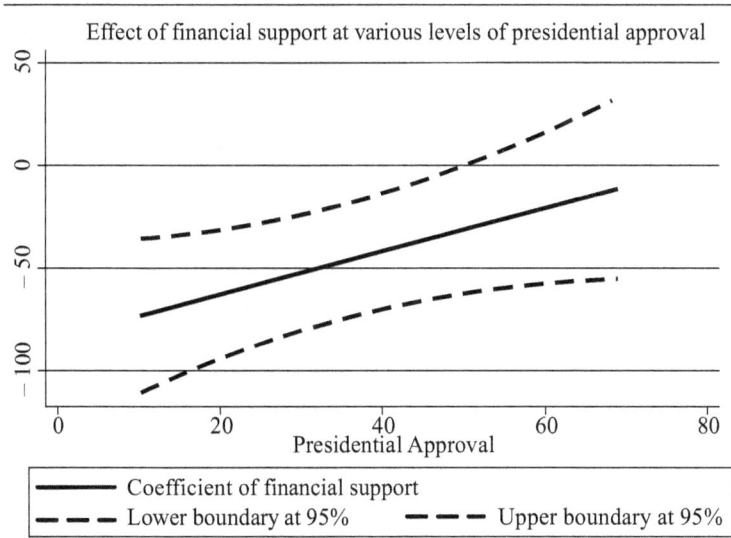

From Model 3 (Column 3) of Table 5.4

Figure 5.4: The results for the interactive term

Table 5.6: Descriptive statistics for the variables in the statistical analysis

Variable	Obser- vations	Mean	Stan. Dev.	Minimum	Maximum
Temporary employees	82	42.79	50.62	.80	183.88
Primaries	82	69.63	19.41	53	100
$\frac{\text{Party Vote} - \text{Governor Vote}}{\text{Governor Vote}}$	82	-.10	.22	-.46	.85
Primaries* $\frac{\text{Party Vote} - \text{Governor Vote}}{\text{Governor Vote}}$	82	-6.70	15.38	-35.55	55.24
Competitiveness	82	19.74	13.75	.34	65.9
Presidential approval	58	32.43	15.00	12.67	69.5
President's party	82	.71	.46	0	1
Gubernatorial elections	82	696.72	397.71	65	1327
Gubernatorial elections squared	82	633339.7	554289.7	4225	1760929
Presidential elections	82	.20	.40	0	1
UCR	82	.22	.42	0	1
Reform	82	.83	.38	0	1
Logged GDP	82	-13.05	.56	-14.20	-12.07
Revenue	82	-.04	.64	-1.21	1.35
Lagged deficit	82	-.08	.10	-.27	.21
Lagged transfers	58	.54	.16	.25	.87
Approval* lagged transfers	58	16.98	8.00	5.79	44.13
Permanent employees	82	433.82	219.12	171.11	847.23
Lagged temporary employees	82	42.58	52.72	.80	229.51

5.4) that uses alternative measurements for the main explanatory variables. As can be seen in Figure 5.4, when the president does not have very high levels of public approval (when the approval rate is less than 51 per cent), the coefficient of transfers is negative (and is statistically significant at 95 per cent). This means that increasing financial dependence of the governor leads to fewer jobs. At the mean approval rate (32 per cent), increasing the transfers with 1 per cent decreases the jobs by half for every 10,000 people. When the President is very strong (for approval rates that are greater than or equal to 51 per cent), that is when her leadership can hardly be challenged by internal opposition, the coefficient of transfers cannot be statistically differentiated from zero. This result supports hypothesis 2 that predicted the leader support to have no effect on patronage when the party leadership position is not open to competition.

The results for the variables suggested by previous literature support some of the expectations. If the governor belongs to the same party as the president, fewer temporary employees seem to be hired in the provincial administration. Whether the governor limits the number of patronage jobs because the president puts pressure on her party members to constrain provincial government deficits, or because the governor thinks that poor national performance would affect his own electoral performance, the statistically significant and quite large coefficient for this variable, -10, suggests that the number of patronage jobs is smaller in provinces that are governed by the president's party. As expected, provincial governments seem to hire more temporary employees right after and before gubernatorial elections. Even though the signs for these coefficients remain the same, they lose statistical significance in the third model where different measurements for the key theoretical variables are used.

Presidential elections and party identity do not seem to have an impact on patronage jobs. The coefficient of presidential elections is negative and statistically significant at 90 per cent in the model presented in column 2, but even the direction of the effect is not robust to changes in model specification. There is some support for the argument that competitiveness of elections matter. As expected, number of employees increases in marginal provinces. None of the socio-economic control variables except permanent employees have an effect.[55]

Conclusion

This chapter analyses public employment at the sub-national level in Argentina to understand how socio-economic and political factors have led to variations in how politicians and parties use public employment to build political support. The most important finding from this analysis concerns the role of political parties. The statistical results support the arguments that I introduced in the previous chapter and that I illustrated with examples earlier in this chapter: Politicians have incentives

---

55. The findings on the key theoretical variables are robust to the exclusion of permanent employees from the analysis. The results are available from the author upon request.

to reduce patronage in the public sector when their party's leadership position is open to competition and when getting the support of their party (leader) is important for their re-election.

The nature of support might vary from symbolic to material resources, but when the gubernatorial candidates rely on their party for their re-election, they seem to have incentives to cut down on the number of temporary jobs that they distribute to build their clientelistic network. In addition, the leaders' threats to condition their support on the observed level of jobs seem to be credible only when they are not dominant or too strong in the party, which allows the party leadership position to be contestable. Competition between the party leader and her potential challengers in the party, under these two conditions, seems to open ways to contain the inflationary tendencies of clientelistic mobilisation.

chapter six | public employment in turkey: an analysis of patronage at the sub-national level

According to the Turkish Minister of Industry and Commerce, Ali Coşkun, there were approximately 800,000 ATM civil servants in the government.[1] They are called ATM civil servants because they withdraw their salaries from cash machines without ever showing up at the office. Coşkun's comment reveals how entrenched the concept of patronage jobs is in Turkish politics, just as it is in Argentina. Again, just as in Argentina, the politics of patronage and the party system are the subject of public political discussion in Turkey, as well as a popular social science research topic.[2]

However, in contrast to Argentina, where civil service employment policy has been mostly static in recent decades, Turkish governments have been reforming the civil service laws.[3] A standardised civil service exam was introduced,[4] and a central state institute – the National Department of Personnel, NDP – became solely responsible for allocating most national and local government jobs to applicants who request to be appointed for the first time to a job in the public sector. Although these reforms reduced local government's independence with regard to hiring, by extending the standardised exam requirement and the NDP's approval to municipal employees (Bozlagan 2003, Arslan 2002)[5], the central government's involvement in the decisions on the size of the municipal personnel was later reversed in 2004 (Mutluer and Oner 2009).

The national government claimed that the reforms of 1999 would improve the quality of public administration, enhance equality of access to the public sector,

---

1. *Hürriyet*, 24 March 2005.

2. For the analysis of political patronage during the pre-1983 Republican period, see Gunes-Ayata (1992), Ozbudun (1981), Sayari (1977), and Sunar (1990). For the later period, see Adaman and Carkoglu (2000), Kalaycioglu (2001), and Heper and Keyman (1998). Sayari (2011) provides a comparative overview of both periods.

3. For background information on the Turkish bureaucracy, see Findley (1980), Ozdemir (2001), Heper (1987), and Heper (1989).

4. The civil service exam requirement was introduced in January 1986. The 1986 code was changed in February 1999 and the exams were centralised. (No. 99/12377) As a result of these changes, civil servants (*memur*), permanent workers (*işçi*) (No. 99/12378) and some contract employees (*sözleşmeli*) are required to take the exam. The extension of the central exam requirement to permanent workers shows that this system is intended to be even more comprehensive than a civil service system.

5. These reforms were introduced between 1999 and 2000 by a coalition government of three parties: the DLP, NAP, and MP.

and constrain the fiscal deficits generated by local governments. However, interviews with politicians and bureaucrats, as well as newspaper reports, suggest that the reforms have failed to achieve these goals: centralising hiring decisions simply changes who is responsible for distributing public jobs. Even if the written exam is fairly administered,[6] the fact is that more applicants pass the exams and qualify for open positions than there are openings.

Therefore, the crucial decision is who to choose from the pool of those that pass the exam, a decision that was made by the NDP. Interviews and newspaper reports suggest that this is where the political element entered the process. For example, a public scandal concerned the hiring of sixteen employees by the Ministry of Health despite the fact that they scored a zero in the placement exam.[7] Although applicants were supposed to be ranked according to their exam scores, the lack of transparency regarding NDP process, and about publicising open positions, imply that it is at this stage that political networks affected the distribution of public jobs. The NDP itself admitted problems at the implementation stage. It cited the lack of clear procedures in the face of unexpected vacancies, the fact that it had to rely on applicants' statements rather than the exam database, and the fact that public institutions could decide to change their by-laws to exempt them from the legislation (NDP 'Cumhuriyetin').

The reforms were spurred by the strength of the main opposition party, the WP[8] (and its successor the VP) in local governments, and the conflicts between coalition partners over the distribution of public jobs. However, the post-reform experience suggests that changing the formal rules did not diminish the role of politics in hiring decisions. Politicians and parties still had incentives to distribute available positions to particular citizens in return for their political support. In fact, the JDP government, formed after the 2002 elections, attempted to abolish the reforms and indeed reduced the role of NDP.[9]

In Chapters Three and Four, I hypothesised that internal and inter-party competition would affect politicians' incentives to use particularistic exchanges of jobs for political support. Although the legal reforms and economic changes have made it more costly for politicians to expand the size of the public sector and hire their

---

6. For the period of analysis in this book, I am not aware of any legal complaints or cases concerning the actual conduct of the exam. I have not seen any newspaper reports about any irregularities in the exam. The ÖSYM (Öğrenci Seçme Yerleştirme Merkezi- Center for Selection and Replacement of Students), which administers the exam, is also responsible for conducting the placement exams at all levels of education. Until very recently it used to be considered independent and fair in administration of the exams. However, there have recently been many complaints, especially about the civil servant placement exam in 2010 (*Milliyet*, 25 August 2010) and the university placement exam in April 2011 (*Radikal*, 2 April 2011).

7. *Hürriyet*, 3 January 2004.

8. See the list of abbreviations.

9. The JDP made some changes to the municipal hiring processes (Mutluer and Oner 2009) and initiated a proposal to reform the personnel system (*Zaman*, 10 December 2004).

supporters for the few available positions, the nature of electoral campaigns and internal party competition in Turkey provides strong incentives for politicians to preserve their efforts to build individual political support through particularistic exchanges of public benefits. The results of the game theoretic analysis in Chapter Four lead me to expect these incentives to be even stronger when the party support is not important for politicians' re-election and when the party leadership is not open to competition. I also test this hypothesis using sub-national level data from Turkey, just as I did in the case of Argentina.

One difference in the case of Turkey is the centralisation of the hiring decisions under the control of the NDP, which falls formally under the jurisdiction of the prime minister. This means that in the period between 1999 and 2004, politicians at the sub-national level needed either their party leader's or the opposition party leader's approval to distribute these jobs.[10] Since the party leader cannot completely block the distribution of patronage jobs, but can control the total number of available jobs, I extend the game theoretic model to incorporate this characteristic of the interaction. I set the level of jobs as equal to $x - x_s$ if the party leader does not support the lower-ranking politician ($s = 0$). However, modifying the model in this way does not change the results concerning the main comparative statics (see Appendix A3).

I first illustrate, with examples from a metropolitan municipality (City of Istanbul), and local municipalities (Beşiktaş and Kartal in the province of Istanbul, City Center and Bozüyük in the province of Bilecik), the mechanisms behind the distribution of patronage jobs, with a focus on the internal competition within parties. Then, I present the results of the statistical analysis of data from sixteen metropolitan municipalities between 1997 and 2001. The results support my hypothesis that politicians limit their efforts to build individual bases of support through particularistic exchanges when there is real competition for the leadership position within their parties, that is, when the party leader is not dominant and when they find the support from their party (leader) valuable for re-election.

Leadership competition and sub-national patronage

In 1984, Law No. 3030 created the administrative unit of metropolitan municipalities for cities with large populations. By 2001, there were sixteen such metropolitan municipalities, including Sakarya.[11] The mayors' control of financial resources and their ability to build an independent political base in these cities have made them important potential candidates for party leadership. As a former legislator

---

10. Even during this period of central government involvement and restrictions, local governments could bypass the central exam requirement and the NDP's allocation decision, by hiring individuals who once entered the public employment system.

11. The metropolitan municipalities are: Adana, Ankara, Antalya, Bursa, Diyarbakir, Erzurum, Eskisehir, Gaziantep, Icel, Istanbul, Izmir, Kayseri, Kocaeli, Konya, Sakarya (2001), and Samsun.

from DLP (Istanbul) stated,[12] '[...] Mayors, after a while, create an independent support base for themselves. With the help of this group, they sever their ties with the party centre. [...] They [mayors], certainly represent a threat to the party leaders'. After the 1983 democratic transition, two mayors challenged and later replaced their party leaders. The current prime minister and the JDP leader, Tayyip Erdoğan, was the mayor of Istanbul between 1994 and 1998. The former leader of SPP (the party that replaced RPP between 1983 and 1992) between 1993 and 1995, and the candidate for the presidency of RPP in 1995, Murat Karayalçın, was elected as the mayor of Ankara in 1989. Therefore, I expect the interaction between mayors of metropolitan municipalities and their *national* party leaders to affect the extent of patronage in these municipalities as modelled in Chapter Four.

As in the case of Argentina, I also expect similar mechanisms of internal party competition and two main political factors, significance of party (leader) support and openness of competition for the *provincial* party leadership post, to affect clientelism at the municipal level in Turkey.

In the rest of this section, I first discuss the examples from the metropolitan municipality of Istanbul and then four local municipalities in Istanbul and Bilecik.

Examples from a metropolitan municipality: Istanbul

Even though the metropolitan municipality's jurisdiction until July 2004 was limited to the borders of the city and did not cover the departments at the outskirts of the province of Istanbul, the municipality's control over vast resources and its responsibility to provide critical services to the people, have made it a significant political force in the whole province. As a consequence, the mayors have been visible in the public and have managed to build a strong political force in the province. Their power and visibility have not only been limited to the province, but most have become important actors in their parties as well as in national politics. The first mayor of Istanbul after the democratic transition, Bedrettin Dalan, formed his own party after his term as the mayor of Istanbul and Recep Tayyip Erdoğan, who was the mayor between 1994 and 1998, is the current prime minister.

The first municipal (local) elections after the democratic transition in 1983 took place one year after the transition on the 25 March 1984. The Motherland Party that became the major opposition party to the military government of 1980–1983, and won 45.1 per cent of the votes in the 1983 legislative elections in the whole country and 45.5 per cent of the votes in Istanbul, got 49.69 per cent of the votes in the local elections in Istanbul against SODEP's 26.28 per cent and MP's candidate, Bedrettin Dalan, became the mayor. Even though MP's share of votes fell in 1987 legislative elections both in the country in general and in Istanbul, to 36.3 per cent and 39.7 per cent consecutively, MP still retained the majority in the national parliament and controlled the national government.

In this period between the 1984 and 1989 local elections, Dalan's perception

---

12. Author's interview (No. 45), February 2004.

was that he had a strong independent support base in Istanbul. According to a former legislator from Istanbul, former vice president of the party, MP, and the inspector of the party in Istanbul before the 1989 elections, 'Dalan did not accept any criticisms. He [Dalan] was saying that he had 62 per cent of the votes in Istanbul, that *he did not want a party* and that he was going to pursue the election effort alone'.[13] Since Dalan had thought that his independent support was very high and that he did not need the party's support for getting re-elected, he did not have any incentives to reduce his efforts to enlarge his support base in the province by distributing more patronage jobs. In addition, in this period starting from 1984 until the unexpected failure of the MP in the local elections of 1989, according to all the interviewed politicians from MP, Turgut Özal, the formal leader of the MP and the prime minister of the time, was the undisputed leader of the party. Therefore, Özal in this period would not have been threatened by Dalan's efforts to establish an independent power base in Istanbul. This provided the second incentive for Dalan (who probably had ambitions for national leadership as his formation of a new party later in the beginning of the 1990s shows), to expand the size of the personnel in his administration through clientelistic networks without any fear of losing the party (leader's) support for his re-election as the mayor of Istanbul. The employment figures in Table 6.1 support this expectation. The number of all types of employees per capita (except the contracted, which formed a minor share of the total administration at the time) as well as the total number of employees per capita in these years were among the highest in the whole period from 1984 until 2003.

The period when the current Prime Minister, Recep Tayyip Erdoğan, controlled the municipality is also helpful in illustrating how internal party dynamics have an impact on patronage jobs. The results of the 1994 municipal elections in Istanbul were a surprise. The Welfare Party that got only 16.7 per cent of the votes in Istanbul in the 1991 general elections and 10.5 per cent of the votes in the 1989 local elections got 25.19 per cent of the votes and their candidate, Recep Tayyip Erdoğan, became the new mayor. Prior to his elections as the mayor, Erdoğan had been the president of the WP's provincial organisation for nine years and was among the party's candidates from Istanbul in the 1991 parliamentary elections. The fact that he later became the president of the JDP is a good indicator that he probably had ambitions to hold a national leadership position. In his first years as the mayor, the party's political support was important for Erdoğan's political success. Especially so, after the RP came out as the leading party in the 1995 parliamentary elections and formed a coalition government that lasted for a year between June 1996 and June 1997, since being part of the national government gave the party leadership access to important financial resources. At the same time, Necmettin Erbakan's leadership in the party was starting to be contested (Yilmaz 2001). Even though in the internal party elections of October 1993 and October

---

13. Author's interview (No. 31), December 2003. Author's emphasis.

1996 Erbakan ran as the single candidate for leadership, he could no longer receive 551 votes of the 552 delegates as he did in the October 1990 national convention. In 1993, he could get only 659 votes out of 982 delegates and in 1996, only 964 delegates out of 1254 voted in the national convention. The 1996 convention was also important because some candidates for the national congress of the party under Erbakan's list were voted out by opposition groups in the party (Yilmaz 2001).

As a result, in the initial years of his term as the mayor of Istanbul, Erdoğan would not want to send a signal of an ambitious type to the party leader, Erbakan. Even before Erdoğan was elected as the mayor, the national party leadership and the provincial organisation of the party under Erdoğan had fallen into opposition with each other, which at the provincial congress of 1992 culminated in an intervention by the national head of the party organisation, Ahmet Tekdal, in the provincial leadership of the party when he forced them to change eight members of the party's provincial congress (Yilmaz 2001). Although Erdoğan remained as the president of the party in Istanbul, this tension between Erbakan's national leadership of the party and the party's provincial branch under Erdoğan's presidency, reveals that the relationship between Erdoğan and Erbakan was already delicate before Erdoğan became the mayor. Yilmaz (2001) even claims that Erdoğan was chosen as the candidate only because the leadership of the party did not expect to win in Istanbul. Therefore, Erdoğan, who needed the support of the party (leadership) before he established his strong independent political base in Istanbul, would not want to sever the relationship with Erbakan by sending signals of intention to move up in the party hierarchy. As such Erdoğan had incentive to curtail his efforts to form a clientelistic network by distributing jobs in the municipal administration.

When we look at the employment figures in Table 6.1 this is partially supported. In 1995 and 1996, the number of civil servants per capita that were employed in the municipal administration is lower than the later years of Erdoğan's term even though it is still higher than the number of civil servants in the previous government of Nurettin Sözen. In contrast to the number of civil servants per capita, the number of workers depicts a different pattern. When we examine Figure 6.1, we can easily observe a decreasing trend in the number of workers per capita. The limited data that is available on the revenue of the municipality between 1997 and 2001 suggests that this decreasing trend might be a result of the loss of total revenue by the municipality of Istanbul. Given their limited resources, the municipality might have been more restricted in its ability to expand the size of the public sector. At this point, data on the number of employees that entered and left the administration is helpful. However, unfortunately this data was made available by the Department of Personnel (Municipality of Istanbul) only for the years between 1995 and 1998. What this information for the years between 1995 and 1998 (see Table 6.2) is telling us is that the number of new people hired both as civil servants and, especially as workers, in 1995 and 1996 was much lower compared to the two later years of Erdoğan's term. Even though the net difference, especially in the number of workers, is smaller given the high number of workers that left the administration, mostly as a result of retirement, there is a large increase in the number of newly hired, potential new patronage jobs, in 1997 and 1998.

Table 6.1: Number of employees per 10,000 people in the metropolitan municipality of Istanbul

Year	Civil Servants	Contracted Employees	Workers	Total	Civil servants/ revenue	Workers/ revenue	Contracted/ revenue	Total/ revenue
1983	13.61	0.57	27.9	42.14				
1984	5.01	0.03	12.7	17.70				
1985	5.74	0.04	12.6	18.41				
1986	5.44	0.04	12.3	17.79				
1987	4.92	0.03	12.0	16.95				
1988	4.72	0.02	10.4	15.16				
1989	4.07	0.02	10.4	14.48				
1990	4.44	0.06	10.0	14.53				
1991	4.23	0.06	9.5	13.77				
1992	4.25	0.05	9.5	13.79				
1993	4.35	0.05	9.1	13.50				
1994	4.45	0.05	8.2	12.70				
1995	5.12	0.04	8.0	13.14				
1996	4.95	0.04	7.7	12.70				
1997	5.68	0.04	7.4	13.16	7.36	9.64	0.05	17
1998	5.88	0.04	7.5	13.37	4.29	5.43	0.03	9.75
1999	5.46	0.04	8.2	13.73	4.51	6.79	0.03	11.3
2000	5.02	0.04	7.5	12.60	3.24	4.87	0.03	8.14
2001	4.72	0.04	6.4	11.16	3.62	4.92	0.03	8.57
2002	4.49	0.04	6.0	10.51				
2003	4.29	0.03	5.3	9.59				

Sources: Metropolitan Municipality of Istanbul on employee data and National Statistics Institute on population and revenue data. The revenue is standardised with the lira/dollar parity and is measured in millions.

This difference between the two early years of Erdoğan's administration and the two later years is expected, given the major changes in the country's political context in these later years. 1997 was a turbulent year of politics in Turkey. In May 1997 a court case was initiated in the Constitutional Court against the Welfare Party claiming that the party's political actions formed a threat to the secular characteristic of the constitution and that these actions were leading the country to a state of civil war.[14] The process culminated in the closure of the party in January 1998. Another court case at the end of 1997 was initiated, this time

---

14. Belgenet, Vural Savas's statement at the press conference on 21 May 1997 http://www.belgenet. com/dava/rpdava_savas.html (accessed 17 November 2011).

against Erdoğan, with the claim that Erdoğan's speech in a public gathering in Siirt, provoked religious hatred. As a result of the court's decision, Erdoğan was sentenced to imprisonment for ten months and his term as the mayor ended in November 1998. Under these extraordinary circumstances, any political or financial support from the party to Erdoğan was not possible. Nor would we expect this type of support (financial or symbolic) to be relevant for Erdoğan towards the end of 1998 when his political career was under threat.

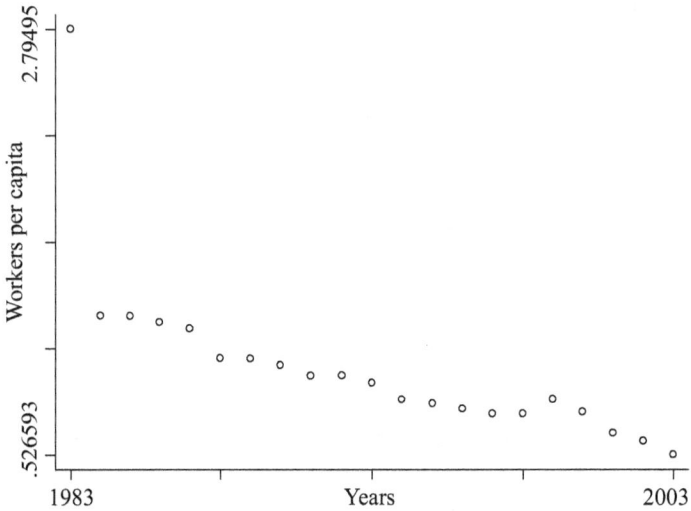

Figure 6.1: Workers per capita in the metropolitan municipality of Istanbul

Table 6.2: Public employees of the metropolitan municipality of Istanbul

	Civil Servant			Worker		
Year	Entrance	Exit	Net Difference	Entrance	Exit	Net Difference
1995	1,491	676	815	1,108	2,642	-1,534
1996	2,128	1,054	1,074	2,609	3,940	-1,331
1997	3,372	1,453	1,919	6,024	5,337	687
1998	4,256	1,829	2,427	10,225	6,873	3,352

Source: Metropolitan Municipality of Istanbul.

Four local municipalities

Istanbul

The administrations of local municipalities provide important resources to politicians, especially mayors in Istanbul, for establishing clientelistic networks. These clientelistic networks, in turn, are not only helpful to incumbent mayors in their competition with other parties in elections, but also assist them in their struggle for power in their own parties. The municipal positions serve as stepping-stones for local politicians who have ambitions to move to higher level positions such as the former mayor of Beyoğlu, Kadir Topbaş, who became the mayor of the metropolitan municipality of Istanbul in 2004, the former mayor of Güngören, Yahya Baş, who became a national deputy from Istanbul in the 2002 elections, or the former mayor of Bakırköy, Ali Talip Özdemir, who became the national president of the MP in 2003. As such, in their efforts to move up in the party hierarchy, mayors of local municipalities pose major threats to those party members who occupy these upper positions.

However, at the same time, these mayors need the support of the national deputies and the mayors of metropolitan municipalities, most importantly for financial resources. As a member of the municipal council from Kartal, RPP, said, 'Every mayor puts effort to increase financial resources channelled to her own municipality through deputies that represent her region'.[15] The metropolitan municipality, in turn, has responsibilities in the departments that are administered by the local municipalities and control more financial resources than local municipalities for investments in public work projects.[16] The politicians who get the credits for these services and public projects initiated by the metropolitan municipality, though, might sometimes be the mayors of local municipalities who are in more direct contact with the citizens. In addition to these financial resources, mayors who want to get re-elected also benefit from the information provided by the national deputies to the national leaders of the party, whose final approval is necessary for candidate nominations if primaries are not held for choosing candidates.[17] As I discussed in Chapter Four, mayors who need and value these different types of support from provincial level party leaders (mayors of metropolitan municipalities and national deputies) might constrain their efforts to expand their clientelistic networks if this could lead to the withdrawal of support from provincial level politicians. This would, in turn, depend on the provincial level politicians' strength in the parties and hence whether the provincial leadership position is open to competition.

---

15. Author's interview with a member of the municipal council from Kartal, RPP (No. 55), March 2005.
16. Author's interview with a member of the municipal council from Kartal, RPP (No. 55), March 2005.
17. Author's interview with one of the vice-presidents of the RPP (No. 51), March 2005.

Table 6.3: Public employees in Beşiktaş

Start date	End date	Total administration			New hires		
		Civil servant	Perm. worker	Temp. worker	Civil servant	Perm. worker	Temp. worker
1/6/1994	31/05/1995	378	502	99		17	8
1/6/1995	31/05/1996	373	493	95			
1/6/1996	31/05/1997	371	481	128			36
1/6/1998	31/05/1999	363	428	204		4	36
1/6/1999	31/05/2000	359	381	197	2 (open)		
1/6/2001	31/05/2002	356	320	206			23
1/6/2002	31/05/2003	345	392	196	4 (open)		

Start date	End date	Transfers to		Resignation		Transfers from		Re-hire
		Civil servant	Perm. worker	Civil servant	Perm. worker	Civil servant	Perm. worker	Civil servant
1/6/1994	31/05/1995	29	4	2	1	17	2	2
1/6/1995	31/05/1996			1	1	3	1	
1/6/1996	31/05/1997	13	3	1		2	4	
1/6/1998	31/05/1999			3	3	3		
1/6/1999	31/05/2000	22		1	13			
1/6/2001	31/05/2002	8		1		3		
1/6/2002	31/05/2003	3				4		

Start date	End date	Retire		Death		End of registration	Proposal	Result
		Civil servant	Perm. worker	Civil servant	Perm. worker	Perm. worker	Total	
1/6/1994	31/05/1995	8	23	2	2	2	36	17
1/6/1995	31/05/1996	2	7	1	1		106	84
1/6/1996	31/05/1997	15	13		2			
1/6/1998	31/05/1999	7	13	1				
1/6/1999	31/05/2000	26	38		2			
1/6/2001	31/05/2002	9	35			28		
1/6/2002	31/05/2003	12	17	1	1	20		

Source: Municipality of Beşiktaş.

In order to analyse whether these two political factors have had an impact on public employment in local municipalities of Istanbul, as in the case of Argentina, I chose two municipalities that contrast in terms of their socio-economic characteristics – Beşiktaş and Kartal (see Appendix B for more information). As in the case of Argentina, the data that is available on public employment at the local municipality level is very limited. For Kartal, I have data only on the current expenditure between 2000 and 2004. In general, expenditure on personnel forms a large part of the current expenditure in municipalities. For example, in 2005, the only year for which I have data on personnel, the spending on personnel in Kartal was 14,857,196 Turkish liras, forming almost one half of the total current expenditure, 30,433,674.[18] Therefore, I use the relative value of current expenditure to investment spending as an indicator of clientelism. For Beşiktaş, I have more detailed data on the number of employees between 1994 and 2003 (with some gaps) and personnel expenditure as a share of revenue for the years between 1994 and 2005.

Beşiktaş

In the case of Beşiktaş, I focus on the period from 1999 until 2005 (the period for which I have data on Kartal) to discuss the role of internal party politics on patronage jobs. The MP won the 1999 local elections in Beşiktaş with 28.95 per cent of the votes just in front of the RPP's 26.54 per cent. This close competition made all the strategies that could increase vote shares in the elections attractive. Indeed if we look at the number of temporary employees that were hired in the twelve month period before the elections, we see that there was an increase of almost 60 per cent (see Table 6.3).

After the election period was over, we see that the new government of Yusuf Namoğlu, from the MP, had an incentive to maintain these high levels until 2001, since his clientelistic efforts would not hurt his political career due to internal party dynamics. Namoğlu was dependent on the party leader's support for re-election since they played a major role in the party's nomination process and since the other centre-right party, TPP, had low levels of support in Beşiktaş (3.34 per cent in the 1999 elections, meaning that Namoğlu would not want to switch to the TPP and run as their candidate in the case that his nomination was not supported by the MP's leadership). However, the political or financial support from the *de facto* provincial leaders of the party, mainly national cabinet ministers who were also deputies representing Istanbul, would not be conditional on Namoğlu's clientelistic efforts. The provincial party congress that had taken place in 1998 indicated that there was no competition for the provincial party leadership. There was just a single list for all the leadership positions and the list was selected with unanimity.[19] Although the candidates for the provincial leadership posts were clearly not

---

18. All the budgetary data was provided by the municipality of Kartal.
19 *Cumhuriyet*, 24th August 1998.

Table 6.4: Spending on personnel as a share of revenue in the local municipality of Beşiktaş

Year	Spending on personnel	Revenue	Share
1994	234,184,639,060	897,544,247,890	0.26
1995	359,816,578,003	997,313,581,223	0.36
1996	688,328,814,921	2,191,593,657,488	0.31
1997	1,212,646,111,007	3,167,775,933,313	0.38
1998	3,035,547,764,591	9,466,269,092,498	0.32
1999	5,938,664,797,031	14,462,434,033,981	0.41
2000	7,687,504,230,436	12,443,156,756,848	0.62
2001	10,778,275,289,218	22,980,569,988,634	0.47
2002	13,672,876,227,877	36,141,470,130,216	0.38
2003	17,876,722,767,924	61,721,293,646,884	0.29
2004	20,730,656,195,810	47,007,570,898,069	0.44
2005*	25,780,474	62,589,410	0.41

* In 2005 a new currency, New Turkish Lira, was used.
Source: The municipality of Beşiktaş.

the cabinet ministers themselves, the competition in the internal elections would have reflected the underlying competition for the *de facto* leadership.

We see a considerable decrease in the levels of spending on personnel in the years 2002 and especially 2003. Even though twenty employees retired from the administration in this year, which opened positions for hiring new employees, we can see that the government did not choose to do so. When we analyse the internal politics of the MP at this period we can see that two conditions for low patronage were met in this period. As in the previous three years, Namoğlu perceived support from his party (leadership) as important. In this new period, though, what changed was that the provincial leadership was not as secure as in the preceding period. The provincial party congress that was held in April 2001, started to show signs of emerging competition for the provincial party leadership. Ahmet Keskin, the former head of the party in Kağıthane and the national deputy candidate, even though he later withdrew his candidacy, formed a major threat to the current president of the party in Istanbul, İbrahim Taşkın.[20]

The 2004 municipal elections gave incentive to the incumbent to increase spending on personnel in order to get re-elected. The MP performed very badly in the 2002 general elections in Beşiktaş, coming third with only 9 per cent of the votes, against RPP's 47 per cent. This major loss of the MP's support by the gen-

---

20. *Akşam* 19 May 2001; *Sabah* 21 May 2002; *Cumhuriyet* 2001.

eral public of Beşiktaş gave an incentive to the incumbent to resort to all types of strategies that could increase vote shares in the short-term before elections, including distributing patronage jobs. Even though no data is available on the number of temporary employees in this year, the increase in the expenditure on personnel supports this expectation (see Table 6.4).

Kartal

Kartal's first government, as most other municipal governments after the transition to democracy, was controlled by the MP. Then in 1991, the SPP took over and starting in 1994 it has been controlled by the WP, VP, and the JDP.[21] In this section, I am going to focus on the political competition between the years 2000 and 2005 for which I have data on the municipal budget. Mehmet Sekmen, the mayor of Kartal, was elected in 1995 from the WP. After the WP was closed down by the constitutional court, he joined the VP. In the 1999 elections, Sekmen was nominated for re-election by the VP. In these elections, the VP's vote shares in Kartal for the parliamentary elections was 21.3 per cent and the party's share for the provincial council was 24.48 per cent against Sekmen's 31.5 per cent for the position of the mayor. Even though Sekmen's individual political support was very high in his own district compared to that of the party, no primary elections have been held either in the WP, VP, or JDP. The VP's ideological position was distant from centre-right parties and hence it was difficult for Sekmen to switch to another party, which made him dependent on the party (leaders) support for getting re-elected. In addition, as the vice-mayor of Kartal (former member of JDP and VP) argued, '[In the municipal budget] there is no space for investment in public works.[...] What do we do? We rely on the support from the metropolitan municipality.'[22] Therefore, financially, too, Sekmen, needed and valued the support from the prominent provincial party members, including the mayor of Istanbul metropolitan municipality at the time, Ali Müfit Gürtuna (VP).

We know that Sekmen had ambition to move to a higher public position, national deputy, since he was elected as one in the 2002 parliamentary elections from the JDP. However, Sekmen had an incentive to constrain his clientelistic efforts because his party's support was important, but this support would be conditional on Sekmen's signs of ambition. During this period, the provincial party leadership was facing internal party competition that originated mostly from competition at the national level between the Traditionalists and Reformists.[23] Therefore, the low

---

21. Both the WP and the VP were closed down by the constitutional court. The VP and JDP are usually considered as the inheritors of the WP due to the continuation of a major share of the political cadre and the similarity of their ideological and policy position (although major changes also have taken place in the last decade. See Carkoglu (1998, 2003)).

22. Author's interview (No. 54), March 2005.

23. Author's interview with a former member of the VP and a national deputy from Istanbul (JDP) (No. 32), February 2003.

Table 6.5: Budget of Kartal municipality

Year	Current Expenditure	Investment	Personnel	Current Expenditure/ Investment
2000	9,377,921,235,587.00	4,182,000,000,000.00		2.24
2001	11,488,145,275,004.00	4,992,000,000,000.00		2.30
2002	17,044,933,705,079.00	6,627,000,000,000.00		2.57
2003	23,628,958,076,662.00	8,042,000,000,000.00		2.94
2004	27,114,537,733,798.00	12,035,000,000,000.00		2.25
2005*	31,439,915.00	18,000,000.00	16,917,333.00	1.75

* In 2005 a new currency, New Turkish Lira, was used.
Source: The municipality of Kartal.

levels of spending on personnel relative to the part of the budget allocated to investment that we observe in Table 6.5 were expected.

Sekmen was nominated and elected as a deputy in the November 2002 elections. After he quit his position of mayor, the council member, Hüsamettin Koçak (JDP) was elected by the municipal council as the mayor until the upcoming elections in 2004. In this period Koçak needed the support of the political party especially since he was not elected as the mayor through elections, but was only substituting for the elected mayor. However, the support from the provincial party leaders in this period would not be withdrawn if Koçak sent signals of intention to take over their positions. In the 2002 parliamentary elections the JDP performed very well and in Istanbul, got 37.2 per cent of the votes. Within the party, too, there was no opposition to the provincial party leadership. In the provincial party congress there was a single list presented by the provincial president of the time, Mehmet Müezzinoğlu.[24] Since there was a strong provincial leadership in the party, Koçak did not have any incentive to curtail clientelistic efforts in the municipal administration as can be seen by high levels of spending in 2003.

High levels of reduction in spending on personnel in 2004, and especially 2005, are surprising given that no obvious changes are observed in these years in terms of internal party dynamics. The fact that municipal elections were held in March 2004 makes this observation even more puzzling. However, one factor that could lead to this outcome is the position of the newly elected mayor of Istanbul, Kadir Topbaş. Before being elected as the mayor of Istanbul, Topbaş was the mayor of Beyoğlu (a densely populated municipality located at the centre of the city) and had won the 1999 elections with 28.5 per cent of the votes. Even though he had considerable popular support [25] the nomination process within the

24. *Hürriyet*, 23 June 2003.

25. *Radikal*, 10 January 2004.

party, before the 2004 local elections, was very competitive. There were six candidates for nomination including Topbaş, the mayor of Pendik, Erol Kaya, mayor
of Tuzla, İdris Güllüce, and the President of DSI (General Directorate of Soil and
Water), Veysel Eroğlu. Even though the national leadership chose Topbaş in the
end, he did not have a dominant position in the party. Given that Kartal needed the
financial support from Topbaş' administration, Arif Dağlar (newly elected mayor
of Kartal, JDP) might have had the incentive not to look ambitious, and limited his
efforts to build an independent power base in Kartal.

Bilecik

As in the case of Buenos Aires and Chaco in Argentina and Istanbul, mayors of local municipalities in Bilecik are potential challengers to provincial level positions.
In Argentina, mayors might take over the position of governor and in Turkey,
mayors are credible threats to the national deputies that represent the province.
In Bilecik, too, as a consequence of the independent financial resources that they
control, and their visibility among the public, mayors have been frequently nominated for the national deputy position. For example, the RPP's deputy from 2002
until 2011, Yaşar Tüzün, was the mayor of the city centre (Bilecik) before being elected as a national deputy; the mayor of the city centre (Bilecik) preceding Tüzün, Mustafa Cinoğlu, later ran for nomination as the TPP's candidate for
the national parliament. The city centre's mayor from the SPP between 1989 and
1994, Akin Olcay, and Bozüyük's mayor Talat Bakkalcıoğlu (SPP, 1989–1999)
also ran for nomination as candidates for the national parliament.

As such, mayors who were in control of the hiring decisions in their local administrations, hence could distribute patronage jobs and could pose as threats to
the national deputies whose political and financial support could be critical for the
mayors' political career. Therefore, I expect two political factors that are related
to inter-and intra-party competition, the importance of party for politicians' re-
election and openness of competition for provincial party leadership posts (in this
case the national deputy or the head of the provincial party organisation), to have
an impact on the level of clientelism in local municipalities. Again, I chose two
municipalities in Bilecik for analysis: the municipality of the city centre (hence-
forth, called Centre) and Bozüyük. However, due to the lack of available data on
public employment in small municipalities, rather than choosing two contrasting
municipalities as I have done in Argentina and Istanbul, I had to choose two municipalities that have the largest share of the population and economic production
in the province.

City Centre

For the municipality of the Centre, I have data on the relative share of current
expenditure and investment in the municipal budget between 1985 and 2002 with
gaps. I focus my analysis on the latter part of this period, from 1996 until 2002, for
which I have data also on Bozüyük. As a result of the 1994 local elections Mustafa

Cinoğlu (TPP) took over the municipal government from Akın Olcay (SPP) with 26.56 per cent of the votes against Olcay's 19.08 per cent. Cinoğlu probably had an ambition to be a national deputy, as he later presented himself as a candidate before the 1999 elections. However, the low levels of current expenditure compared to investment in 1994, 1995, and 1997 (see Table 6.6) are puzzling given that the internal politics of the TPP in this period would not give Cinoğlu any incentive to constrain his clientelistic efforts. Bahattin Şeker's position as the national deputy and his leadership at the provincial party organisation were not at all disputed.[26] Even though Cinoğlu might have needed the financial resources that Şeker could channel to the province (such as the relocation of a public liquor company or the building of a stadium) or the political support that could help Cinoğlu to get re-elected as a mayor, Şeker's political dominance in the province meant that this support would be provided to Cinoğlu whether or not Cinoğlu sent signs of having ambition to be elected as a national deputy from Bilecik. In 1998, our expectations are fulfilled and the spending on personnel sky-rockets. Şeker did not present himself as a candidate for the 1999 elections and there was tight competition for the party nomination. The TPP decided to hold indirect primaries where 2,600 delegates selected at the departmental party congresses would vote. Five candidates including Cinoğlu competed for the two positions.[27] Cinoğlu ended up second behind Kemal Eğilmez with a large difference of 374 votes.[28]

In the 1999 elections when the RPP performed extremely poorly both in the parliamentary and local elections, its candidate for the municipality of the Centre, Yaşar Tüzün, won the elections with 42.91 per cent of the votes. The RPP's vote share for the parliamentary elections in the Centre was only 9.8 per cent and for the provincial council the RPP's share was 14.92 per cent. Tüzün was elected as a municipal council member in the 1994 elections after getting the largest number of votes in the primary elections for this position.[29] He was also the head of the provincial party organisation before he presented his candidacy for the position of the mayor in 1999. Tüzün was the single candidate and was automatically nominated by the RPP for the position of mayor.[30] In 2002, Tüzün ran for the parliamentary elections. The provincial party leadership nominated two (including Tüzün in the first position) out of four pre-candidates without any open disagreement about Tüzün's nomination. The relatively low levels of current expenditure in 2000 and 2001 after Tüzün's election as the mayor can be explained by this lack of competition for the parliamentary membership nomination. In contrast to the lack of internal party competition, competition between parties in the general elections was fierce. The RPP, with Tüzün as its candidate, ended with the third largest vote

---

26. *Yarın*, 3 November 1995.
27. *Yarın*, 3 February 1999.
28. *Yarın*, 22 February 1992.
29. *Yarın*, 1 February 1994.
30. *Yarın*, 28 January 1999.

Table 6.6: Budget of municipality, City Center of Bilecik

Bilecik Centre	Current expenditure	Investment expenditure	Revenue	Current/ investment
1985	177,340,258.00	70,514,644.00	296,934,265.25	2.51
1986	207,100,977.00	251,177,881.00	678,094,240.03	0.82
1990	2,055,010,364.00	435,530,132.00	3,106,477,555.00	4.72
1991	4,015,398,482.00	647,578,200.00	4,402,521,856.00	6.20
1992	7,353,529,400.00	1,864,663,800.00	7,670,120,626.00	3.94
1994	22,323,232,907.00	9,698,209,000.00	33,036,869,316.00	2.30
1995	48,291,178,262.00	21,397,497,000.00	84,099,404,391.00	2.26
1997	204,840,180,171.00	98,059,512,500.00	262,993,566,316.00	2.09
1998	386,298,743,139.00	40,383,507,000.00	446,101,825,636.00	9.57
2000	1,107,612,979,770.00	307,753,927,432.00	285,441,395,155.00	3.60
2001	1,566,859,158,780.00	350,563,089,000.00	1,905,303,763,397.00	4.47
2002	1,975,904,985,037.00	86,917,240,767.00	2,693,476,575,784.00	22.73

Source: The municipality of City Center, Bilecik.

share of 20.3, after JDP's 27.5 and the TPP's 24.1 per cent. This close competition between the RPP and the TPP, that fought for the second deputy position, gave the incentive to Tüzün to increase the share of current expenditure in his municipal administration in 2002, as can be observed in Table 6.6.[31]

Bozüyük

In 1984, Bozüyük was one of the few municipalities where the MP did not win the elections for the mayor. The first municipal government was controlled by the TPP, then there were two terms by the SPP, and the following two elections were won by the NAP. Since I have data on personnel spending between 1996 and 2004, I discuss only this period. In 1996, the mayor of Bozüyük was Mehmet Talat Bakkalcıoğlu from the SPP, who was elected for the second time in 1994. As he later presented himself as a candidate for the position of the national deputy in 1999, he probably had an ambition for this position. The internal party dynamics in this period did not put any constraints on Bakkalcıoğlu to limit his clientelistic efforts. The party did not have any representatives in the national parliament and hence support from the provincial leadership was hardly critical for Bakkalcıoğlu's political career. Instead, he could rely on his own efforts and financial resources in Bozüyük to win political support in the 1999 primary elections. Indeed, in the indirect primaries he got 163 out of 511 of his total votes in Bozüyük. Olcay, his

---

31. The economic crisis is also likely to have contributed to the decrease in investment expenditure.

Table 6.7: Budget of municipality, Bozüyük

Year	Spending on personnel	Revenue	Personnel/ Investment	Investment
1996	72,643,740,600	149,319,365,791	2.34	31,049,245,600
1997	157,949,605,000	302,477,724,946	2.61	60,503,848,700
1998	305,729,665,500	652,138,910,993	1.44	212,770,092,200
1999	521,967,711,120	1,311,715,741,368	1.20	433,256,499,300
2000	765,442,714,000	3,825,650,981,500	0.48	1,593,927,301,000
2001	1,093,770,544,000	4,909,659,538,000	0.39	2,774,737,970,000
2002	1,810,551,342,000	5,487,008,173,000	0.58	3,112,576,722,000
2003	2,400,431,909,000	6,990,445,320,000	0.90	2,660,232,639,000
2004	3,495,343,948,000	10,065,998,253,000	1.20	2,907,958,899,000

Source: The municipality of Bozüyük.

runner-up, could get votes from only 8 delegates in Bozüyük.[32] As expected, the levels of spending on personnel between 1996 and 1998 were much higher compared to latter years.

In the 1999 elections, the RPP lost the municipality to the NAP. In the initial years of Ahmet Berberoğlu's term as the mayor, we see a substantial drop in spending on personnel (see Table 6.7). The party had a representative, Hüseyin Arabacı, in the national parliament. His support and the centralised nomination procedures in the NAP made the party support important for Berberoğlu's political career. At the same time, the NAP's vote share for parliamentary elections in the whole province was slightly above the TPP's with a margin of only 0.2 per cent. With only 200 votes of difference, the NAP received the second parliamentary seat from Bilecik. Although the small margin is not a direct indicator of intra-party support for Arabacı, it is a sign that his position as national deputy was not that secure. This made it important for Beberoğlu not to send signs of ambition so that support from Arabacı would not be withdrawn. As such we would expect low levels of spending on personnel in Berberoğlu's initial term as mayor and this is exactly what we observe in Table 6.7. However, the NAP lost a lot of public support generally in Turkey as a result of the catastrophic economic crisis under their national coalition government. In turn, they could not pass the 10 per cent national threshold and could not win any national deputy seats in the 2002 elections. Accordingly, the NAP label did not carry much value, either. Therefore, support from the provincial leadership no longer was crucial for Berberoğlu, which eliminated the constraints that internal party politics enforced on Berberoğlu to limit his clientelistic efforts and we see an increase in personnel spending between 2002 and 2004[33] (see Table 6.7).

32. *Yarın*, 16 February 1999.

33. This increase can also partly be influenced by the general economic recovery in Turkey.

Statistical analysis of employment in the metropolitan municipalities:

Unfortunately I have access to very limited data on the number of personnel for Turkey. Therefore, I use the data on personnel spending (as a share of revenue) as a proxy to measure the extent of patronage in public employment. This data exists for 1997–2001 in the case of Turkish metropolitan municipalities.

Just as in Argentina, political factors are more likely to influence the hiring of temporary and contracted personnel than tenured civil servants. This is because politicians are more willing to manipulate temporary jobs since each new government can replace the previous government's temporary employees with their own supporters. In the aftermath of the 1999 reforms, we would expect to see political factors having a different effect on temporary workers and contract personnel because the latter were required to pass centralised exams.[34]

Unlike temporary employees who, by the very nature of their jobs, have short-term contracts, permanent workers are supposed to enjoy job security.[35] However, in practice, politicians and governments do fire these workers illegally, or find some kind of legal excuse to fire them (Akinci 1999), or pressure them to take early retirement. The permanent workers' positions are more attractive to aspiring politicians for patronage purposes than the civil service jobs because the Civil Service Law (No. 657) bans civil servants from joining political parties. As a result, politicians cannot use civil service jobs to reward their party loyalists for services rendered. In response to my question about how public employees contribute to the parties' campaign efforts, a WP legislator from Kocaeli said that permanent workers are not bound by Law No. 657.[36] Therefore, ideally I would want to run regressions for different types of employees. Given the lack of data, I use the aggregate measure. This can reveal a weaker link, but I do not expect the results to be biased.

Explanatory variables[37]

In order to capture how internal party rivalries affect patronage in public employment, I first look at whether the politician needs and values the party (leader's) support to be re-elected, that is, the importance of party support. Since I analyse metropolitan municipalities, where I expect the interaction between mayors and

---

34. Unfortunately, the lack of data on different types of employees means this hypothesis cannot be analysed. According to a later law on municipalities (No. 5395/13.7.2005), some contract personnel employed in the municipalities are not required to take the centralised exam.

35. Under Law No. 667, public employees are categorised into four groups: civil servants (*memur*), contracted employees (*sözleşmeli personel*), temporary employees (*geçici personel*), and workers (*işçiler*). According to Article No. 4 of this legislation, (permanent) workers are defined as the ones that do not fit any of the previous three categories. Legislation No. 1475 defines the rights and obligations of the workers (in the private and public) sector.

36. Author's interview (No. 28), January 2004.

37. See Table 6.10 for descriptive statistics and Appendix C for sources of data.

their party leaders to have an impact on patronage, I use a similar measure to the one I used to measure the importance of party support for Argentine governors: I look at the difference between the mayors' vote shares and the vote shares of their parties in the legislative elections. I divide this difference by the mayor's vote share in local elections in order to control for the smaller impact that the same amount of difference might have when the mayor's vote share is already high in the district.

The second variable related to internal party competition is the openness of party leadership competition. Just like in Argentina, I expect that the party leader's support for her fellow party members (mayor of the metropolitan municipality) will not endanger her leadership when she (the party leader) is dominant in the party. If she is not, however, she will probably lose her leadership position if she supports her challengers. I therefore expect the lower level politician (mayor of the metropolitan municipality) to reduce particularistic job distribution when his party leader is not dominant, since rivals would then know that the leader's support would be conditional on the extent of their effort to build individual political bases. I look at the results of indirect elections for party leadership to measure the leader's strength and hence the openness of party leadership competition. When there is only one candidate for the leadership position, I code the results as one.

Since, just as in Argentina, I expect the importance of party support to reduce particularistic exchanges in public sector employment only when the party leadership position is open to competition, I include an interactive term of these two variables in the analysis. (See Figure 5.1 in Chapter Five for a more detailed discussion of this interaction effect.) The model in Chapter Four predicts the importance of party support to have no effect when the party leadership is not open to competition.

Then, I control for some other political variables: I expect that in Turkey the party's ideological position might affect the particularistic distribution of public jobs. In Argentina, the provincial governments in the analysis were all controlled by the Peronists or Radicals. I had taken out those that were controlled by provincial parties since the main hypotheses that I introduced in Chapter Four are relevant only for parties where competition with a national party leader might make a difference for patronage. As such, for Argentina I could use a simple party identification variable to control for a potential difference between parties. In Turkey, rather than having indicator variables for each separate party, I control for the underlying dimension that might make a difference, the ideological position of the politicians' party. I include an indicator variable that takes on the value of one when the politician is from a rightist party.

In order to decide whether or not the party is rightist, I use Carkoglu's (1998) analysis of party manifestos, a spatial analysis of party discourse during the 1995 election campaigns (Secor 2001), and the results of a post-election election survey (Carkoglu 2003). Carkoglu's analysis of the manifestos follows the Manifesto Research Group's method and the manifestos are assigned positions on the left-right ideological spectrum according to the policies proposed by parties. However, Carkoglu's 1998 analysis covers only the period between 1946 and 1995. Since none of these studies cover the entire period of my research, I cannot assign a different position for a party in each election year. Instead, I use an average combined measure from these three studies. In all three works, zero represents the centre on the ideological dimension. I code those parties that have been to the right of zero all the time from 1983 (the time of democratic transition) to 2001 in all three works as one. Then, I code those that have been on the left as zero. In this period only one party, the DLP, moved from the left of zero to the right. In order to take this into account, I run one regression where I code DLP as one and another where I code it as zero.

Another political variable I include is the competitiveness of the local elections. To measure competitiveness, I take the absolute value of the difference between the vote shares of the incumbent party and the leading opposition party in the district. I also include two indicator variables that take the value of one when the mayor belongs to a party in national government and when (local or general) elections are held in that year. The socio-economic control variables included in the analysis are logged GDP per capita (measured in US dollar equivalents) and logged population. I also control for the share of transfers (special aids and funds) in their revenue. I include an indicator variable that takes on the value of one for the years 2000 and 2001, to capture the effect of legal reforms that concern public employment. I expect to observe fewer employees, hence a smaller share of revenues allocated to personnel spending, after the introduction of these reforms.

Analysis and findings

This section presents the results from the analysis of Turkish metropolitan municipalities. The data is cross-sectional time series for the years between 1997 and 2001. The unit of analysis is one metropolitan municipality per year for sixteen metropolitan municipalities. I estimate the model with OLS, fixed unit effects for the municipalities, and panel corrected standard errors. My analysis of municipal public employment reveals no indication of temporally dependent standard errors (see Table 6.9).

The results are presented in Table 6.8. The findings support the main hypothesis that importance of party support (party-mayor vote/mayor vote) reduces spending on personnel when the party leadership position is open to competition. Where the party leader won less than 85 per cent of the votes in the internal leadership elections, the coefficient of party support is negative and statistically significant at 95 per cent. To discuss the substantive impact, we can look at the coefficient of party support when the internal election result is 60 per cent: -0.08. Let's say that the mayor won the elections with 30 per cent (the mean in the data is 32 per cent). and his party also won 30 per cent in the general elections. If the party had won, instead, 33 per cent of the votes, indicating that the party support is now more important for the mayor, this would have decreased the share of personnel spending in the revenue with 0.008 where the mean is 0.39. As expected, we do not find an effect of party support on personnel spending when the leadership position is not open to competition; that is, where the party leader got more than 84 per cent of the votes (see Figure 6.2).

As in the statistical analysis of employees in Argentina, I find that politicians

Effect of party support at various levels of internal election results

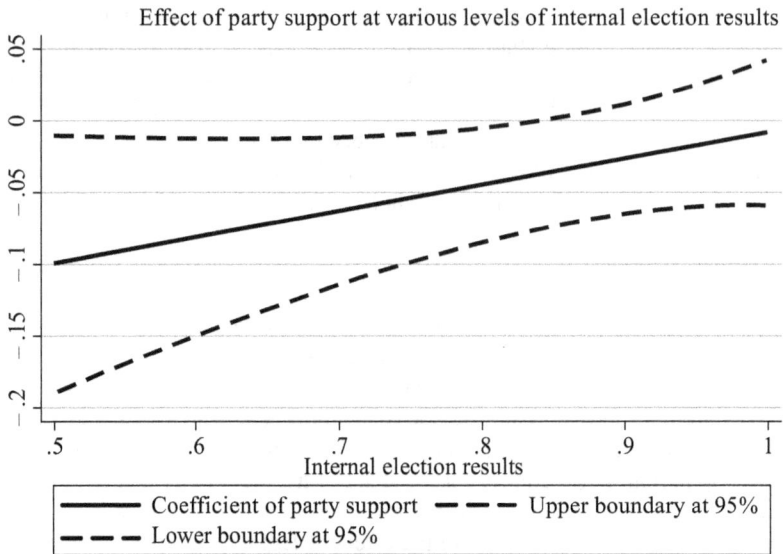

From Model 1 (Column 1) in Table 6.8

Figure 6.2: The results for the interactive term

do indeed spend less on personnel when they belong to a party in government, but more in election years. There is a weak finding that competitiveness of the district matters. The results actually show a positive association between personnel spending and the distance between the mayor's vote share and the competitor's vote. However, the coefficient is statistically significant only at 90 per cent and the finding is not robust to changes in the specification of the model. When the lagged dependent variable is not included in the analysis, the coefficient is no longer statistically significant. The direction of the effect, though, does not change.

In contrast to the analysis of Argentine data, where I did not find any effect of socio-economic variables, here we can see that more populated municipalities spend more on personnel.[38] However, the finding is not robust to changes in the model specification and the coefficient is only statistically significant at 90 per cent. The administrative reforms that were introduced in 1999 and came to effect starting in 2000, also seemed to increase the share of personnel spending. However, as in the previous finding, the result is not robust to changes in model specification. When the lagged dependent variable is included, the coefficient of this of variable is no longer statistically different from zero.

In contrast to the expectations of the previous literature, the municipalities that depend more on transfers seem to spend less on personnel. According to the common pool argument, governments or administrations that can externalise their

---

38. Since the dependent variable in the Argentine case is the number of temporary employees per 10,000 people, population is not included separately as an independent variable.

Table 6.8: OLS Parameter estimates for models predicting personnel spending (1997–2001)

	(1)	(2)	(3)
Intra-Party Competition Effects			
Internal party elections	0.07	0.06	0.07
	(0.03)*	(0.03)+	(0.07)
Party-mayor vote/mayor vote	-0.19	-0.19	-0.21
	(0.10)+	(0.10)+	(0.12)+
Party-mayor vote/mayor vote * internal party elections	0.18	0.18	0.22
	(0.12)	(0.12)	(0.20)
Government party	-0.05	-0.05	-0.10
	(0.01)**	(0.01)**	(0.05)*
Inter-Party Competition Effects			
Competitiveness	0.0004	0.0004	0.004
	(0.0008)	(0.001)	(0.002)+
Elections (1999)	0.10	0.10	0.11
	(0.01)**	(0.02)**	(0.02)**
Right parties	0.0003	-	-0.01
	(0.02)		(.05)
Right (2)	-	0.01	
		(0.01)	
Socio-Economic Controls			
Reform	0.04	0.04	0.04
	(0.02)*	(0.02)*	(0.03)
Logged GDP	-0.01	-0.01	-0.002
	(0.01)	(0.01)	(0.01)
Logged population	0.15	0.15	0.16
	(0.10)	(0.10)	(0.10)+
National transfers	-1.27	-1.25	-1.95
	(0.47)**	(0.45)**	(0.72)**
Lagged dependent variable	-	-	0.01
			(.28)
Municipality dummies	yes	yes	yes
Number of observations	76	76	60
Number of municipalities	16	16	15

Standard errors in parentheses + significant at 10%; * significant at 5%; ** significant at 1%

Table 6.9: Check for serial correlation. Residuals from the analysis of personnel spending in metropolitan municipalities

Lagged residuals	-0.29
	(0.38)
Party-mayor vote/mayor vote	-0.03
	(0.11)
Internal election results	0.04
	(0.07)
Party-mayor vote/mayor vote * internal election results	0.07
	(0.18)
Government dummy	-0.02
	(0.05)
Competitiveness	0.002
	(0.003)
Elections (1999)	0.01
	(0.02)
Right parties	-0.01
	(0.05)
Reform	0.01
	(0.02)
Logged GDP	0.008
	(0.008)
Logged population	0.004
	(0.08)
National transfers	-1.27
	(0.83)
Municipality dummies	yes
Number of observations	60
Number of municipalities	15

Standard errors in parentheses * significant at 5%; ** significant at 1%

Table 6.10: Descriptive statistics for the variables in the statistical analysis

Variable	Obs.	Mean	Std. Dev.	Min	Max
Personnel spending (as a share of revenue)	76	.39	.21	.05	1.20
Internal election results	76	.85	.19	51	1
Party-mayor vote/mayor vote	76	-.36	.39	-.97	.48
Government's party	76	.43	.50	0	1
Competitiveness	76	10.91	9.27	.21	38.18
Elections	76	.20	.40	0	1
Right	76	.59	.50	0	1
Right 2	76	.75	.44	0	1
Reform	76	.41	.50	0	1
Logged population	76	14.25	.74	12.51	16.15
Logged GDP per cap.	76	-5.79	.64	-7.52	-3.92
Transfers	76	.03	.03	.0002	.14
Lagged spending	60	.39	.22	.05	1.20

cost of spending through their access to the resources that originate from a common pool, such as the national government budget, tend to spend more (Remmer and Wibbels 2000). I might be finding the opposite effect, because having a larger share of revenue as transfers might be an indication of the municipality's dependence on the national government. If the national government is concerned about inefficient spending in the municipalities, they might be more effectively putting pressure on dependent municipalities to restrain their spending. I use the share of (lagged) national transfers as an indicator for the importance of party support in the case of Argentine provinces controlled by the national incumbent party to test the main theoretical hypotheses of this book. Unfortunately the small number of cases (thirty-three observations), and the lack of data that measures the strength of the prime minister, prevent me from conducting a similar analysis for the Turkish data.

Conclusion

Both resource (economic) constraints and legal reform of public employment in Turkey have limited politicians' ability to distribute public jobs in a particularistic manner. However, the statistical analysis of subnational employment suggests that these legal reforms have not been successful in lowering personnel spending at the sub-national level. Moreover, the results also indicate that these reforms have not eliminated particularistic exchanges of jobs between politicians and their supporters.

As in Argentina, the findings from the empirical analyses highlight the importance of party politics. Even with limited abilities to employ their supporters in the public sector, politicians seem to resort to particularistic exchanges in order to build a strong political support base in the public as well as in their own party. Leadership competition within the party, however, puts pressure on politicians to restrict their efforts to establish such individual power bases through particularistic distribution of jobs. Such pressures from the party leadership seem to have an impact under two conditions: when politicians need and value their party's support for re-election and when there is open competition for the party leadership; that is, when the leader is not dominant in the party.

In Turkey, the mayors of metropolitan municipalities are potential rivals to the party leader. The statistical analysis in this chapter shows that when a mayor's individual support base in his district is weak relative to his party's popularity, and when his party leader is not dominant in the party, he will spend less on personnel in order to signal to the party leader that he is not a rival, and hopes to secure his party's support in the elections.

chapter seven | conclusion

Argentina and Turkey are two developing countries that are, after their transition to democracy in 1983, still facing problems with the quality of democracy, rule of law, and economic, as well as *de facto* political, inequalities. Particularistic relationships between state and citizens, where citizens' demands from the state and their rights are met through their personal and particular networks with some state actors, are closely related to these major problems that challenge these two countries, as well as many others throughout the world. The prevalence of particularism is partly a consequence of these problems, such as the inability of the state to enforce its impartial rules and unequal economic opportunities that are available to citizens. At the same time, they partly contribute to the persistence and even growth of these problems by violating further the application of universal rules and preventing access to state resources by some citizens.

In this book I attempted to improve our understanding of the political factors that shape these particularistic relationships between citizens and state actors by trying to fill in some of the gaps and to answer some of the puzzles in the current literature. By narrowing down the analysis to the particularistic exchanges of public jobs between elected office holders and citizens, I tried to achieve more accuracy in the theoretical explanations of the mechanisms behind these exchanges. This has led me to focus on an additional stage of political competition that the previous literature has mostly ignored: competition within political parties. By examining patronage jobs and politics in two countries that have different cultural backgrounds and formal political institutions, I was able to point to two key characteristics of the parties and the party system as the political factors that have an impact on particularistic hirings in public employment. These two characteristics are the importance of party support for politicians' careers and openness of competition for the party leadership post.

Internal party politics gives incentives to politicians to increase the size of their clientelistic networks because these clientelistic networks also help them in the first stage of electoral competition, that is, for nominations and leadership. Politicians distribute public jobs to party activists in order to mobilise them for their campaigns or to receive their votes in internal party elections. The analysis of internal party politics in Argentina and Turkey showed that competition within the party at the same time can help limit the extent of politicians' clientelistic efforts. The interdependence of party members for the electoral success of the party and the ambiguity about politicians' intentions behind the allocation of patronage jobs – whether they distribute jobs with the purpose of improving their electoral performance in general elections or for internal party competition – allows this to happen.

If there is real competition for party leadership positions, one of the key determinants of this being open and participatory selection mechanisms, the party leader feels threatened by potential challengers to her power in the party. At the same time, though, her challengers might rely on political or financial support from this party leader. For example, leaders might play a critical role in nomination procedures (as in the case of all Turkish parties), or they might control significant campaign resources that they can channel to their party members. If both of these conditions hold, politicians, whether they are governors in Argentina or mayors in Turkey, hesitate to appear as challengers and would constrain their clientelistic efforts since their efforts, which would be signalled by the size of patronage jobs, are easily observable by their leaders. This behaviour would be a credible signal compared to, for example, verbal statements of supporting the party leader and hence provide reliable information about their intentions to move up in the party hierarchy.

Thus, the analysis of party competition and public employment in Argentina and Turkey reveals that when party leadership is open to competition and when parties provide important advantages to the politicians, we are less likely to observe particularism in public employment at the sub-national level. This finding suggests that more participatory forms of leadership selection, such as open primaries with high turn-out, and important role for parties in general elections, such as state campaign contributions that are directed from parties to decentralised branches of parties, would help reduce patronage within parties.

These mechanisms would be expected to work under democratic systems where multiple number of parties compete and have real chances of participating in the government as well as the single party dominant democracies such as India during Congress Party period or the LDP period in Japan. Although there are some works in the literature that focused on internal party competition, especially among factions (see Zuckerman 1979; Bettcher 2005; Benton 2007 as examples that focus on factions and clientelism), and the effect of *intra-party competition* on policy choice and implementation, a large part of this literature has examined countries in the period when a single party dominated politics. (See Golden and Chang 2001 on Italian Christian Democrats and corruption, McCubbins and Thies 1997 on LDP factions and fiscal policy, and Jacob 2005 on Indian economic development as examples.) What this book argues is that even though in single party dominant systems intra-party competition, especially in the form of competition among factions, is more visible, some degree of competition and struggle for power exists in all parties and such internal party politics might also have an effect on policy formulation and implementation in competitive party systems.

A notable example that initiated the analysis of intra-party competition in the context of multi-party systems is Laver and Shepsle's (1996) study of coalition formation. An interesting point that emerges out of their relaxation of the unitary actor assumption for parties is that just the existence of factions in a party can lead to different outcomes even when these factions do not have decision-making power within their parties. This book's theoretical arguments and empirical findings also highlight the importance of potential conflicts among politicians (groups) of the same party even when one of these actors does not have a formal role in the decision making process. In the case of patronage jobs at the sub-national level, even when national party leaders do not have formal power over the hiring decisions, they can have an impact on the extent of patronage. The national leaders' control over the distribution of incentives (Panebianco 1988) allows the interaction with the national leader to be consequential for hiring decisions.

As in any other organisation, leaders in a political party are faced with delegation problems. Policy-making in various administrative levels is transferred to other party members. However, such delegation brings with it the possibility of two problems that exist in any principle-agent relationship: moral hazard (Alesina and Spear 1988) and adverse selection. For example, governors or mayors can have different preferences than the national party leader about the optimal number of patronage jobs or they might not have the capability to effectively run these administrations. One additional dimension that is highlighted in this book is that leaders might face the threat of losing their own position if their fellow organisation members get powerful enough to challenge them, mostly as a result of the responsibilities that are delegated to them. What this book argues and empirically supports is that this potential threat or delegation problem, in turn, has consequences for the distribution of resources in the organisation.

One critical point regarding internal party competition that emerged out of the analysis of patronage politics within parties is the interdependence of the political actors who are involved. Since politicians within the same party care about the party's performance, they sometimes have to rely on each other. An interesting question is how this interdependence, compared to the lack of it in inter-party competition, would affect other types of policy choices and their implementation. An obvious direction for future research is to look at other types of benefits that can be distributed in a particularistic manner. For example, in the case of state contacts, do we see similar mechanisms of intra-party politics? If politicians are exchanging contracts in return for campaign contributions (Fleischer 1997; Samuels 2000), does competition with higher level party members affect the extent of this corruption? Could contract awarding in exchange for illegal financial contributions (that is supposedly less visible) serve as signals about the intention of politicians and hence its levels be constrained by internal competition? Or if the contracts cannot signal politicians' intentions, could it lead to the opposite outcome where fierce internal party competition would accelerate the illegal awarding of contracts?

Narrowing the research question to just one type of benefit that is exchanged, in this case public jobs, was clearly helpful for analytical purposes. However, clearly there is a link between clientelistic exchanges that involve benefits of different types. A party member who received a job in the public sector through her clientelistic network can and probably *does* obtain other benefits such as better services in the public hospital of the neighbourhood or easier access to public offices through the same clientelistic network to which she belongs. What do the findings from this book tell us about the prevalence of these broader clientelistic networks in a polity?

Electoral competition among parties has long been argued to have an effect on the politicisation of the state. As I mentioned in the introduction, there are conflicting views on this: Some authors have argued that more intense competition increases the level of clientelism (Remmer 2007), others claim that competition actually restrains the discretionary use of state resources by parties (Grzymala-Busse 2007; Geddes 1994). Shefter (1994) argues that the relative timing of democratisation and bureaucratisation matters. This book illustrates that *intra-party competition* can constrain clientelism in public employment when the party is important for electoral chances of politicians and when leadership selection process is competitive.

One critical aspect of clientelism in public employment is that patronage jobs facilitate the expansion of other clientelistic exchanges by politicising the services in the public administration. Party supporters who are hired to public positions through clientelistic networks, rather than impartial bureaucrats, are more likely to prioritise the needs and demands of others in their own clientelistic networks before those that are excluded from the networks. Even if the final decision about the identity of the recipient of a public benefit such as a subsidy or a contract might be taken by a politician, for example the governor or the mayor, party supporters in the administration are helpful when carrying out these decisions in the actual distribution stage of material goods. Therefore, the higher the level of clientelism in public employment, the more widespread other types of clientelistic linkages between the state and citizens are expected to be, even if spill over effect might not be direct, linear or immediate.

In addition, as Piattoni (2001) argues, the perceptions of citizens about patron-client relationships, such as about the identity of potential patrons (or brokers such as *punteros* in the case of Argentina), or about the likelihood of having access to a service through particularistic relationships, affect the formation of actual clientelistic networks through potential clienteles' decisions about, in the first place, whether to engage in a clientelistic relationship and second, about their choice of the patron. Calvo and Murillo (2008) indeed find through surveys that individuals who are more connected to party members expect to receive more clientelistic benefits. Therefore, widespread existence of clientelism in public employment would be expected to lead to the spread, or at least persistence, of clientelism in other areas by making citizens believe that they are more likely to have access to public benefits if they are part of a powerful politician's clientelistic network, that is by maintaining or increasing the demand for particularistic exchanges.

In this book I have focused on the supply side of the particularistic exchanges; that is, the incentives of politicians to expand their clientelistic networks. However, even though focusing on either the demand or supply side is useful for analytical purposes, they are interrelated and the widespread supply of patronage jobs would be expected to affect the demand from citizens for these particularistic exchanges. The supply of patronage jobs are likely to lead to the persistence of demand from citizens for these particularistic exchanges of not only jobs, but potentially of other benefits. One of the implications of this book is that polities where the party system has open and participatory leadership selection procedures and where the parties play an important role in electoral competition would be expected to have lower levels of such particularistic relationships between principals and their elected representatives.

| appendices

The follower maximises his utility function with respect to x and subject to four constraints: $\sigma_1 s + \sigma_2 x \le 1, \alpha_1 s + \alpha_2 x \le 1, x \ge 0, x \le 1.$

When $t = 1$ the objective function to maximise is

$$[(\sigma_1 s + \sigma_2 x)M + (\alpha_1 s + \alpha_2 x)R - vx^2].$$

Then, the Lagrangian is

$$(\sigma_1 s + \sigma_2 x)M + (\alpha_1 s + \alpha_2 x)R - vx^2 - \lambda_1(\sigma_1 s + \sigma_2 x - 1) - \lambda_2$$

$$(\alpha_1 s + \alpha_2 x - 1) + \lambda_3 x - \lambda_4(x - 1)$$

and $\frac{\partial L}{\partial x} = \sigma_2 M + \alpha_2 R - 2vx - \lambda_1 \sigma_2 - \lambda_2 \alpha_2 + \lambda_3 - \lambda_4.$

If the constraints are not binding ($\lambda_1, \lambda_2, \lambda_3, \lambda_4 = 0$), the

value of x that gives the maximum utility is $\frac{\sigma_2 M + \alpha_2 R}{2v}$ where

$$0 < \sigma_2 M + \alpha_2 R < 2v, \sigma_2^2 M + \alpha_2 \sigma_2 R < 2v(1 - \sigma_1 s), \text{ and}$$

$$\sigma_2 \alpha_2 M + \alpha_2^2 R < 2v(1 - \alpha_1 s).$$

If $\sigma_1 s + \sigma_2 x \le 1, \alpha_1 s + \alpha_2 x \le 1, x \le 1$ constraints are binding, the follower's

utility is maximised when x is equal to $\frac{1 - \sigma_1 s}{\sigma_2}, \frac{1 - \alpha_1 s}{\alpha_2}$ and 1 respectively for each

constraint.

When the constraint that $x \ge 0$ is binding, that is $x = 0$ and $\lambda_3 > 0, \lambda_4 = 0,$

$\sigma_2 M + \alpha_2 R = \lambda_1 \sigma_2 + \lambda_2 \alpha_2 - \lambda_3.$ Then, either $\alpha_1 s = 1$ or $\lambda_2 = 0.$ And

either $\sigma_1 s = 1$ or $\lambda_1 = 0.$ If $\lambda_1, \lambda_2 = 0,$ then $\sigma_2 M + \alpha_2 R = -\lambda_3,$ but

$\sigma_2 M + \alpha_2 R > 0$ (according to the model's assumptions) and this cannot be

true.

If $\lambda_1 = 0$ and $\sigma_1 s = 1$, the follower's utility function is maximised at $x = 0$, but theoretically this is not an interesting case since the maximum probability of re-election is achieved by s (the support from the leader) and x (patronage jobs) plays no role.

If $\lambda_2 = 0$ and $\alpha_1 s = 1$, the follower's utility function is maximised at $x = 0$, but again theoretically this is not an interesting case since the maximum probability of taking over the leadership position is achieved by s and x plays no role.

When $t = 0$, if the constraints are not binding ($\lambda_1, \lambda_2, \lambda_3, \lambda_4 = 0$), the value of x that gives the maximum utility is $\frac{\sigma_2 M}{2v}$

where $0 < \sigma_2 M < 2v, \sigma_2^2 M < 2v(1 - \sigma_1 s)$, and $\sigma_2 \alpha_2 M < 2v(1 - \alpha_1 s)$.

Therefore, for the rest of the analysis I assume that $\sigma_2 M + \alpha_2 R < 2v$.

Appendix A.1: The Leader's best response function under complete information:

For the case when P_F is a challenger, that is $t = 1$, when $s = 1$, the utility of P_L is $U_{P_L} = (\beta_1 s + \beta_2 x)G + [1 - (\alpha_1 s + \alpha_2 x)]Q$ and when $s = 0$ the utility of P_L is $U_{P_L} = (\beta_2 x)G + (1 - \alpha_2 x)Q$. $U_L(s = 1) \geq U_L(s = 0)$ only when $\frac{G}{Q} \geq \frac{\alpha_1}{\beta_1}$.

For the case when P_F is not a challenger, that is $t = 0$, when $s = 1$, the utility of P_L is $U_{P_L} = (\beta_1 s + \beta_2 x)G + Q$

and when $s = 0$ the utility of P_L is $U_{P_L} = (\beta_2 x)G + Q$.

Therefore, $U_L(s = 1) \geq U_L(s = 0)$ is always true given that by assumption $\beta_1 s > 0$ and $G > 0$.

Appendix A.2: Formal derivations of Equilibria under incomplete information:

Let $\mu : X \to \Delta(T)$ be the updated beliefs of P_L about P_F's type given x, where for a finite set D, $\Delta(T)$ denotes the set of probability distributions over D and $\mu(t \mid x)$ is P_L's belief about the likelihood that P_F is type $t \in \{1, 0\}$ given that x is observed by P_L.

A strategy for P_F is a function $z : T \to \Delta(X)$ where $z(x \mid T)$ is the probability that P_F sends the signal x given that his type is $t \in \{1, 0\}$. Type $t \in \{1, 0\}$ chooses $x \in X$ according to $z(.)$ if $z(x \mid T) > 0$. The strategy for P_L is defined by a function such that $r : X \to \Delta(S)$ where $r(s \mid x)$ denotes the probability that P_L takes action s upon observing x.

Pure strategy separating equilibria:

Let the level of x that is chosen by type 1 be x' and the level of x that is chosen by type 0 be x'', then $x' \neq x''$.

First, I consider the case where $x' > x''$.

Trivially, the updated beliefs on the equilibrium path are $\mu^*(1 \mid x = x') = 1$ and $\mu^*(0 \mid x = x'') = 1$.

For the follower's actions that are off-the equilibrium path, any posterior beliefs are possible. In the rest of the analysis, for off-the equilibrium path actions, I consider the beliefs $\mu(t = 1 \mid x) = 1$ for all $x > x''$ so that posterior beliefs are monotonic in x.

Then, expected payoffs from P_L's actions are:

$$E(s = 1 \mid x > x'') = (\beta_1 s + \beta_2 x)G + [1 - (\alpha_1 s + \alpha_2 x)]Q,$$
$$E(s = 0 \mid x > x'') = (\beta_2 x)G + [1 - \alpha_2 x]Q,$$
$$E(s = 1 \mid x \leq x'') = (\beta_1 s + \beta_2 x)G + Q, \quad E(s = 0 \mid x \leq x'') = (\beta_2 x)G + Q.$$

$E(s = 1 \mid x > x'') \geq E(s = 0 \mid x > x'')$ if $\frac{G}{Q} \geq \frac{\alpha_1}{\beta_1}$ and

$E(s = 1 \mid x \leq x'') \geq E(s = 0 \mid x \leq x'')$ when $(\beta_1 s)G \geq 0$. Since by

assumption $\beta > 0$ and $G > 0$, $(\beta_1 s)G \geq 0$ is always true.

Therefore, if $\frac{G}{Q} > \frac{\alpha_1}{\beta_1}$, $r^*(s = 1 \mid x) = 1 \quad \forall x \in X$.

Given $r^*(s = 1 \mid x) = 1 \quad \forall x \in X$, $\forall t \in \{0,1\}, z^*(x \mid t) > 0$ only if

$x \in \arg\max_{x \in X} U_{P_F}(t, x, r^*(x))$. $\quad \arg\max_{x \in X} U_{P_F}(t = 1, x, r^*(x))$

$= \arg\max_{x \in X}[(\sigma_1 s + \sigma_2 x)M + (\alpha_1 s + \alpha_2 x)R - vx^2] = \frac{\sigma_2 M + \alpha_2 R}{2v}$.

$\arg\max_{x \in X} U_{P_F}(t = 0, x, r^*(x)) = \arg\max_{x \in X}[(\sigma_1 s + \sigma_2 x)M - vx^2] = \frac{\sigma_2 M}{2v}$.

Since $\frac{\sigma_2 M}{2v} < \frac{\sigma_2 M + \alpha_2 R}{2v}$ the assumption that $x' > x''$ is fulfilled. Therefore,

we get a pure strategy separating PBE where $\frac{G}{Q} > \frac{\alpha_1}{\beta_1}$; $r^*(s = 1 \mid x) = 1$

$\forall x \in X$; $z^*(t = 1, x = \frac{\sigma_2 M + \alpha_2 R}{2v}, r^*(x)) = 1$, $z^*(t = 0, x = \frac{\sigma_2 M}{2v}, r^*(x)) = 1$

and $\mu^*(t = 1 \mid x = \frac{\sigma_2 M + \alpha_2 R}{2v}) = 1$ and $\mu^*(t = 0 \mid x = \frac{\sigma_2 M}{2v}) = 1$.

If $\frac{G}{Q} < \frac{\alpha_1}{\beta_1}$, $r^* = \begin{cases} s = 0 \text{ if } x > x'' \\ s = 1 \text{ if } x \leq x'' \end{cases} = 1$. Given

$r^* = \begin{cases} s = 0 \text{ if } x > x'' \\ s = 1 \text{ if } x \leq x'' \end{cases} = 1$, $\forall t \in \{1,0\}, z^*(x \mid t) > 0$ only if

$x \in \arg\max_{x \in X} U_{P_F}(t, x, r^*(x))$. The follower of type 1 either can

choose x that maximises his utility function when $s = 0$ which is

$\arg\max_{x \in X} U_{P_F}(t = 1, x, r^*(x)) = \arg\max_{x \in X}[(\sigma_2 x)M + (\alpha_2 x)R - vx^2] = \frac{\sigma_2 M + \alpha_2 R}{2v}$

or choose $x \leq x''$ and get support $s = 1$. The follower of type 0

would choose x that maximises his utility function when $s = 1$;

$\arg\max_{x \in X} U_{P_F}(t = 0, x, r^*(x)) = \arg\max_{x \in X}[(\sigma_1 s + \sigma_2 x)M - vx^2]; x = \frac{\sigma_2 M}{2v}$.

Therefore, we also get a pure strategy separating PBE where

$$\frac{G}{Q} < \frac{\alpha_1}{\beta_1}; \quad r^* = \begin{cases} s = 0 \text{ if } x > x'' \\ s = 1 \text{ if } x \le x'' \end{cases} = 1; \quad z^*(t = 1, x = \frac{\sigma_2 M + \alpha_2 R}{2v}, r^*(x)) = 1,$$

$$z^*(t = 0, x = \frac{\sigma_2 M}{2v}, r^*(x)) = 1, \quad \mu^*(t = 1 \mid x = \frac{\sigma_2 M + \alpha_2 R}{2v}) = 1,$$

$$\mu^*(t = 0 \mid x = \frac{\sigma_2 M}{2v}) = 1$$

and when $U_F(t = 1, x = \frac{\sigma_2 M}{2v}, s = 1) - U_F(t = 1, x = \frac{\sigma_2 M + \alpha_2 R}{2v}, s = 0) \le 0$.

The condition is simplified as $\sigma_1 M + \alpha_1 R - \frac{\alpha_2^2 R^2}{4v} \le 0$.

When P_L is indifferent between $s = 1$ and $s = 0$, that is when $\frac{G}{Q} = \frac{\alpha_1}{\beta_1}$,

the condition for the follower's decision to forego patronage becomes

$(1-k)\sigma_1 M + \alpha_1 R - \frac{\alpha_2^2 R^2}{4v} \le 0$ where k is the probability of the P_L choosing

$s = 1$.

The case where $x' < x''$: We know that $\mu^*(t = 1 \mid x = x') = 1$ and

$\mu^*(t = 0 \mid x = x') = 1$.

For the inequalities $x < x', x > x''$ and the interval $x' < x < x''$ any posterior

beliefs are possible.

Expected payoffs from P_L's actions are:

$$E(s = 1 \mid x = x') = (\beta_1 s + \beta_2 x)G + [1 - (\alpha_1 s + \alpha_2 x)]Q,$$

$$E(s = 0 \mid x = x') = (\beta_2 x)G + [1 - (\alpha_2 x)]Q,$$

$$E(s = 1 \mid x = x'') = (\beta_1 s + \beta_2 x)G + Q, \quad E(s = 0 \mid x = x'') = (\beta_2 x)G + Q.$$

$E(s = 1 \mid x = x') \ge E(s = 0 \mid x = x')$ when $\frac{G}{Q} \ge \frac{\alpha_1}{\beta_1}$ and

$E(s = 1 \mid x = x'') \ge E(s = 0 \mid x = x'')$ when $(\beta_1 s)G \ge 0$ and we know

that this condition always holds. Therefore, if $\frac{G}{Q} > \frac{\alpha_1}{\beta_1}$, $r^*(s = 1 \mid x) = 1$

where

$$x \in \{x', x''\}, \ r^* = \begin{cases} s = 0 \text{ if } x = x' \\ s = 1 \text{ if } x = x'' \end{cases} = 1 \text{ if } \frac{G}{Q} < \frac{\alpha_1}{\beta_1}, \text{ and } r^*(s = 1 \mid x) = k$$

if $\frac{G}{Q} = \frac{\alpha_1}{\beta_1}$.

We still need to consider off-the equilibrium path actions. If we let the posterior belief of the leader that the follower is a challenger if $x < x'$ is observed be ρ, then ρ can take on the value of only 1 since $x' < x''$.

Then, the expected payoffs from P_L's actions are:

$$E(s = 1 \mid x < x') = (\beta_1 s + \beta_2 x)G + [1 - (\alpha_1 s + \alpha_2 x)]Q,$$

$$E(s = 0 \mid x < x') = (\beta_2 x)G + [1 - (\alpha_2 x)]Q.$$

Therefore, if $\frac{G}{Q} > \frac{\alpha_1}{\beta_1}$, $r^*(s = 1 \mid x < x') = 1$. If $\frac{G}{Q} < \frac{\alpha_1}{\beta_1}$,

$$r^*(s = 0 \mid x < x') = 1.$$

If we let the posterior belief of the leader that the follower is a challenger if $x > x''$ is observed be γ, then γ can take on the value of only 0 since $x' < x''$.

Then, the expected payoffs from P_L's actions

are: $E(s = 1 \mid x > x'') = (\beta_1 s + \beta_2 x)G + Q$,

$E(s = 0 \mid x > x'') = (\beta_2 x)G + Q$. Therefore, $r^*(s = 1 \mid x > x'') = 1$.

For an observed x in the interval $x' < x < x''$ let the posterior belief that the follower is of type 1 be δ. Then the posterior belief that the follower is of type 0 is $1 - \delta$. Expected payoffs from P_L's actions are:

$$E(s = 1 \mid x' < x < x'') = \delta[(\beta_1 s + \beta_2 x)G + [1 - (\alpha_1 s + \alpha_2 x)]Q] +$$

$$(1 - \delta)[(\beta_1 s + \beta_2 x)G + Q] = (\beta_1 s + \beta_2 x)G + [1 - \delta(\alpha_1 s + \alpha_2 x)]Q,$$

$$E(s = 0 \mid x' < x < x'') = \delta[(\beta_2 x)G + [1 - (\alpha_2 x)]Q] +$$

$$(1 - \delta)[(\beta_2 x)G + Q] = (\beta_2 x)G + [1 - \delta(\alpha_2 x)]Q.$$

As such, $E(s = 1 \mid x' < x < x'') \geq E(s = 0 \mid x' < x < x'')$ when $\beta_1 G \geq \delta \alpha_1 Q$.

Therefore, if $\frac{G}{Q} > \frac{\delta\alpha_1}{\beta_1}$, $r^*(s=1\,|\,x' < x < x'') = 1$.

If $\frac{G}{Q} < \frac{\delta\alpha_1}{\beta_1}$, $r^*(s=0\,|\,x' < x < x'') = 1$.

Then the best response of the leader to x is : When $\frac{G}{Q} > \frac{\alpha_1}{\beta_1}$, $r^*(s=1\,|\,x) = 1$

$\forall x \in [0,1]$.

When $\frac{\alpha_1}{\beta_1} > \frac{G}{Q} > \frac{\delta\alpha_1}{\beta_1}$, $r^* = \begin{cases} s=0 \text{ if } x \le x' \\ s=1 \text{ if } x > x'' \end{cases} = 1$ and when $\frac{G}{Q} < \frac{\delta\alpha_1}{\beta_1}$

$r^* = \begin{cases} s=0 \text{ if } x < x'' \\ s=1 \text{ if } x \ge x'' \end{cases} = 1$.

Given these best response actions of the leader, $\forall t \in \{1,0\}, z^*(x\,|\,t) > 0$

only if $x \in \arg\max_{x \in X} U_{P_F}(t,x,r^*(x))$.

When $\frac{G}{Q} > \frac{\alpha_1}{\beta_1}$, $\arg\max_{x \in X} U_{P_F}(t=1,x,r^*(x)) = \arg\max_{x \in X}[(\sigma_1 s + \sigma_2 x)$

$M + (\alpha_1 s + \alpha_2 x)R - vx^2] = \frac{\sigma_2 M + \alpha_2 R}{2v}$

and $\arg\max_{x \in X} U_{P_F}(t=0,x,r^*(x)) = \arg\max_{x \in X}[(\sigma_1 s + \sigma_2 x)M - vx^2] = \frac{\sigma_2 M}{2v}$.

However, since $\frac{\sigma_2 M}{2v} < \frac{\sigma_2 M + \alpha_2 R}{2v}$ the assumption that $x' < x''$ is not fulfilled.

Therefore, a pure strategy separating PBE where $x' < x''$ cannot exist when

$\frac{G}{Q} > \frac{\alpha_1}{\beta_1}$.

When $\frac{\alpha_1}{\beta_1} > \frac{G}{Q} > \frac{\delta\alpha_1}{\beta_1}$, P_{P_F} either chooses $x > x'$ and gets $s=1$ or chooses

$x \le x'$ and gets $s=0$. Since for type 0 his utility is greater when $s=1$, $P_{P_F}^0$

chooses $x > x'$. If $P_{P_F}^1$'s utility is higher when he deviates from x',

and gets $s=1$, there is no pure strategy PBE under these conditions. If his

utility is higher when $s=0$ and $x = x'$, he chooses x that maximises his

utility function, $(\sigma_2 x)M + (\alpha_2 x)R - vx^2$, which is $x = \frac{\sigma_2 M + \alpha_2 R}{2v}$. $P_{P_F}^0$ chooses

$\arg\max_{x \in X} U_{P_F}(t=0,x,r^*(x)) = \arg\max_{x \in X}[(\sigma_1 s + \sigma_2 x)M - vx^2]$ given that he chooses x greater than x'.

Therefore, $P^0_{P_F}$ chooses $x = \frac{\sigma_2 M}{2v}$. However, since $\frac{\sigma_2 M}{2v} < \frac{\sigma_2 M + \alpha_2 R}{2v}$ the assumption that $x' < x''$ is not fulfilled.

Therefore, a pure strategy separating PBE where $x' < x''$ cannot exist when

$$\frac{\alpha_1}{\beta_1} > \frac{G}{Q} > \frac{\delta\alpha_1}{\beta_1}.$$

When $\frac{G}{Q} < \frac{\delta\alpha_1}{\beta_1}$, P_F either chooses $x < x''$ and gets $s = 0$ or chooses $x \geq x''$ and gets $s = 1$. Since for type 0 his utility is greater when $s = 1$, P^0_F chooses $x \geq x''$. P^1_F gets $s = 0$ if he chooses $x = x'$ and gets $s = 1$ if he deviates to $x \geq x''$. Therefore, if his utility is higher when he deviates from x', and gets $s = 1$, there is no pure strategy PBE under these conditions. If his utility is higher when $s = 0$ and $x = x'$, he chooses x that maximises his utility function, $(\sigma_2 x)M + (\alpha_2 x)R - vx^2$, which is $x = \frac{\sigma_2 M + \alpha_2 R}{2v}$. P^0_F chooses $\arg\max_{x \in X} U_{P_F}(t = 0, x, r^*(x)) = \arg\max_{x \in X}[(\sigma_1 s + \sigma_2 x)M - vx^2]$ given that he chooses x greater than x''. Therefore, P^0_F chooses $x = \frac{\sigma_2 M}{2v}$. However, since $\frac{\sigma_2 M}{2v} < \frac{\sigma_2 M + \alpha_2 R}{2v}$ the assumption that $x' = x''$ is not fulfilled. Therefore, a pure strategy separating PBE where $x' < x''$ cannot exist when $\frac{G}{Q} < \frac{\delta\alpha_1}{\beta_1}$, either. Since all possible conditions for the posterior beliefs of the leader are covered, there is no pure strategy separating PBE where $x' < x''$.

Pooling equilibria:

The first condition that must be satisfied is $x' = x''$. Therefore, for PBE to exist

$$z^*(x' \mid t) = 1, \forall t.$$

With the prior belief that $p(t = 1) = p$, $\mu^*(t = 1; x = x') = p$. Let q be the probability that $t = 1 \mid x > x'$. Then, the expected payoffs from P_L's actions are:
$$E(s = 1 \mid x > x') = q[(\beta_1 s + \beta_2 x)G + [1 - (\alpha_1 s + \alpha_2 x)]Q] + (1 - q)[(\beta_1 s + \beta_2 x)$$
$$G + Q]$$

and $E(s = 0 \mid x > x') = q[(\beta_2 x)G + [1 - (\alpha_2 x)]Q] + (1 - q)[(\beta_2 x)G + Q]$,

$$E(s = 1 \mid x \le x') = p[(\beta_1 s + \beta_2 x)G + [1 - (\alpha_1 s + \alpha_2 x)]Q] + (1 - p)$$

$$[(\beta_1 s + \beta_2 x)G + Q]$$

and $E(s = 0 \mid x \le x') = p[(\beta_2 x)G + [1 - \alpha_2 x]Q] + (1 - p)[(\beta_2 x)G + Q]$.

Then $E(s = 1 \mid x > x') \ge E(s = 0 \mid x > x')$ when $\frac{G}{Q} \ge \frac{q\alpha_1}{\beta_1}$

and $E(s = 1 \mid x \le x') \ge E(s = 0 \mid x \le x')$ when $\frac{G}{Q} \ge \frac{p\alpha_1}{\beta_1}$.

Therefore, if $\frac{G}{Q} > \frac{q\alpha_1}{\beta_1}$, $r^*(s = 1 \mid x) = 1 \; \forall x \in X$,

$z^*(x \mid t) > 0$ only if $x \in \arg\max_{x \in X} U_{P_F}(t, x, r^*(x))$.

$\arg\max_{x \in X} U_{P_F}(t = 1, x, r^*(x)) = \arg\max_{x \in X}[(\sigma_1 s + \sigma_2 x)M + (\alpha_1 s + \alpha_2 x)$

$R - vx^2] = \frac{\sigma_2 M + \alpha_2 R}{2v}$ and

$\arg\max_{x \in X} U_{P_F}(t = 0, x, r^*(x)) = \arg\max_{x \in X}[(\sigma_1 s + \sigma_2 x)M - vx^2] = \frac{\sigma_2 M}{2v}$.

Since $x(t = 1) \ne x(t = 0)$, we do not get a pure strategy PBE when $\frac{G}{Q} \ge \frac{q\alpha_1}{\beta_1}$.

If $\frac{p\alpha_1}{\beta_1} < \frac{G}{Q} < \frac{q\alpha_1}{\beta_1}, r^* = \begin{cases} s = 0 \text{ if } x > x' \\ s = 1 \text{ if } x \le x' \end{cases} = 1, \; z^*(x \mid t) > 0$

only if $x \in \arg\max_{x \in X} U_{P_F}(t, x, r^*(x))$. The follower of type 1 either

can choose x that maximises his utility function when $s = 0$ which is

$\arg\max_{x \in X} U_{P_F}(t = 1, x, r^*(x)) = \arg\max_{x \in X}[(\sigma_2 x)M + (\alpha_2 x)R - vx^2] = \frac{\sigma_2 M + \alpha_2 R}{2v}$

or choose $x \leq x''$ and get support $s = 1$.

The follower of type 0 would choose x that maximises his utility function when

$s = 1$: $\arg\max_{x \in X} U_{P_F}(t = 0, x, r^*(x)) = \arg\max_{x \in X}[(\sigma_1 s + \sigma_2 x)M - vx^2] = \frac{\sigma_2 M}{2v}$.

Therefore, we get a pure strategy pooling PBE where $\frac{q\alpha_1}{\beta_1} > \frac{G}{Q} > \frac{p\alpha_1}{\beta_1}$;

$$r^* = \begin{cases} s = 0 \text{ if } x > x' \\ s = 1 \text{ if } x \leq x' \end{cases} = 1;$$

$z^*(\forall t \in \{1,0\}, x = \frac{\sigma_2 M}{2v}, r^*(x)) = 1$ and $\mu^*(t = 1 \mid x = \frac{\sigma_2 M}{2v}) = p$ when

$U_{P_F}(t = 1, x = \frac{\sigma_2 M + \alpha_2 R}{2v}, s = 0) - U_{P_F}(t = 1, x = \frac{\sigma_2 M}{2v}, s = 1) < 0.$

If $\frac{p\alpha_1}{\beta_1} > \frac{G}{Q}$, $r^*(s = 0 \mid x) = 1$ $\forall x \in X$ and we do not get a pooling equilibrium.

Semi-separating (hybrid) equilibria:

P_F^0 never randomises because $x = \frac{\sigma_2 M}{2v}$ always maximises his utility. P_F^1 randomises with ω to make P_L indifferent between $s = 1$ and $s = 0$. The updated beliefs are

$$\mu^*(t = 1 \mid x = \frac{\sigma_2 M}{2v}) = \frac{P(x = \frac{\sigma_2 M}{2v} \mid t=1)p}{P(x = \frac{\sigma_2 M}{2v} \mid t=1)p + P(x = \frac{\sigma_2 M}{2v} \mid t=0)(1-p)} = \frac{\omega}{1-p+\omega p}.$$

Then, the expected payoffs that P_L gets are:

$$E(s = 1 \mid x \le \frac{\sigma_2 M}{2v}) = \frac{\omega}{1-p+\omega p}[(\beta_1 s + \beta_2 x)G + [1 - (\alpha_1 s + \alpha_2 x)]Q] +$$

$$\frac{1-p}{1-p+\omega p}[(\beta_1 s + \beta_2 x)G + Q]$$

$$E(s = 0 \mid x \le \frac{\sigma_2 M}{2v}) = \frac{\omega}{1-p+\omega p}[(\beta_2 x)G + [1 - \alpha_2 x]Q] + \frac{1-p}{1-p+\omega p}[(\beta_2 x)G + Q]$$

When $E(s = 1) = E(s = 0)$,

$$\frac{\omega}{1-p+\omega p}(G\beta_1 s) - \frac{\omega}{1-p+\omega p}(Q\alpha_1 s) + \frac{1-p}{1-p+\omega p}(G\beta_1 s) = 0 \text{ and } \omega = \frac{(1-p)G\beta_1}{Q\alpha_1 - G\beta_1}.$$

The leader randomises, then, with ϕ:

$$\phi[(\sigma_2 \frac{\sigma_2 M + \alpha_2 R}{2v})M + (\alpha_2 \frac{\sigma_2 M + \alpha_2 R}{2v})R - v(\frac{\sigma_2 M + \alpha_2 R}{2v})^2] +$$

$$(1 - \phi)[(\sigma_1 s + \sigma_2 \frac{\sigma_2 M + \alpha_2 R}{2v})M + (\alpha_1 s + \alpha_2 \frac{\sigma_2 M + \alpha_2 R}{2v})R - v(\frac{\sigma_2 M + \alpha_2 R}{2v})^2] =$$

$$[(\sigma_1 s + \sigma_2 \frac{\sigma_2 M}{2v})M + (\alpha_1 s + \alpha_2 \frac{\sigma_2 M}{2v})R - v(\frac{\sigma_2 M}{2v})^2];$$

$$\phi = \frac{[\sigma_2 \frac{\alpha_2 R}{2v}M + \alpha_2 \frac{\alpha_2 R}{2v}R - \frac{2\sigma_2 M \alpha_2 R + \alpha_2 R^2}{4v}] + (\sigma_1 sM + \alpha_1 sR)}{(\sigma_1 sM + \alpha_1 sR)}$$

Appendix A.3: Extension to the case of the leader having an effect on hiring at the sub-national level (as exemplified in Turkey)

In this version I assume that the level of jobs is equal to $x - x_s$ if the party leader does not support the follower ($s = 0$).

Pooling equilibria

The first condition that must be satisfied is $x' = x''$ Therefore, for PBE to exist $z^*(x' \mid t) = 1, \forall t$. With the prior belief of p,

$$\mu^*(t = 1; x = x') = \frac{p}{p+(1-p)} = p.$$

Let q be the probability that $t = 1 \mid x > x'$. Then, the expected payoffs from P_L's actions are:

$$E(s = 1 \mid x > x') = q[(\beta_1 s + \beta_2 x)G + [1 - (\alpha_1 s + \alpha_2 x)]Q] +$$
$$(1-q)[(\beta_1 s + \beta_2 x)G + Q];$$

$$E(s = 0 \mid x > x') = q[\beta_2(x - x_s)G + [1 - (\alpha_2(x - x_s))]Q] +$$
$$(1-q)[\beta_2(x - x_s)G + Q]$$

For $E(s = 1 \mid x > x') \geq E(s = 0 \mid x > x')$;

$$q[(\beta_1 s + \beta_2 x)G + [1 - (\alpha_1 s + \alpha_2 x)]Q] + (1-q)[(\beta_1 s + \beta_2 x)G + Q] \geq$$
$$q[\beta_2(x - x_s)G + [1 - (\alpha_2(x - x_s))]Q] + (1-q)[\beta_2(x - x_s)G + Q],$$

$$\beta_1 G + \beta_2 x_s G \geq q\alpha_1 Q + q\alpha_2 x_s Q$$

That is, $\frac{G}{Q} \geq \frac{q(\alpha_1 + \alpha_2 x_s)}{\beta_1 + \beta_2 x_s}$.

For $E(s = 1 \mid x \leq x') \geq E(s = 0 \mid x \leq x')$; $E(s = 1 \mid x \leq x') =$

$$p[(\beta_1 s + \beta_2 x)G + [1 - (\alpha_1 s + \alpha_2 x)]Q] + (1 - p)[(\beta_1 s + \beta_2 x)G + Q] =$$

$$(\beta_1 s + \beta_2 x)G + [1 - p(\alpha_1 s + \alpha_2 x)]Q; \quad E(s = 0 \mid x \leq x') =$$

$$p[\beta_2(x-x_s)G+[1-\alpha_2(x-x_s)]Q]+(1-p)[\beta_2(x-x_s)G+Q]=$$

$$\beta_2(x-x_s)G+[1-p\alpha_2(x-x_s)]Q;$$

$$(\beta_1 s+\beta_2 x)G+[1-p(\alpha_1 s+\alpha_2 x)]Q \ge \beta_2(x-x_s)G+[1-p\alpha_2(x-x_s)]Q.$$

That is, $\frac{G}{Q} \ge \frac{p(\alpha_1+\alpha_2 x_s)}{\beta_1+\beta_2 x_s}$.

Therefore, if $\frac{G}{Q} \ge \frac{q(\alpha_1+\alpha_2 x_s)}{\beta_1+\beta_2 x_s}$, $r^*(s=1\,|\,x)=1$ $\forall x \in X$.

Given $\mu^*(t=1\,|\,x')=p$ and $r^*(s=1\,|\,x)$ $\forall x \in X$, what is $z^*(x,t)$?

$\forall t \in \{1,0\}$, $z^*(x\,|\,t)>0$ only if $x \in \arg\max_{x\in X} U_{P_F}(t,x,r^*(x))$.

$\arg\max_{x\in X} U_F(t=1,x,r^*(x)) = \arg\max_{x\in X}[(\sigma_1 s+\sigma_2 x)M +$

$(\alpha_1 s+\alpha_2 x)R - vx^2]$; $x=\frac{\sigma_2 M+\alpha_2 R}{2v}$ $\arg\max_{x\in X} U_F(t=0,x,r^*(x)) =$

$\arg\max_{x\in X}[(\sigma_1 s+\sigma_2 x)M - vx^2]$; $x=\frac{\sigma_2 M}{2v}$.

Since $x(t=1) \ne x(t=0)$, we do not get a pure strategy PBE when

$\frac{G}{Q} \ge \frac{q(\alpha_1+\alpha_2 x_s)}{\beta_1+\beta_2 x_s}$

If $\frac{p(\alpha_1+\alpha_2 x_s)}{(\beta_1+\beta_2 x_s)} < \frac{G}{Q} < \frac{q(\alpha_1+\alpha_2 x_s)}{\beta_1+\beta_2 x_s}$, $r^* = \begin{cases} s=0 \text{ if } x>x' \\ s=1 \text{ if } x \le x' \end{cases} = 1$

Given $\mu^*(t=1\,|\,x')=p$ and $r^* = \begin{cases} s=0 \text{ if } x>x' \\ s=1 \text{ if } x \le x' \end{cases} = 1,$

what is $z^*(x\,|\,t)$? $\forall t \in \{1,0\}$, $z^*(x\,|\,t)>0$ only if

$x \in \arg\max_{x\in X} U_{P_F}(t,x,r^*(x))$. The follower of type 1 either can

choose x that maximises his utility function when $s=0$ which is

$\arg\max_{x\in X} U_F(t=1,x,r^*(x)) = \arg\max_{x\in X}[(\sigma_2(x-x_s))M + (\alpha_2(x-x_s))$

$R - v(x-x_s)^2]$; $x=\frac{\sigma_2 M+\alpha_2 R+2vx_s}{2v}$

or choose $x \le x'$ and get support $s=1$. The follower of type 0

would choose x that maximises his utility function when $s=1$;

$$\arg\max_{x \in X} U_F(t=0, x, r^*(x)) = \arg\max_x [(\sigma_1 s + \sigma_2 x)M - vx^2];$$

$$x = \frac{\sigma_2 M}{2v}$$

Therefore, we get a pure strategy pooling PBE where

$$\frac{p(\alpha_1 + \alpha_2 x_s)}{(\beta_1 + \beta_2 x_s)} < \frac{G}{Q} < \frac{q(\alpha_1 + \alpha_2 x_s)}{\beta_1 + \beta_2 x_s} \quad r^* = \begin{cases} s = 0 \text{ if } x > x' \\ s = 1 \text{ if } x \le x' \end{cases} = 1$$

$$z^*(\forall t \in \{1, 0\}, x = \frac{\sigma_2 M}{2v}, r^*(x)) = 1 \text{ and } \mu^*(t = 1 \mid x = \frac{\sigma_2 M}{2v}) = p$$

when $U_F(t = 1, x = \frac{\sigma_2 M + \alpha_2 R + 2vx_s}{2v}, s = 0) - U_F(t = 1, x = \frac{\sigma_2 M}{2v}, s = 1) < 0.$

The condition,

$$U_F(t = 1, x = \frac{\sigma_2 M}{2v}, s = 1) - U_F(t = 1, x = \frac{\sigma_2 M + \alpha_2 R + 2vx_s}{2v}, s = 0) \ge 0$$

is simplified as $\sigma_1 M - \frac{\alpha_2^2 R^2}{4v} + \alpha_1 R + vx_s^2 \ge 0$

If $\frac{p(\alpha_1 + \alpha_2 x_s)}{(\beta_1 + \beta_2 x_s)} > \frac{G}{Q}$, $r^*(s = 0 \mid x) = 1 \ \forall x \in X$ and we do not get a pooling equilibrium.

From the analysis of the pooling equilibria, it can be seen that the comparative statics that are derived from this version of the model are the same as in the original model.

Appendix B: Socio-economic Characteristics of Cases

Argentina

Provinces of Buenos Aires and Chaco

In terms of economic development, we can compare the two provinces in terms of two indicators: GDP per capita and the role of manufacturing industry in provincial production. First of all, Buenos Aires throughout the 1990s had a GDP per capita of twice that of Chaco. In 1991, the GDP per capita in Buenos Aires was 50,676 thousand pesos, and was 23,859 thousand pesos in Chaco.[1] The relative size of the GDP per capita has remained more or less the same in the 1990s and when we look at the figures for 2000, we can see that Buenos Aires had a GDP per capita of 69,709 thousand pesos and Chaco 27,833 thousand pesos. When we examine the composition of the economic production in the two provinces, the contrast is more striking. If we compare the corresponding shares of manufacturing industry in the provinces' total economic production, we can see that in Buenos Aires the relevant figure is 32 per cent while in Chaco it is only 12 per cent. In addition, Chaco's economy for a long period has depended on the production of one agricultural raw material – cotton. Even though, as I will discuss below in more detail, the province has gone through a major economic restructuring and the role of cotton production has decreased immensely, in 1990 cotton production constituted 12.57 per cent of the province's total GDP (*Norte Economia y Negocios*, September 30, 2003).

The province of Buenos Aires is responsible for a large part of economic production in Argentina. The share of this province in the country's GDP ranged from 32 per cent to 36 per cent in the period from 1984 to 2000 (Provinfo). In contrast to Buenos Aires, Chaco contributes a much smaller amount of the country's total economic production. In the period between 1984 and 2000, its share in the GDP was around 1 per cent. This is partly a consequence of its size and population being rather small.

---

1. The data is available on the Ministry of Interior's website.

Appendix B: Table 1: Evolution of GDP and unemployment

| | Buenos Aires | | Chaco | |
year	GDP growth rate	Unemployment	GDP growth rate	Unemployment
1980	-		-	2.1
1981	-1.13	4.2	-14.82	4.3
1982	-3.32	6.7	3.66	5.2
1983	7.53		-3.84	6.3
1984	2.28		5.81	5.4
1985	-3.84	6.5	-0.37	5.4
1986	9.35		-3.58	
1987	-1.98	5.9	-1.78	10.5
1988	2.28	7.4	19.99	9.7
1989	-7.66	8.7	-15.24	8.4
1990	-	10.2	-	5.1
1991*	161.16	6.7	123.06	5.7
1992	24.65	7.3	27.18	4.5
1993	13.33	11.2	5.87	6.4
1994	8.76	11.9	-2.17	7.2
1995	-2.51	22.6	0.04	12.5
1996	1.64	20.4	3.48	11.9
1997	6.20	18.6	3.54	13.2
1998	1.74	15.8	2.01	10.4
1999	-5.11	17.5	-0.33	9.5
2000	-4.14	17.9	-6.22	10.4
2001	-6.00	18.7	-8.97	13.0

Sources: Provinfo on GDP data and INDEC on unemployment data.

*A new methodology for calculating GDP was adopted in 1991.

Another major difference between the two provinces is the economic dependence of citizens on the state. One indicator that would measure this dependence is the relative size of public sector employment to private sector employment. Since the size of the public sector is also affected by the levels of particularistic exchanges between politicians and their supporters, this indicator cannot reveal the independent effect that citizens' dependence has on particularistic linkages between politicians and citizens. Yet, looking at these figures is still helpful in terms of showing us the extent to which economic life is dominated by the state's role in the province of Chaco. In the period between 1994 and 2000, the average ratio of the number of public employees to employees in the private sector in Chaco was 0.97. The corresponding figure for the province of Buenos Aires was 0.31. As can be seen from these figures, citizens in Chaco are much more dependent on the state for their income when compared to Buenos Aires. The alternative to getting a job in the public sector; that is, private sector employment, is quite low in Chaco, which would be expected to increase the motivation for citizens to engage in particularistic networks with politicians in order to have access to public jobs. According to the census data that is provided by INDEC, the number of employees working in the private sector in the province of Buenos Aires was 2,011,615 in 1980, 2,144,607 in 1991, and 2,155,682 in 2001. In Chaco, the corresponding figures were 86,982, 104,807, and 86,469. As these figures show, the private sector in neither province was successful in generating alternative employment opportunities to jobs provided in the public sector. As can be seen in Table 1, unemployment in both provinces has increased to very high levels.

Demographic characteristics of the province are also expected to have an impact on the clientelistic relationships between politicians and their supporters. The density of the population is the most crucial aspect. However, there is disagreement in the literature about the direction of its impact. While some argue that urbanisation (higher density) would decrease clientelistic exchanges because the poor (workers) would then be able to pursue collective action through organisations and associations rather than forming particularistic dependent relationships (Gunes-Ayata 1992), others argue that higher density would actually increase these particularistic exchanges because it would then be easier to mobilise the receivers of the benefits for political action (Mayhew 1986). Whatever direction in which the effect operates, there is a major difference between these two provinces in terms of urbanisation. According to the 2001 census, in the province of Buenos Aires the population that lives in the Conurbano area, that is, in the area surrounding the city of Buenos Aires which is composed of 24 municipalities, constitute 67.09 per cent of the total population. In Chaco, the capital of the province, Resistencia, and the surrounding municipalities, Grand Resistencia, in turn, constitute 36.48 per cent of the provincial population.

In contrast to Buenos Aires where the levels of foreign investment in the Conurbano area increased from 181,305 thousand dollars in 1993 to 1,499,503 thousand dollars in 1998 (the increase in the total province was slower, but still substantial: from 976,271 thousand dollars in 1993 to 3,579,813 thousand dollars in 1998 (Provinfo[2])) foreign investment in Chaco was not a factor that could alleviate the province's economic problems. From 1993 to 1999, the increase was minimal, from 22,450 thousand dollars to 40,367 thousand dollars and it decreased to 5,955 thousand dollars in 2000. Trade openings did not lead to short-term improvement, either. However, their long term effects are yet to be seen as a consequence of major restructuring in the raw agricultural materials that are produced

---

2.   While some of this investment is a consequence of the privatisation process, such as the 771,400 thousand dollars that went into the production of electric energy in the whole province, other sectors such as construction and mechanical equipment also benefited from these investments.

in the province. As I have already mentioned, cotton production has historically played a large role in Chaco's economic life. However, a parallel development of the textile industry did not take place. Most of the raw material was either exported or sent to other provinces, especially Buenos Aires province (Panaia and Ramos 2004). For example, in 1982 only 11 out of 2,008 textile companies that were affiliated with the AOT (The Textile Worker Association) were located in the province of Chaco. The corresponding figures for 1992 are 19 out of 3,252, and for 1995, 18 out of 2,388.[3]

In the 1990s, the demand for cotton started to decrease. The domestic textile industry had to compete with imports, whose levels reached 112,000 tons in 1996[4] and the number of textile companies in the country decreased from 3,075 in 1980 to 2,259 in 1996, and in the crisis period of 2002 to 2,065. These changes in the textile industry had a major impact on the province's economy. The fact that Chaco did not process raw cotton in the province itself allowed it to be more flexible when the conditions of the international market changed. As a result of the fall in demand for cotton, soya production started to replace cotton. However, this transition took place gradually: the amount of land that was used to cultivate soya in 1995 was 76,000 hectares while only in 2001 it rose to 550,000 (*Norte*, September 30, 2003). In the meantime, the size of land in which cotton was cultivated, in turn, decreased from 611,930 to only 93,000. Even though the effect of this restructuring on economic production in Chaco is yet to be seen, what is important from our stand-point is that citizens in this transition period remained dependent on the state for economic resources. As the preceding discussion illustrates, the economic changes of the 1990s have not reduced, but even amplified the dependence of citizens on state resources in both states, but this dependence remained much higher than the average in the province of Chaco.

Two municipalities in the Province of Buenos Aires: La Matanza and Pilar

There is a major divide among the municipalities of the province Buenos Aires between those belonging to the Conurbano area, that is, the area surrounding the City of Buenos Aires and composed of 24 municipalities, and the rest of the province. The municipalities of the Conurbano are populated more densely and on average they are more developed economically. Since the challenge from the mayors in the Conurbano area to the provincial party leaders has played an important role in the internal politics of parties at the provincial level, I selected one municipality from that area. La Matanza is the most populated municipality of the province with 1,250,715 inhabitants (2001 Census, INDEC). The principal activity in economic production is the manufacturing industry and a large part of the labour force works

---

3. The data on the number of textile companies were provided by the AOT.
4. Interview with a professor of Economics (No. 21), University of the Northeast, September 2003.

in the informal sector without getting any formal salaries.[5]

In contrast, Pilar is a much smaller municipality. I chose Pilar among other smaller municipalities of the province due to data accessibility. According to the 2001 census (INDEC), the population of Pilar is only 231,120. Its economic structure is complicated by the fact that it hosts an Industrial Park that has attracted high levels of private investment (domestic and international) in the 1990s and a growing construction sector that appeals to the upper classes of the City of Buenos Aires with its large gated communities (*barrios cerrados*).[6] Although these developments without doubt have helped the economic situation in the municipality by creating employment, the income levels and living conditions of the registered residents of the municipality (who voted within the borders of Pilar) have remained poor[7]. For example, according to the 2001 Census, the percentage of the population whose basic needs, such as portable water and sewer system, were satisfied was only around 20 per cent. The corresponding figure for La Matanza was much higher, approximately 50 per cent.

Two municipalities in Chaco: Resistencia and Fontana

Resistencia is the capital of the province. While the population of Resistencia in 1991 was 229,960, Fontana had only 16,166 inhabitants. As in the case of Pilar in the province of Buenos Aires, the choice of Fontana among small municipalities of Chaco was shaped by the availability of information on the political process in Fontana. The respective electoral weights of each municipality in the province are 29 per cent and 2.26 per cent (Sotelo n.d.). It is harder to compare the two municipalities economically because the data is available only for administrative units. Only limited data exists at the municipal level. We can compare them in terms of the composition of economic activities and the difference is striking. While the relative size of the population working in the commercial and service sectors to the manufacturing sector in Resistencia is 8.9, the corresponding figure in Fontana was only 0.7 in 1994 (Ministry of Interior website).

---

5. Statistics provided by the municipality of La Matanza and author's interviews with the president of the municipal council (No. 24), October 2003 and May 2005.

6. Further information is available on the Municipality's website, http://www.pilar.gov.ar.

7. Author's interview with a municipal council member from Pilar (No. 67), May 2005.

Turkey

Provinces of Istanbul and Bilecik

Istanbul is the province with the largest population in the country with approx-imately 10 million inhabitants as of 2000 (DPT 2003). According to the 2007 Census, this figure has risen to 12,573,836.[8] It also had the highest population density among the eighty one provinces (the number of people per every kilometre square in 2000 was 1,928. In 2007 this was calculated as 2,420). In contrast, the size of the population in Bilecik was only around 200,000 in 2000 (DPT 2003), and it was more or less the same, 203,777, in 2007. The density shows a major contrast, as well. In 2000 the number of people per every kilometre square was only 45 (DPT 2003). The urbanisation levels, even if not that strikingly different as the previous figures, also show quite dissimilar characteristics. While in Istanbul the percentage of the population living in the urbanised areas was 91 per cent, in Bilecik only 64 per cent of the people lived in urban areas in 2000 (DPT 2003).

If we analyse only the GDP per capita in these two provinces, Istanbul and Bilecik would have similar levels that are above the average GDP per capita of the country. In 2000 the GDP per capita was 2,750 million Turkish liras in Istanbul and 2,204 in Bilecik. However, as interviews with politicians and bureaucrats in Bilecik suggested these figures are more concealing than revealing. The fact that Bilecik is geographically close to major centres of industrial production such as Istanbul, İzmit, Bursa, and Eskişehir, makes it a popular location for establishing small companies that pursue auxiliary production for major enterprises that are located in other provinces and raises the aggregate share of Bilecik in the country's total production. However, the share of the income and revenue that remains in the province ends up being quite small compared to the more economically developed provinces. One statistical figure that can support this argument is the per capita tax income that each province contributes to the national budget. In 1997, the corre-sponding levels were 42,658 Turkish liras for Bilecik and 250,508 Turkish liras for Istanbul. In addition, the data on the composition of economic production displays clearly the striking difference in the structure of economic production in these two provinces. The share of the labour force that works in the agricultural sector in Bilecik was 46.5 per cent in 2000 while in Istanbul the share is as low as 8.1 per cent. The large part of the labour force in Istanbul works in the manufacturing (32.2 per cent) and commercial (18.7 per cent) sectors. In Bilecik the correspond-ing figures were 19.3 per cent and 5.9 per cent in 2000.

The third socio-economic dimension that would be expected to have an impact on patron-client relationships, and hence needs to be considered, is the economic dependence of citizens on public resources. As I have already discussed in the pre-

---

8.   The 2007 Census figures are available at the TUIK's website, http://tuikapp.tuik.gov.tr/adnksdag-itapp/adnks.zul.

vious section on Argentina, one figure that can be used to compare the two provinces in terms of this dimension is the size of the public employment. Even though the size of the public sector is clearly endogenous to the prevalence of particularism in the allocation of public jobs, the relative importance of the public sector in the economic production in the province is a good indicator of the dependence of citizens on the state. When we compare Istanbul and Bilecik according to the 1994 survey of public employment, we can see that the share of public employees in the whole population is quite large, 0.08, in Bilecik compared to Istanbul where the corresponding figure is 0.03.

Two Municipalities in Istanbul: Beşiktaş and Kartal

Beşiktaş is located at the center of the city, with a population of 191,776 (2000 Census). The population is largely composed of middle, upper-middle class professionals who are older than the average population in Istanbul,[9] and major commercial centres and headquarters of corporations are located within the borders of the municipality. In contrast, Kartal lies at the outskirts of the city, and has a population of 405,392, which is mostly composed of workers in the private sector.

Two Municipalities in Bilecik: City Center and Bozüyük

The total population of the Center and Bozüyük are 52,929 and 60,863 consecutively, (the third largest municipality population-wise, Osmaneli, lags much behind with a population of 21,070) (IAV 2003). Forty-three per cent of the labour force in the whole province in 2003 was located in the City Centre and 36 per cent in Bozüyük (Bilecik Valiligi 2003). The shares of the Centre's and Bozüyük's production in the provincial exports were 23 per cent and 68 per cent respectively (Bilecik Valiligi 2003).

---

9. Author's interviews with party members from RPP and JDP in Besiktas (No. 48; No. 53).

Appendix C: Sources of Data

Argentina

Temporary and permanent employees: The data are gathered by the author. With the exception of Santa Fe province, which publicises its personnel data on its web page (www.santafe.gov.ar), I had to use provincial appropriations bills, which are published in their respective official bulletins. Unfortunately, provincial bulletins are not centralised in any one place, and what does exist varies with respect to the amount of detail on personnel. As a result, some cases lack data. The appropriation bills for the province of Buenos Aires, Chaco, Mendoza, and for Federal Capital can be found in their provincial legislative libraries. The data for the rest of the provinces were gathered from the official bulletins that are available either on their web pages or in their provincial government offices in the city of Buenos Aires. (The dataset includes: Buenos Aires 1984-2000; Catamarca 1994, 1996, 2000, 2001; Chaco 1984–1991, 1996–2001; Capital Federal 1999; Formosa 1985–87, 1994–2001; Jujuy 1991; La Rioja 1993–96; Mendoza 1984–5, 1988–2001; Río Negro 1999–2001; Salta 1988, 1990, 96, 97, 2001; San Juan 1992; San Luis 2000-01; Santa Cruz 1990–2001; Santa Fe 1992–2001; Tierra del Fuego 2000–01.) *Electoral data*: The data are available at the National Electoral Chamber and the website, Atlas Electoral de Andy Tow (http://www.towsa.com/andy/index.html). *Primaries:* The information was collected through the analysis of the Argentine newspaper, *La Nación*, except one case. The information on the Radical presidential nomination in 1983 was taken from Rock (1987: 387). *Presidential approval:* The opinion polls are conducted by *Nueva Mayoria*. I thank Ernesto Calvo for providing these data. *GDP and Population:* The information was available on the PROVINFO's website (http://www.mininterior.gov.ar/provinfo/inicio.asp) *Revenue, Deficit and National Transfers*: The data are published by the Ministry of Economy on its website (http://www.mecon.gov.ar/hacienda/info_fin.htm).

Turkey

Personnel spending, revenue and national transfers in metropolitan municipalities: The information is provided by TUIK. Publication title: Final Accounts of Municipalities (http://www.tuik.gov.tr) *Electoral data*: The information is provided by TUIK, Turkish Statistical Institute (Publication title: Election results, http://www.tuik.gov.tr), Belgenet (http://www.belgenet.com), and Yerelnet (http://www.yerelnet.org.tr) *Internal elections:* The information on the results of internal party elections was collected through the analysis of Turkish newspapers, *Milliyet, Cumhuriyet, Radikal*, and *Hürriyet*, except one case. The information on the TPP's internal elections was provided by the party. *GDP:* The information is provided by TUIK. Publication title: National Accounts (http://www.tuik.gov.tr) *Population:* The information is provided by TUIK. Publication title: Census (http://www.tuik.gov.tr) *Revenue of municipalities*: The information is provided by TUIK. Publication title: Final Accounts of Municipalities (http://www.tuik.gov.tr).

Appendix D: List of Interviews

Interview Number	Position	Location	Date
1	Former Legislator, Istanbul, SPP/RPP (1987–1999), Former Minister of Justice, Former Minister of Labour and Social Security	Istanbul, Turkey	Jun-02
2	Commissioner Of Revenue Administration, (Post-interview) Legislator, Trabzon, RPP (2002–)	Ankara, Turkey	Jun-02
3	Department Head, General Directorate of Budget and Fiscal Control	Ankara, Turkey	Jun-02
4	Treasury expert, General Directorate of Incentive and Implementation (Undersecretariat of Treasury)	Ankara, Turkey	Jun-02
5	Head of Department, General Directorate of State Owned Enterprises, Undersecretariat of Treasury	Ankara, Turkey	Jun-02
6	Bureaucrat, Department of Personnel, Ministry of Interior	Ankara, Turkey	Jun-02
7	Director of the ARI block	Cordoba, Argentina	Jul-02
8	Provincial Legislator, Vice-president of the UCR Block	Cordoba, Argentina	Jul-02
9	Provincial Legislator, UCR	Cordoba, Argentina	Jul-02
10	President of the Electoral Tribunal, UCR	Cordoba, Argentina	Jul-02
11	Provincial Legislator, PJ	Cordoba, Argentina	Jul-02
12	Secretary of the Press and Propaganda, Trade Union of Public Employees	Cordoba, Argentina	Jul-02
13	Bureaucrat, Ministry of Interior	Capital Federal, Argentina	Aug-02
14	Party member, PJ	Capital Federal, Argentina	Aug-02

Interview Number	Position	Location	Date
15	Former Mayor of Fontana (UCR), Sub-secretary of Social Development (Provincial Government of Fontana), (Post-interview) National Legislator (UCR) (2003–)	Chaco, Argentina	Oct-03
16	Former Mayor of Quintilipi (UCR), President of the Provincial Congress of Deputies (UCR)	Chaco, Argentina	Oct-03
17	First Council Member of the City of Resistencia (UCR), (Post-interview) Mayor of Resistencia (2003–)	Chaco, Argentina	Oct-03
18	President of the Electoral Tribunal, UCR	Chaco, Argentina	Oct-03
19	Former Governor of Chaco (AC)	Chaco, Argentina	Oct-03
20	Party member, PJ, Member of the Constitutional Convention (1994)	Chaco, Argentina	Oct-03
21	Professor of Economics, University of Northeast	Chaco, Argentina	Oct-03
22	Advisor to the national deputy of UCR, Federico Storani, Advisor (Ministry of Interior)	phone interview	Oct-03
23	Former Pre-candidate for the Mayor of La Matanza (PJ), Member of the Municipal Council, La Matanza (PJ)	Buenos Aires, Argentina	Oct-03
24	President of the Municipal Council, La Matanza (PJ), (Post-interview) Appointed as the Mayor of La Matanza	Buenos Aires, Argentina	Oct-03 & May 2005
25	President of the Municipal Council, Pilar (PJ)	Buenos Aires, Argentina	Oct-03
26	Director of Commerce, La Matanza	Buenos Aires, Argentina	Oct-03
27	Former President of the SPP, Canakkale	Canakkale, Turkey	Nov-03
28	Former mayor of Korfez, Kocaeli (RP), Legislator, Kocaeli, (JDP)	Ankara, Turkey	Dec-03

Interview Number	Position	Location	Date
29	Former member of the National Congress, RPP, Former candidate for the Mayor of Istanbul, SPP, Legislator, Istanbul (RPP)	Istanbul, Turkey	Jan-04
30	Head of Personnel Department, Municipality of Istanbul	Istanbul, Turkey	Jan-04
31	Former vice-president of MP, Former legislator (MP), Rize (1987–1991), Istanbul (1991–2002)	Istanbul, Turkey	Jan-04
32	Former mayor of Gungoren, Legislator, Istanbul (JDP)	Istanbul, Turkey	Jan-04
33	Former president of the provincial party branch, Bilecik (RPP), Former National Convention Delegate (RPP), Candidate for the mayor of Bilecik (RPP)	Bilecik, Turkey	Jan-04
34	President of the provincial party branch, Bilecik (RPP), Former National Convention Delegate (RPP)	Bilecik, Turkey	Jan-04
35	Party member, Bozuyuk, (RPP)	Bilecik, Turkey	Jan-04
36	Mayor of Bilecik (RPP), Candidate for the mayor of Bilecik (RPP)	Bilecik, Turkey	Jan-04
37	Former mayor of Bilecik (RPP), Legislator, Bilecik (RPP)	Bilecik, Turkey	Jan-04
38	Legislator, Bilecik (JDP)	Bilecik, Turkey	Jan-04
39	President of the local party organisation, Bilecik City Center (TPP)	Bilecik, Turkey	Jan-04
40	Former president of the provincial party branch, Bilecik (MP), President of the Bilecik Chamber of Industry and Commerce, (Post-interview) Candidate for the mayor of Bilecik (MP)	Bilecik, Turkey	Jan-04
41	Former local party officer, Bakirkoy (TPP)	Istanbul, Turkey	Feb-04
42	Former party member (WP), President of the local party organisation, Bakirkoy, JDP	Istanbul, Turkey	Feb-04

Interview Number	Position	Location	Date
43	Vice-president of provincial party organisation, Istanbul, MP	Istanbul, Turkey	Feb-04
44	Former president of the provincial party organisation, Istanbul, MP	Istanbul, Turkey	Feb-04
45	Former legislator, Istanbul, DLP, (1999–2002), party member, NTP	Istanbul, Turkey	Feb-04
46	President of the provincial party organisation, Istanbul, NAP	Istanbul, Turkey	Feb-04
47	President of Provincial Party Organisation, Istanbul (DLP)	Istanbul, Turkey	Feb-04
48	Secretary of Party Organisation, Besiktas (RPP)	Istanbul, Turkey	Feb-04
49	Former Minister of Economy and Production (PJ)	Boston, USA	May-04
50	Former president of the local party branch, Bakirkoy (Istanbul), Former president of the provincial party organisation (Istanbul), Legislator, Istanbul (RPP, post-interview SPP)	Ankara, Turkey	Mar-05
51	Vice-president of RPP	Ankara, Turkey	Mar-05
52	Vice-president of RPP	Ankara, Turkey	Mar-05
53	President of the local party organisation, Besiktas (JDP)	Istanbul, Turkey	Mar-05
54	Former party member (JDP), Vice-mayor of Kartal	Istanbul, Turkey	Mar-05
55	Municipal Council member, Kartal (RPP)	Istanbul, Turkey	Mar-05
56	Former Secretary of Economic Planning (UCR)	Capital Federal, Argentina	May-05
57	Former minister of labour and social security (PJ)	Capital Federal, Argentina	May-05
58	Secretary of the UCR Block in the National Senate	Capital Federal, Argentina	May-05
59	Provincial Legislator, Buenos Aires (UCR), General Secretary of the UCR Block in the Chamber of Deputies	Buenos Aires, Argentina	May-05
60	Provincial Legislator, La Matanza (Buenos Aires) (PJ)	Buenos Aires, Argentina	May-05

Interview Number	Position	Location	Date
61	Provincial Legislator, Junin (Buenos Aires) (PJ)	Buenos Aires, Argentina	May-05
62	Provincial Legislator, Buenos Aires (PA.U.FE)	Buenos Aires, Argentina	May-05
63	Provincial Legislator, Buenos Aires (MST-IU)	Buenos Aires, Argentina	May-05
64	Provincial Legislator, Buenos Aires (Social Ecologist Block, President)	Buenos Aires, Argentina	May-05
65	Provincial Legislator, Buenos Aires (ARI)	Buenos Aires, Argentina	May-05
66	Provincial Senator, Buenos Aires (Popular Encounter Block)	Buenos Aires, Argentina	May-05
67	Municipal Council member, Pilar (PA.U.FE)	Buenos Aires, Argentina	May-05
68	President of the Provincial Electoral Tribunal, UCR	Buenos Aires, Argentina	May-05

| bibliography

Acuña, C., Galiani, S. and Tommasi, M. (2004) 'Understanding reform: the case of Argentina', Universidad San Andreas.

Adaman, F., Carkoglu, A. and Senatalar, B. (2001) *Turkiye'de Yolsuzlugun Nedenleri ve Onlenmesine Iliskin Oneriler,* Istanbul: TESEV Yayinlari.

Akinci, U. (1999) 'The Welfare Party's municipal track record: evaluating islamist municipal activism in Turkey', *Middle East Journal*, 53(1): 75–94.

Alesina, A. and Spear, S. E. (1988) 'An overlapping generations model of electoral competition', *Journal of Public Economics*, 37: 359–79.

Anderson, L. (2009) 'The Problem of Single-Party Dominance in an Unconsolidated Democracy: The Example of Argentina', *Perspectives on Politics*, 7(4): 767–784.

Arslan, A. R. (ed.) (2002) *Kamu Personel Rejimi ve Reform Calismalari Semineri,* Ankara: Turk Agir Sanayii ve Hizmet Sektoru Kamu Isverenleri Sendikasi Yayini.

Auyero, J. (2001) *Poor People's Politics: Peronist Survival Networks and the Legacy of Evita*, Durham: Duke University Press.

Baland, J. and Robinson, J. (2007) 'How does vote buying shape the economy?', in F. C. Schaffer (ed.) *Elections for Sale*, Boulder: Lynn Rienner.

Beck, N. and Katz, J. N. (1995) 'What to do and not to do with time-series cross-section data', *American Political Science Review*, 893: 634–47.

— (2001) 'Throwing out the baby with the bathwater: a comment on Green, Yoon and Kim', *International Organizations*, 55: 487–95.

Benton, A. L. (2007) 'The strategic struggle for patronage: political careers, state largesse, and factionalism in Latin American parties', *Journal of Theoretical Politics*, 19: 155–82.

Bettcher, K. E. (2005) 'Factions of interest in Japan and Italy: the organizational and motivational dimensions of factionalism', *Party Politics*, 11(3): 339–358.

Bhagwati, J. and Srinivasan, T. N. (2002) 'Trade and poverty in the poor countries', *American Economic Review*, Papers and Proceedings, 92: 2180–83.

Boissevain, J. (1966) 'Patronage in Sicily', *Man*, 1: 18–33.

— (1979) 'Towards a social anthropology of the Mediterranean', *Current Anthropology*, 20: 81–93.

Boratav, K., Yeldan, E. and Kose, A. (2001) 'Globalization, Distribution and Social Policy in Turkey: 1980–98' in L. Taylor (ed.) *External Liberalization, Economic Performance and Social Policy*, New York: Oxford University Press.

Bozlagan, R. (2003) *Belediyelerde Orgut Gelistirme Istanbul Buyuksehir Belediyesi Ornegi*, Istanbul: Hayat Yayincilik.

Brambor, T., Clark W. R. and Golder, M. (2006) 'Understanding Interaction

Models: Improving Empirical Analyses', *Political Analysis*, 14(1): 63–82.

Brusco, V., Nazareno M. and Stokes, S. C. (2001) 'Clientelism and democracy: an analysis of ecological data from Argentina', paper presented at the American Political Science Association Annual Conference, San Francisco, September 2001.

— (2007) 'Poverty, risk and clientelism', paper presented at the Latin American Studies Association Conference, Montreal, September 2007.

Cakir, R. (1994) *Ne Seriat Ne Demokrasi*, Istanbul: Metis Yayinlari.

Calvo, G. and Mendoza E. (2000) 'Capital-markets crisis and economic collapse in emerging markets: an informational-frictions approach', *American Economic Review*, 90: 59–64.

Calvo, E. (2007) 'The responsive legislature: public opinion and law making in a highly disciplined legislature', *British Journal of Political Science*, 37: 263–280.

Calvo, E., and Murillo, M. V. (2004) 'Who delivers? Partisan clients in the Argentine electoral market', *American Journal of Political Science*, 48: 742–57.

— (2008) 'When parties meet voters: partisan networks and distributive expectations', paper presented at the American Political Science Association Annual Conference, Boston, August 2008.

Carkoglu, A. (1998) 'Turkish party system in transition: party performance and agenda change', *Political Studies*, 46: 544–71.

— (2003) 'The rise of the new generation pro-islamists in Turkey: The Justice and Development Party phenomenon in the November 2002 elections in Turkey', *South European Society & Politics*, 7: 123–56.

— (2011) 'Turkey's 2011 General Elections: Towards a Dominant Party System?', *Insight Turkey*, 13(3): 43–62.

Chandra, K. (2004) *Why Ethnic Parties Succeed: Patronage and Ethnic Headcounts in India*, Cambridge: Cambridge University Press.

Chubb, J. (1982) *Patronage, Power, and Poverty in Southern Italy : A Tale of Two Cities*, New York: Cambridge University Press.

Coppedge, M. (1994) *Strong Parties and Lame Ducks: Presidential Partyarchy and Factionalism in Venezuela*, Stanford: Stanford University Press.

Dahlberg, M. and Johansson, E. (2002) 'On the vote-purchasing behavior of incumbent governments' *American Political Science Review*, 85(1): 46–57.

Daughters, R. and Harper, L. (2007) 'Fiscal and political decentralization reforms' in E. Lora (ed.) *The State of State Reform in Latin America*, Washington, D. C.: The Inter-American Development Bank.

Davis, S. J., Haltiwanger, J. C. and Schuh, S. (1996) *Job Creation and Destruction*, Cambridge, MA: MIT Press.

Deichmann J., Karidis, S. and Sayek, S. (2003) 'Foreign direct investment in Turkey: regional determinants', *Applied Economics,* 35 (16): 1767–1778.

De Luca, M. (2008) 'Political recruitment and candidate selection in Argentina:

presidents and governors, 1983–2006', in P. M. Siavelis and S. Morgenstern (eds) *Pathways to Power Political Recruitment and Candidate Selection in Latin America*, University Park: The Pennsylvania State University Press.

De Luca, M., Jones, M. and Tula, M. I. (2002) 'Back rooms or ballot boxes: candidate nomination in Argentina', *Comparative Political Studies*, 354: 413–36.

— (2008) 'Revisando las consecuencias políticas de las primarias: un estudio sobre las elecciones de gobernador en la Argentina', *PostData*, 13: 81–102.

Denemark, D. (2000) 'Partisan Pork Barrel in Parliamentary Systems: Australian Constituency-Level Grants', *Journal of Politics*, 62(3): 896–915.

Desposato, S. (2003) 'How informal electoral institutions shape the legislative arena', *manuscript*.

Dinçer, B., Özaslan, M. and Satılmış, E. (1996) *İllerin Sosyo-Ekonomik Gelişmişlik Sıralaması Araştırması*, Ankara: DPT.

Dixit, A. and Londregan, J. (1996) 'The determinants of success of special interests in redistributive politics', *The Journal of Politics*, 58: 1132–1155.

DPT (2003) 'Illerin ve bolgelerin sosyo-ekonomik gelismislik siralamasi', paper no. DPT 2671.

Dunning, T. and Stokes, S. S. (2008) 'Clientelism as persuasion and mobilization', paper presented at the American Political Science Association Annual Conference, Boston, August 2008.

Eaton, K. (2004) *Politics Beyond the Capital*, Stanford: Stanford University Press.

— (2005) 'Menem and the governors: intergovernmental relations in the 1990s', in S. Levitsky and M. V. Murillo (eds), *The Politics of Institutional Weakness Argentine Democracy*, University Park: The Pennsylvania University Press.

Edwards, E. (1995) *Crisis and Reform in Latin America: From Despair to Hope*, New York: Oxford University Press.

Eisenstadt, S. N. and Roniger, L. (1984) *Patrons, Clients and Friends: Interpersonal Relations and the Structure of Trust in Society*, New York: Cambridge University Press.

Epstein, L. D. (1986) *Political Parties in the American Mold*, Madison: University of Wisconsin Press.

Erlat, G. (2000) 'Measuring the impact of trade flows on employment in the Turkish manufacturing industry', *Applied Economics*, 32: 1169–1180.

Etchemendy, S. (2001) 'Constructing reform coalitions: the politics of compensations in Argentina's economic liberalization', *Latin American Politics and Society*, 43: 1–36.

Fanelli J. M. and Machinea, J. L. (1994) 'Capital movements in Argentina', Biblioteca Virtual Sala De Lectura Consejo Latinoamericano De Ciencias Sociales CLACSO, *documento CEDES/99 serie economia*.

Findley, C. V. (1980) *Bureaucratic Reform in the Ottoman Empire: The Sublime Porte, 1789–1922*, Princeton: Princeton University Press.

Fleischer, D. (1997) 'Political corruption and campaign financing: Brazil's slow shift towards anti-corruption laws', paper presented at the Latin American Studies Association Annual Conference, Guadalajara, April 1997.

Fontdevila, P. A. (1994) 'Downsizing the state: The Argentina experience', in S. A. Chaudhry, G. J. Reid, and W. H. Malik (eds) *Civil Service Reform in Latin America and the Caribbean*, Washington, D. C.: The World Bank.

Freedman, A. E. (1994) *Patronage: An American Tradition*, Chicago: Nelson-Hall.

Frenkel, R. and M. G. Rozada (2001) 'Argentina: balance of payments liberalization: effects on growth, employment and income' in L. Taylor (ed.) *External Liberalization, Economic Performance and Social Policy*, New York: Oxford University Press.

Garcia-Zamor, J.-C. (1968) *Public Administration and Social Changes in Argentina: 1943–1955*, Rio de Janeiro: Mory.

Geddes, B. (1994) *Politicians Dilemma Building State Capacity in Latin America*, Berkeley: University of California Press.

Geddes, B. and Neto, A. R. (1992) 'Institutional sources of corruption in Brazil', *Third World Quarterly*, 13: 641–61.

Gellner, E. (1977) 'Patrons and Clients' in E. Gellner and J. Waterbury (eds) *Patrons and Clients in Mediterranean Societies*, Hanover: Center for Mediterranean Studies of the American Universities Field Staff.

Gellner, E. and Waterbury, J. (eds) (1977) *Patrons and Clients in Mediterranean Societies*, Hanover: Center for Mediterranean Studies of the American Universities Field Staff.

Genckaya, O. F. (2000) 'Siyasi partilere ve adaylara devlet destegi, bagislar ve secim giderlerinin sinirlandirilmasi', in A. Carkoglu (ed.) *Siyasi Partilerde Reform*, Istanbul: TESEV Yayinlari.

Gerchunoff, P. and Coloma, G. (1993) 'Privatization in Argentina', in M. Sanchez and R. Corona (eds) *Privatization in Latin America*, Baltimore: Johns Hopkins University Press.

Gibson, E. (1997) 'The populist road to market reform: policy and electoral coalitions in Mexico and Argentina', *World Politics*, 49: 32–55.

Gobel, C. (2001) 'Towards a consolidated democracy? Informal and formal institutions in Taiwan's political process', paper presented at the American Political Science Association Annual Conference, San Francisco, September 2001.

Golden, M. A. and Chang, E. C. C. (2001) 'Competitive corruption factional conflict and political malfeasance in postwar Italian Christian democracy', *World Politics*, 53: 558–622.

Gordin, J. P. (2002) 'The political and partisan determinants of patronage in Latin America 1960-1994: A comparative perspective', *European Journal of Political Research* 41: 513–549.

— (2006) 'Intergovernmental fiscal relations, "Argentine style"', *Journal of Public Policy*, 26: 255–277.

Greene, K. F. (2007) *Why Dominant Parties Lose Mexico's Democratization in Comparative Perspective*, New York: Cambridge University Press.

Gryzmala-Busse, A. (2007) *Rebuilding Leviathan Party Competition and State Exploitation in Post-Communist Democracies*, New York: Cambridge University Press.

Gunes-Ayata, A. (1992) *CHP Orgut ve Ideoloji*, Ankara: Gundogan Yayinlari.

— (1994) 'Clientelism: premodern, modern, postmodern', in L. Roniger and A. Gunes-Ayata (eds) *Democracy, Clientelism and Civil Society*, Boulder: Lynne Rienner.

Halperin-Donghi, T. (1993) *Contemporary History of Latin America*, Durham: Duke University Press.

Helmke, G. (2003) 'Checks and balances by other Means: strategic defection and Argentina's supreme court in the 1990s', *Comparative Politics*, 352: 213–30.

Henry, P. B. (2003) 'Capital accounts liberalization, the cost of capital, and economic growth', *manuscript*.

Heper, M. (1987) 'State, democracy, and bureaucracy in Turkey', in M. Heper (ed.) *The State and Public Bureaucracies A Comparative Perspective*, Westport: Greenwood Press, Inc.

— (1989) 'Country report: motherland party governments and bureaucracy in Turkey, 1983–1988', *Governance: An International Journal of Policy and Administration*, 2: 457–68.

Heper, M. and Keyman, E. F. (1998) 'Double- faced state: political patronage and the consolidation of democracy in Turkey', *Middle Eastern Studies*, 34: 259–77.

Huber, J. D. and Ting, M. M. (2009) 'Redistribution, Pork and Elections', *manuscript*.

Huntington, S. (2002) 'Modernization and Corruption', in Heidenheimer, A. J. and Johnston, M. (eds) *Political Corruption Concepts and Contexts*, New Brunswick: Transaction Publishers.

IAV (2003) *Bilecik Ilinin Ekonomik Gelismesi*, Istanbul: IAV.

Ignazi, P., Farrell, D. M. and Römmele, A. (2005) 'The prevalence of linkage by reward in contemporary parties', in A. Römmele, D. M. Farrell and P. Ignazi (eds) *Political Parties and Political Systems The Concept of Linkage Revisited*, Westport: Praeger.

Jacob, S. (2005) 'Intra-party competition and policy change: an explanation of India's development trajectory', *manuscript*.

James, S. (2005) 'Patronage regimes and American party development from 'The Age of Jackson' to the progressive era', *British Journal of Political Science*, 36: 39–60.

Jaspersen, F. (1996) 'Capital flows to Latin America 1982–1992: trends and prospects', in R. Corona, and W. Glade (eds) *Bigger Economies, Smaller Governments Privatization in Latin America*, Boulder: Westview Press.

Jones, M. P. (1997) 'Evaluating Argentina's presidential democracy: 1983–1995', in S. Mainwaring and M. S. Shugart (eds) *Presidentialism and Democracy in Latin America*, New York: Cambridge University Press.

Jones, M. P., Sanguinetti, P. and Tommasi, M. (2000) 'Politics, institutions, and fiscal performance in a federal system: an analysis of the Argentine provinces', *Journal of Development Economics*, 61: 305–33.

Jones, M. P., Saiegh, S., Spiller, P. T. and Tommasi, M. (2001) 'Keeping a seat in congress: provincial party bosses and the survival of Argentine legislators', *manuscript*.

Kalaycioglu, E. (2001) 'Turkish democracy: patronage versus governance', *Turkish Studies*, 2: 54–70.

Kaufman, R. R. (1974) 'The patron-client concept and macro-politics: prospects and problems', *Comparative Studies in Society and History*, 16: 284–308.

Keele, L. and Kelly, N. J. (2004) 'Dynamic models for dynamic theories: the ins and outs of lagged dependent variables', *manuscript*.

Keeling, D. (1997) *Contemporary Argentina*, Boulder: Westview Press.

Kessler, T. P. (1998) 'Political capital: Mexican financial policy under Salinas', *World Politics*, 51: 36–66.

Kim, S. (1999) 'Patronage politics as an obstacle to democracy in South Korea: regional networks and democratic consolidation', in H. Handelman and M. Tessler (eds) *Democracy and Its Limits: Lessons from Asia, Latin America, and the Middle East*, Notre Dame: University of Notre Dame Press.

Kitschelt, H. (2000) 'Linkages between citizens and politicians in democratic polities', *Comparative Political Studies*, 33: 845–879.

Kitschelt, H. and Wilkinson, S. I. (eds) (2007) *Patrons, Clients, and Policies Patterns of Democratic Accountability and Political Competition*, New York: Cambridge University Press.

Krishna, P., Mitra, D. and Chinoy, S. (2001) 'Trade liberalization and labor demand elasticities: evidence from Turkey', *Journal of International Economics*, 55 (2): 391–409.

Kristensen, I. P. and Wawro, G. J. (2004) 'Lagging the dog?: the robustness of panel corrected standard errors in the presence of serial correlation and observation specific effects', *manuscript*.

Krueger A. *et al.* (eds) (1983) *Trade and Employment in Developing Countries*, Chicago: University of Chicago Press.

Laver, M. and Shepsle, K. A. (1996) *Making and Breaking Governments: Government Formation in Parliamentary Democracies*, New York: Cambridge University Press.

Lawson, K. (1980) *Political Parties and Linkage: A Comparative Perspective*, New Haven: Yale University Press.

Lemarchand, R. (1988) 'The state, the parallel economy, and the changing structure of patronage systems', in D. Rothchild and N. Chazan (eds) *The Precarious Balance: State and Society in Africa*, Boulder: Westview Press.

Lemarchand, R. and Legg, K. (1972) 'Political clientelism and development', *Comparative Politics*, 4(2): 149–178.

Levinsohn, J. (1999) 'Employment responses to international liberalization in Chile', *Journal of International Economics*, 47: 321–44.

Levitsky, S. (2003) *Transforming Labor-Based Parties in Latin America: Argentine Peronism in Comparative Perspective*, New York: Cambridge University Press.

— (2005) 'Argentina: Democratic Survival amidst Economic Failure', in F. Hagopian and S. Mainwaring (eds) *The Third Wave of Democratization in Latin America: Advances and Setbacks,* New York: Cambridge University Press.

Lloyd-Sherlock, P. (1997) 'Policy, distribution, and poverty in Argentina since redemocratization', *Latin American Perspectives*, 24: 22–55.

Lyne, M. (2007) 'Rethinking economics and institutions: the voter's dilemma and democratic accountability', in H. Kitschelt and S. Wilkinson (eds) *Patrons, Clients and Policies: Patterns of Democratic Accountability and Political Competition*, New York: Cambridge University Press.

— (2008) *The Voter's Dilemma and Democratic Accountability Latin America and Beyond*, University Park: The Pennsylvania State University Press.

Magaloni, B. (2006) *Voting for Autocracy Hegemonic Party Survival and Its Demise in Mexico*, New York: Cambridge University Press.

Magaloni B., Diaz-Cayeros, A. and Estevez, F. (2007) 'Clientelism and portfolio diversification: a model of electoral investment with applications to Mexico' in H. Kitschelt and S. I. Wilkinson (eds) *Patrons, Clients, and Policies Patterns of Democratic Accountability and Political Competition,* New York: Cambridge University Press.

Mainwaring, S. P. (1999) *Rethinking Party Systems in the Third Wave of Democratization: The Case of Brazil*, Stanford: Stanford University Press.

Manin, B. (1997) *The Principles of Representative Government*, New York: Cambridge University Press.

Manzetti, L. (1993) *Institutions, Parties, and Coalitions in Argentine Politics*, Pittsburgh: University of Pittsburgh Press.

Mayhew, D. R. (1986) *Placing Parties in American Politics: Organization, Electoral Settings, and Government Activity in the Twentieth Century*, Princeton: Princeton University Press.

McCubbins, M. D., and Thies, M. F. (1997) 'As a matter of factions: the budgetary implications of shifting factional control in Japan's LDP', *Legislative Studies Quarterly,* 22(3): 293–328.

McGuire, J. W. (1997) *Peronism without Peron: Unions, Parties and Democracy in Argentina*, Stanford: Stanford University Press.

Medina, L. F. and Stokes, S. (2002) 'Clientelism as political monopoly', *manuscript*.

Michels, R. (1962 [1915]) *Political Parties: A Sociological Study of the Oligarchical Tendencies of Modern Democracy*, New York: Free Press.

Miguez, D. P. (1995) 'Democracy, political machines and participation in the surroundings of Buenos Aires', *European Review of Latin American and Caribbean Studies*, 58: 91–106.

Mouzelis, N. P. (1978) *Modern Greece: Facets of Underdevelopment*, London: Macmillan.

Murillo, M. V. (2001) *Labor Unions, Partisan Coalitions and Market Reforms in Latin America*, New York: Cambridge University Press.

Mutluer, K. M. and Oner, E. (2009) *Teoride ve Uygulamada Mahalli Idareler Maliyesi*, Istanbul: Istanbul Bilgi Universitesi Yayinlari.

Nas, T. and Odekon, M. (1998) 'Economic Liberalization and the Turkish Labor Market' in P, Dabir-Alai and Odekon, M. (eds) *Economic Liberalization and Labor Markets*, Westport, CT: Greenwood Publishing Group.

NDP publication (n.d.) 'Cumhuriyetin Ilanindan Gunumuze Devlet Personel Rejiminin Gelisimi', http://www.basbakanlik-dpb.gov.tr (5/1/2005)

Nichter, S. (2008) 'Vote buying or turnout buying? machine politics and the secret ballot', *American Review of Political Science*, 102(1): 19–31.

Novaro, M. and Palermo, V. (1998) *Los caminos de la centroizquierda Dilemas y desafíos del Frepaso y de la Alianza*, Buenos Aires: Editorial Losada.

O'Donnell, G. (1996) 'Illusions about consolidation', *Journal of Democracy*, 7(2): 34–51.

Ollier, M. M. (2001) *Las coaliciones politicas en la Argentina El caso de la Alianza*, Buenos Aires: Fondo de Cultura Economica.

Onis, Z. (1998) 'The state and economic development in contemporary Turkey: etatism to neoliberalism and beyond', in Z. Onis (ed.) *State and Market The Political Economy of Turkey in Comparative Perspective*, Istanbul: Bogazici University Press.

Ozbudun, E. (1981) 'Turkey: the politics of political clientelism', in S. N. Eisenstadt and R. Lemarchand (eds) *Political Clientelism, Patronage, and Development, Sage studies in Contemporary Political Sociology*, vol.3, Beverly Hills: Sage Publications.

—— (2000) *Contemporary Turkish Politics: Challenges to democratic consolidation*, Boulder, Colo.: Lynne Rienner Publishers.

Ozbudun, S. (2005) 'The reproduction of clientelism in regressing rural Turkey or "why I became an erect ear"', *Dialectical Anthropology*, 29: 241–72.

Ozdemir, H. (2001) *Osmanli Devletinde Burokrasi*, Istanbul: Okumus Adam Yayinlari.

Ozkul, E. (1996) *Clientelism in Bureaucracies: A Case Study in a Turkish State Enterprise*, unpublished master of arts thesis, Bogazici University.

Panaia, M. and Ramos M. (2004) 'El mercado de trabajo en la articulacion rural-urbana del nordeste Argentino', in M. Panaia (ed.) *Crisis Fiscal, Mercado de Trabajo y Nuevas Territorialidades en el Nordeste Argentino*, Buenos Aires: La Comena.

Panebianco, A. (1988) *Political Parties: Organization and Power*, New York: Cambridge University Press.

Piattoni, S. (2001) *Clientelism, Interests and Democratic Representation the European Experience in Historical and Comparative Perspective*, Cambridge: Cambridge University Press.

Powell, G. B. (2001) *Elections and Elements of Democracy: Majoritarian and Proportional Visions*, New Haven: Yale University Press.

Przeworski, A., Stokes, S. C. and Manin, B. (1999) *Democracy, Accountability, and Representation*, New York: Cambridge University Press.

Rahat, G. and Hazan, R. Y. (2001) 'Candidate selection methods: an analytical framework', *Party Politics*, 73: 297–322.

Remmer, K. (2007) 'The Political Economy of Patronage Expenditure Patterns in the Argentine Provinces, 1983–2003', *Journal of Politics*, 69(2): 363–377.

Remmer, K. and Wibbels, E. (2000) 'The subnational politics of economic adjustment provincial politics and fiscal performance in Argentina', *Comparative Political Studies*, 33(4): 419–51.

Rinne, J. (2003) 'The politics of administrative reform in Menem's Argentina: the illusion of isolation', in B. R. Schneider and B. Heredia (eds) *Reinventing Leviathan: The Politics of Administrative Reform in Developing Countries*, Boulder: Lynne Rienner.

Roberts, K. (1996) 'Economic crisis and the demise of the legal left in Peru', *Comparative Politics*, 29: 69–92.

Roberts, M. J. and Tybout, J. R. (1996) *Industrial Evolution in Developing Countries: Micro patterns of turnover, productivity, and market structure*, New York: Oxford University Press.

Robinson, J. A. and Verdier, T. (2002) 'The political economy of clientelism', Centre for Economic Policy Research Discussion Papers Series No. 3205.

Rock, D. (1975) *Politics in Argentina, 1890–1930: The Rise and Fall of Radicalism*, Cambridge: Cambridge University Press.

— (1987) *Argentina, 1516–1987: From Spanish Colonization to Alfonsín*, Berkeley: University of California Press.

Rodrik, D. (1992) 'The limits of trade policy reform in developing countries', *The Journal of Economic Perspectives*, 61: 87–105.

Romero, L. A. (2002) *A History of Argentina in the Twentieth Century*, University Park, PA: Pennsylvania State University Press.

Römmele, A., Farrell, D. and Ignazi, P. (2005) *Political Parties and Political Systems*, Westport CN: Praeger/Greenwood.

Rose-Ackerman, S. (1999) *Corruption and Government Causes, Consequences and Reform*, New York: Cambridge University Press.

— (2005) *From Elections To Democracy: Building Accountable Government in Hungary and Poland*, New York: Cambridge University Press.

Samuels, D. (2000) 'Does money matter? Credible commitments and campaign finance in new democracies: theory and evidence from Brazil', *manuscript*.

Sayari, S. (1977) 'Political patronage in Turkey', in E. Gellner and J. Waterbury (eds) *Patrons and Clients in Mediterranean Societies*, London: Duckworth.

— (2002) 'The Changing Party System' in S. Sayari and Y. R. Esmer (eds) *Politics, Parties and Elections in Turkey*, Lynne Rienner Publishers.

— (2011) 'Clientelism and Patronage in Turkish Politics and Society' in F. Birtek and B. Toprak (eds) *The Post-Modern Abyss and the New Politics of Islam: Assabiyah Revisited*, Istanbul Bilgi University Press.

Schaffer, F. C. (2007) (ed.) *Elections for Sale: The Causes and Consequences of*

Vote Buying, Boulder: Lynne Riener Publishers.

Schinelli, D. A. and Vacca, C. A. (1999) 'Problematica a nivel de provincia', in A. Salvia (ed.) La *Patagonia de los noventa: sectores que ganan, sociedades que pierden*, Buenos Aires: Editorial La Colmena.

Schuler, H. (1999) *Turkiye'de Sosyal Demokrasi Particilik Hemsehrilik Alevilik*, Istanbul: Iletisim Yayinlari.

Schumpeter, J. A. (1975) *Capitalism, Socialism, and Democracy*, New York: Harper and Row.

Scott, J. (2002) 'Corruption, machine politics and political change', in A. J. Heidenheimer and M. Johnston (eds) *Political Corruption Concepts and Contexts*, New Brunswick: Transaction Publishers.

Secor, A. J. (2001) 'Ideologies in crisis: political cleavages and electoral politics in Turkey in the 1990s', *Political Geography*, 20: 539–560.

Simga-Mugan, C. and Yuce, A. (2003) 'Privatization in emerging markets: the case of Turkey', *Emerging Markets Financa and Trade*, 39(5): 83–110.

Shefter, M. (1994) *Political Parties and the State The American Historical Experience*, Princeton: Princeton University Press.

Smulovitz, C. and Peruzotti, P. (2002) *Controlando a La Politica. Ciudadanos Y Medios En Las Nuevas Democracias Latinoamericanas*, Buenos Aires: Editorial Temas.

Sotelo, S. O. (n. d.) 'Breve Historia Electoral: Provincia del Chaco', *manuscript*.

Steed, R. P. (ed.) (1998) *Party Organization and Activism in the American South*, Tuscaloosa: University of Alabama Press.

Stokes, S. (2005) 'Perverse accountability: a formal model of machine politics with evidence from Argentina', *American Political Science Review*, 99(3): 315–327.

— (2007) 'Is vote buying undemocratic?', in F. C. Schaffer (ed.) *Elections for Sale: The Causes and Consequences of Vote Buying*, Boulder: Lynne Riener Publishers.

Sunar, I. (1990) 'Populism and patronage: the Demokrat Party and its legacy in Turkey', *Il Politico*, 4: 745–57.

Tommasi, M. (2002) 'Federalism in Argentina and the reforms of the 1990s', Working Paper N 147, Center for Research on Economic Development and Policy Reform, Stanford University.

Unamuno, M. and Bortnik, R. (1986) *La reforma constitucional en el siglo XX*, Buenos Aires: Centro Editor de América Latina.

Vacs, A. C. and Renwick, T. J. (1998) 'Argentina Neoliberal Restructuring and Its Impact on Employment' in P, Dabir-Alai and M. Odekon (eds) *Economic Liberalization and Labor Markets*, Westport, CT: Greenwood Publishing Group.

Vicente, P. C. (2007) 'Is vote buying effective? Evidence from a field experiment in West Africa', paper presented at the American Political Science Association Annual Conference, Chicago, September 2007.

Wantchekon, L. (2003) 'Clientelism and voting behavior evidence from a field experiment in Benin', *World Politics*, 55: 399–422.

Ware, A. (1992) 'Activist-leader relations and the structure of political parties:

'exchange' models and vote-seeking behaviour in parties', *British Journal of Political Science*, 22: 71–92.

— (1996) *Political Parties and Party Systems*, Oxford: Oxford University Press.

Waterbury, J. (1993) *Exposed to Innumerable Delusions: Public Enterprise and State Power in Egypt, India, Mexico, and Turkey*, New York: Cambridge University Press.

Weingrod, A. (1968) 'Patrons, patronage and political parties', *Comparative Studies in Society and History*, 7: 377–400.

White, C. (1980) *Patrons and Partisans: A Study of Politics in Two Southern Italian Comuni*, New York: Cambridge University Press.

Wolfinger, R. E. (1972) 'Why political machines have not withered away and other revisionist thoughts', *Journal of Politics*, 34(2): 365–398.

Wylde, C. (2011), 'State, Society and Markets in Argentina: The Political Economy of Neodesarrollismo under Néstor Kirchner, 2003–2007', *Bulletin of Latin American Research*, 30(4): 436–452.

Yavuz, H. (2002) 'Politics of fear: the rise of the Nationalist Action Party (MHP) in Turkey', *The Middle East Journal*, 56(2): 200–21.

Yilmaz, T. (2001) *Tayyip: Kasimpasa'dan Siyasetin On Saflarina*, Ankara: Umit Yayinlari.

Zuckerman, A. (1979) *The Politics of Faction: Christian Democratic Rule in Italy*, New Haven: Yale University Press.

| index

Beck, N. 93
Benton, A. L. 43 n.1, 55, 128
Berberoğlu, A. 118
Beşiktaş 11, 105, 111–13, 151
  JDP and 151 n.9
  MP and 111, 112, 113
  public employment data *112,*
    111–13
    internal party politics, role of
      111-13
    patronage jobs and 111, 112, 113
  RRP and 111, 112, 151 n.9
Bettcher, K. E. 128
Beyoğlu 109, 114
Bhagwati, J. 22 n.11
Bilecik 11, 35, 38, 44 n.4, 116, 118,
  150, 151
  City Centre municipality 11, 103,
    115-16, 151
    budget (1985–2002) 115, *117*
    political competition and 115
  economic development in 150
  employment figures *32, 36*
  labour force in 150
  mayors, political competition and
    115
    personnel spending and 115
  party financing in 46
  population statistics 150
  public sector jobs and 151
  see also Bozüyük
Bittel, D. F. 73, 89
Bivort, S. 80
Boissevain, J. 4 n.4, 14
Boratav, K. 26 n.15
Bordón, J. O. 71
Bortnik, R. 67 n.1
Bozlagan, R. 101
Bozüyük 11, 103, 115, 117-18, 151
  municipal budget (1996–2004) 117,
    118
    political competition and 117
    personnel spending and 117, *118*
Brambor, T. 93
Brazil 21

brokers 130
  see also Argentina, *punteros* and
Brown, C. 70
Brusco, V. 16, 21, 43
Buenos Aires, City of (Capital Federal)
  28, 30, 44, 68 n.4, 92, 149, 152
Buenos Aires, province of 11, 18, 44,
  52 n.27, 69, 81, 145–7, 148
  Co-Participation agreement and 70
  demographic characteristics of 147
    clientelistic exchanges and 147
  economic development of 145
    GDP per capita 145, *146*
  election results 53, 89 n.48
  electorate statistics 69
  employment in *24, 28,* 29–30, *146*
    particularistic exchanges and 35
    public and private sector differ-
      ences 29–30, *146,* 147
  Federal League and 72
  Federal Union and 73
  governor challengers to national
    leaders 69
    Duhalde and Menem 69, 70,
      71–3
    employment data and 71, *72,* 73
    party leader networks and 69
    patronage jobs and 70, 71, 73
  patronage jobs 68, 69–72
  PJ (Peronists) 53
    budget analysis 47
  UCR 69
    budget analysis 47
  unemployment in *146,* 147
  urbanisation and 147
  see also La Matanza; Pilar

Cafiero, A. F. 69, 70, 89 n.48
Calvo, E. xi, 5, 16, 43, 68, 91, 130,
  152
Calvo, G. 21
Camara Nacional Electoral *39,* 47
Çanakkale *32, 36,* 45
Capital Federal *see* Buenos Aires, City
  of

www.ingramcontent.com/pod-product-compliance
Lightning Source LLC
Chambersburg PA
CBHW072131020426

42334CB00018B/1746